The Meek Shall Inherit the *Earth*

A Matter of Inheritance

The crucial truth of Israel - Islam and the Church

Author

Renate Vinje

Copyright © 2006 by Renate Vinje
Revised June 2006

The Meek Shall Inherit the Earth
by Renate Vinje

Printed in the United States of America

ISBN 1-59781-556-X

All rights reserved solely by the author. The author guarantees all contents are original and do not infringe upon the legal rights of any other person or work. No part of this book may be reproduced in any form without the permission of the author. The views expressed in this book are not necessarily those of the publisher.

Unless otherwise indicated, Bible quotations are taken from NIV Bible. Copyright © 1985 by Zondervan publishing.

www.xulonpress.com

To Mark,

Renate Viinje
Lude 13:30

Dedication

To my LORD and Savior, Jesus Christ.

To my husband who models Him daily and promised, "I will never leave you nor forsake you."

To my sons who teach me more than I ever taught them.

To true friends who love me for who I am in good times and in bad.

To the American soldier who fought for my freedom that I might be raised in a free Germany and now live in the Unites States of America.

To a free country that permits me to write this book and worship God.

Thank you!

Renate Vinje

Contents

Prologue: Why me?.. ix

1. What is all this fuss about Israel?...................................13
2. The mind of Satan 17
3. In the middle 23
4. What is all that fuss about Jerusalem? 35
5. Who rules from the Temple Mount? 45
6. The mind of Christ 53
7. The choosing of the firstborn 57
8. The rejection of the firstborn..67
9. From last to first 79
10. Religious deception in Israel, we are first!...................93
11. Deception in Christianity, we are first! 103
12. More religious arrogance 115
13. Deception in Nazi Germany, we are first!..................119
14. Islam, Satan's masterpiece, we are first!....................125
15. Islam, Peace - or Anti Christ religion?.......................135
16. Who is the true prophet like Moses?...........................143
17. Who is your neighbor?...151
18. If the shoe fits wear it! 159
19. Babylonian kingdoms, or God's Kingdom on earth?...167
20. Beast Kingdoms that rule the earth 175
21. European Union or Eurabia?..183
22. Woe to the Great city! 195

23. September 11 and the number 11 213
24. The seat of Satan 219
25. Exempt from tribulation or God's wrath? 235
26. The wrath of God 247
27. Six days 255
28. In my Father's house 259
29. An everlasting love 269

Bibliography 275

Index for:
    Covenant land Grant 277
    Warning of dispersions 277
    Restoration 277
    Arab nations, Judgments and Destructions 278

PROLOGUE

Why me?

In the first century stiff-necked theologians had their minds made up. In turn God chose common Jewish fishermen to accomplish His plan. How about today?

You may ask "what qualifies me to write this book, where is my degree, or where did I go to seminary?" I have one simple answer. God indeed chooses the foolish things to shame the wise. (1 Corinthians 1:18-31). Although I deeply value and respect education, I lost my opportunity for higher education due to family tragedy.

Born and educated in Germany shortly after WWII, I had minimal lessons in English. I am therefore self-taught and have no clue or understanding of proper grammar, and simply write by what seems to look and feel right. Until God gave me the gift in 1993, I had never known how to express my thoughts on paper, and to this day cannot type because my eye and hand coordination just does not cooperate. Prior to my conversion at age 37, I never opened the Bible, was disinterested in history, and as a result uneducated in these areas.

God hates outward perfectionism, at the expense of inner purity of heart. He condemns the arrogant who think they are first, and despises those who won't humble themselves who dare to destroy the *least*. Since I myself abhor the perfection in which I was raised that almost destroyed me, I therefore did not wish to have my sentences professionally edited nor corrected, but rather reflect my German heritage, my inadequacies, my lack of knowledge in grammar, so that the glory may go to God. If this book is a success, God has indeed exalted the *last to first place*. This work is the result of His gift to me and my intense spiritual battle of 57 years to survive Satan's attacks.

God has used tremendous pain and loss, and a heart for hurting people to give me insight into His Word. I am proud and yet humble to say that I have graduated from "the school of trials" to be an overcomer, and present my diploma with honors from God.

God has deemed it worthy to use:

1.) The stealing of birthrights
2.) The rejection and abandonment of my birth father
3.) Living with abuse, terror, fear, and further abandonment by my adoptive father
4.) Death of my adoptive mother which resulted in total abandonment at a young age
5.) Deception and abandonment by my knight in shining armor.
6.) Total emotional collapse resulting in the loss of my son
7.) In order to marry the man that I met and who loved me, it meant leaving my country, culture, and traditions which were precious to me. Not realizing the severity of my identity crisis, I even changed my name from Renate to Renee, ignored the pain and "stuffed" it. For years I never spoke of my past nor used my mother tongue.
8.) In addition, I discovered I was unable to have anymore children.
9.) I missed the opportunity to care for my beloved mother's grave. When I finally returned after ten years, I discovered it no longer existed. Graves are not purchased but leased, requiring a minimal annual fee for upkeep. After ten years of non-payment and no family member found to keep it, it was considered abandoned, cleared out, and reused. I was horrified and utterly broken to realize that the only person that I loved as a child, the woman I honored and cherished, had been abandoned in the grave, her skull somewhere on a

shelf, numbered and marked "abandoned". I wept as I had lost all of my identity.

10.) In 1986, Jesus Christ found me. He wanted me, the one He had created in His image and likeness, not the one I was deceived to accept and created to survive. I confessed my willful sins, forgave those who sinned against me, but was in need of deep emotional healing. To face the truth of the past I fell into deep depression. At times the anguish was utterly unbearable. I begged God to let me die. He didn't, but rather used those years to drive me deep into His Holy Word, where much healing came. After years of being childless, we decided to adopt two orphans from Romania. If ever anyone knew about abuse, rejection, and abandonment, it was me. I knew I would understand their pain and be able to identify with them and be able to help. But little did I know how their pain was going to drive me deeper into my own. More depression came with anxiety attacks, and wished I was dead, but knew I had to go on for the sake of my sons. God continued to drive me more deeply into the Scriptures.

11.) Then the LORD prompted me to relinquish my German citizenship. With intense anxiety and fear I replied: *"My citizenship gives me the right to return. I can get retirement, full medical and dental insurance in Germany. We have hopes to retire there and live part of the time in the USA and abroad. In case something should happen to my husband I would be more secure there. Just the thought of relinquishing my citizenship makes me terrified. No Lord you can't mean it? Besides, this paper is the only thing left of my past that says who I am. "*

Again He drove me deeper into His Word. With great joy through my study, I discovered God's everlasting Covenant promises and love for Israel, but realized that most believers did not share my enthusiasm. In my search for understanding of the Holocaust I discovered Christian history was filled with blood, murder, anti-Semitism, and stealing God's promises from Israel for the church.

Soon after that time God gave me a vision. As I looked upon the city crest of Berlin, the "Black Bear", this beast moved towards me as if to attack and devour, but stopped just in time right before my face. In terror I trembled, ran and cried out: "Not again LORD not again!" I knew from that moment on that Germany would once again be a major player in the persecution of the Jewish people during the Great Tribulation to come.

Although unaware of any Jewish heritage in my family, this vision gave me the faith to relinquish my German citizenship in obedience to my Savior, the ultimate Jew from the tribe of Judah, the King of Israel whom I love with all of my heart. It meant renouncing any identity of my past, and giving up my security blanket in all that Germany had to offer. By faith, I truly left my country, my people, my father's household, and declared my citizenship was in heaven alone.

I knew from that day forward that God had chosen me to speak out about the everlasting hatred of Satan, versus God's everlasting love for Israel, as they are the nation and people whom God chose to accomplish His eternal purposes for the whole earth, to save even me. But most of all, I have learned this; while" beast" nation after nation has sought to control the earth and destroy Israel, God always has and always will save a remnant of Israel, because - *"The meek shall inherit the earth."*

CHAPTER 1

What is all this fuss about Israel?

Turn on your radio, TV, or read your newspaper and magazines, there is Israel on the daily news. Why would a nation the size of Vancouver Island carry such importance? What is all this fuss about Israel?

The Bible declares that Israel would become a great nation, and blessings were to flow from her to all nations, and curses to any who hated her. Then why do so many hate Israel and her people with such drive and determination even seeking her extermination? Search as far and wide as you wish, find excuse after excuse, but it simply cannot be explained outside of the *demonic*. What we see here on earth, in the physical realm, is merely a reflection of the battle in the spiritual realm and has been since the beginning of time, even from eternity.

The world does not recognize the only true God of Abraham, Isaac and Jacob, never mind His sovereignty that decreed to provide His mercy and love to mankind, and bless us through this very nation, Israel, to redeem mankind. What does it mean to be blessed by God? It simply means He places His goodness upon that life. It is God's will to bestow blessings from and through Israel to the world and therefore making her the focus of Satan's unswerving deception and hate. The adversary of God is committed with all of his might to oppose His will. From the beginning, Satan has tried to thwart the plan of redemption by either corrupting or destroying the chosen lineage, out of which the Messiah of Israel and Savior of the world would come. Anytime you read the will of God, you can count on Satan's consequent opposition.

God's seven-fold will and promise to Abraham. (Genesis 12)
I will make you into a great nation.
I will bless you.
I will make your name great.
You will be a blessing.
I will bless those who bless you.
Whoever curses you I will curse.
And through you all peoples of the earth will be blessed.

Through Abraham came the chosen lineage of Isaac and Jacob (Israel) through whom the Messiah would come to restore all things.

The opposition
In turn Satan has decreed Israel's destruction. Let's write the above seven-fold promise to Abraham in reverse, to gain insight into the satanic will and opposition of the enemy of Israel and all of mankind.
I will erase the memory of Israel forever.
I will curse you.
I will make your name hated.
I will make them hate you.
I will curse those who bless you.
Whoever blesses you I will curse.
I will make you the scorn of the nations.

Try as he may, God chose Abraham, blessed him and made a Covenant cut in blood and guaranteed the Promised Land through his descendants Isaac, and Jacob (Israel), *forever.* (Genesis 12:1-3; 15:15-18; 17*)* It is through this Covenant that we, the believing Gentiles are grafted in, as God assured blessings to all nations. Those who hate Israel cannot love the God of Abraham, Isaac and Jacob and her people, as she is the nation through whom:
1.) God revealed Himself.

2.) Established His Word and Covenants.
3.) Preserved His Word.
4.) Produced His Son Jesus Christ, the redeemer of Israel and the world.
5.) Established His church.
6.) Brought us Gentiles the Gospel.
7.) Will come back to Jerusalem to deliver the nation of Israel, whose timing is inseparably linked with the ultimate deliverance of the church by the Resurrection and Rapture, and the redemption and ultimate re-creation of the earth.

Humble hearts of gratitude to God for His eternal purposes in and through Israel, and His beloved Son Jesus the Christ, will want to bless Israel. No true Christian can claim to love the Messiah of Israel and hate Israel or the Jewish people. It's rather simple, you either have a heart of gratitude or not. But the question remains, why did God choose this very particular piece of Land, Israel, to accomplish His plan? It's rather simple as well. Often we cannot "see the forest for the trees". It all began there and it will end there. So let us begin.

CHAPTER 2

The mind of Satan

Many are conformed into the image of Satan. They exemplify his mind and consequent behavior, as he disguises himself as an "angel of light", but in reality is the "prince of darkness". He has managed to distort the role of leadership in all areas from governments to religious leaders, even in marriage and families. He is the "father of lies" who produces tyrants like himself that confuse leadership with domination and control. In their ruthless quest to rule, they even kill and destroy the very gift God has given them, whether it was to govern nations, lead churches, or protect their lovely bride and family. Rather than shepherds they are ravenous wolves!

How did all this distortion begin?
God's creation was His perfect plan and will, as He declared it good in every aspect. (Genesis 1)

But something went terribly wrong. While numerous scholars teach Lucifer's rebellion against God, his unwillingness to serve Him, the question that has haunted me for years was "why?" What was it that made Lucifer so utterly discontent, full of hate and revenge, unwilling to serve God, and demanding to rule? What was it that caused 1/3 of the angels to follow him and rebel against God and refuse to serve Him as well? What was it that made Lucifer hate mankind the way he does?

Insight is given as we discover that God created the heavens *first* and the Earth *last*. (Gen.1: 1). Thus everything in heaven was created *before* God created the earth and man.

Angels

Angels predate man. *(Job 38:1-7; Ps.148: 2-5).*
Angels are more powerful than man. (2 Peter 2: 11)
Angels do not have authority to declare anything different from God's Word. (Galatians 1: 8)
Angels are free moral agents. (2 Peter 2: 4; Genesis 2, 3)
Angels are supernatural light beings, who may not receive worship. (Col. 2:18; Revelation 22:8-9. Col 1:16, Job 38: 1-7)
Lucifer was God's most beautiful and powerful angel. (Isaiah 14: 12. Ezekiel 28:16-19)

Man

After God created the earth, He made Adam in His own image *from the earth* and placed him in the Garden of Eden. (Gen.1; 2; Hebrews 2) He made Eve from Adam's side and blessed them both to enjoy His creation. God decreed the earth as their *inheritance and gave them rule and dominion over it.* (Genesis 1: 28) By creating mankind in God's image, we are children of God, sons and daughters, His rightful children and *heirs* to live with Him. By creating us from the earth God has forever identified us with our *inheritance*.

The Eternal hatred

I believe that the major key that unlocks much of scripture is to understand that Lucifer's heart was enraged when he, the *first created* did not receive the *inheritance of the earth*, and was furthermore appointed to *serve* man *below* him, specifically those who *inherit salvation.* (Hebrews 1:14) In his arrogant rage, I believe he said something like this to God:

"I was created first, yet you created man in your own image, why not me?"

"I was created first, yet you gave man the earth as their inheritance, and told them to multiply, why not me?" Where is my wife and my heirs?

"I was created first, yet you gave them the earth to rule, why not me?"

"I was created first, am above man, am more powerful, yet you expect me to serve them?"

"I was created *first* they were created *last*, so they should serve me!"

"Forget it! I am not serving YOU either!"

"I will be first and rule from your throne in HEAVEN!"

"I will be first and rule from your throne on EARTH!"

"I will deceive and destroy mankind so none will receive your inheritance! *I AM THE HEIR!"*

The eternal hatred: (Genesis 3)

With unswerving determination, fueled by satanic jealousy and rage, Lucifer appeared in the form of a serpent to deceive man to steal the inheritance. Eve, rather than seek out her God appointed king (husband) for guidance and protection, listened to the snake and ate the forbidden fruit. Adam, rather than protect his wife, crush Satan's head and kill him and claim his authority as king of the earth, ate as well. So much for the inheritance, it was gone, stolen, and so was man's relationship with God.

Man's cover-up: (Gen.3: 7)

For the first time, Adam and Eve knew they were naked. Rather than go to God asking for forgiveness and covering, they hid and covered their own nakedness with leaves. When God asked them questions, Adam blamed Eve, even blamed God for giving her to him. Eve was honest enough to say, "The serpent deceived me and I ate." Neither of them admitted that they had rebelled against God, and His clear instructions not to eat of the fruit of that tree. Eden is a stark reminder that Satan is a deceiver and thief, and that man is a "cover-up", never satisfied, and when given a chance will take more.

God cursed Satan (Gen.3:14-15)

God determined to fulfill His will for mankind, cursed Satan on the spot for his rebellion and deception, and declared that He will redeem man through the seed of a woman that will crush the serpents

(Satan's) head. A **seed** is clearly an heir. This **chosen heir** of God would be inflicted by a wound from Satan's seed, (first coming of Christ) but He will ultimately prevail by giving Satan a blow in the head that will crush his head.(Second coming) When God says **"I will"** it is an oath, a vow, it cannot be changed. Count on it! It is **HIS WILL**! God clearly told Satan that the inheritance would never be his, because an inheritance is given to His rightful heir, not stolen. That is why God's promises are recorded in His WILL and Old Testament, confirmed and fulfilled in His WILL and New Testament. That is why you are to have your own WILL and Last Testament to appoint your own heirs so the inheritance will not be stolen.

God's provision (Genesis 3: 21; John 1:29)

God made it very clear to Adam and Eve, no cover- ups! You come to "ME" naked, with all your sin and I will cover you. He alone is the author of Grace, the Way, the Truth and the Life, the Redeemer of all that was lost. He extended His grace and provided redemption by covering Adam and Eve with "garments of skin", thus causing the first death of an innocent animal. So from the beginning, we see that God established the concrete truth that no man comes to Him without His provision. God is the Savior! This pointed to the temporary sacrificial system that He would establish with His chosen lineage, until the once and for all, **ultimate sacrifice** would come, *"The Lamb of God that takes away the sins of the world."*

666

In the meantime let us remember that it was **day 6,** the last day of creation when Lucifer rebelled, and said something like this:

"I HATE day **6**!

"I HATE your heirs! **6**

"I HATE you God! **6**

"From now on it will be **666**! Do you hear me?"

"I am god and I will have heirs in my own image!" **6**

"I will destroy your heirs!" **6**

"I will establish my kingdom to oppose your kingdom!" **6**

God cursed him! To this day the battle rages on! It is God, His Son and His kingdom, verses Satan, his seed and his kingdom.

The test

God always tests the **first with the last.** The divine principle was laid down before the foundations of the earth. The question is "Who will exemplify the mind of Satan or the mind Christ? Who will hate, is unwilling to serve the *least*, and arrogantly asserts first place even if it means to kill and destroy them like a ruthless beast? Who will love and willingly become last, like He who made Himself nothing, who even died on a cross for mankind?" In His first coming Jesus said:

> *"Indeed there are those who are last who will be first,*
> *and first who will be last."*
> (Luke 13:30).

First position does not mean domination, but rather, the awesome, God ordained role, as protector and lover of those *under* their care. That is why God is called the "Good Shepherd" and we are His sheep. A good shepherd does not abuse his sheep, nor abandons them, fleeces them for his own gain, or lets them eat inferior grain, but provides still water, green pasture, anoints them with oil to protect them from pests, and kills the wolves who dare to destroy the flock. God gives the same responsibility to all in first position:

"Angels, love and serve mankind!"
"Husbands, love and serve your wife and children!"
"Pastors, love and serve your flock!"
"Kings, love and serve your citizens!
"Managers, love and serve your employees!"
"Teachers, love and serve your students!"
"Rich, love and serve the poor!"
"Healthy, love and serve the sick!"
"Firstborn, love and serve your younger siblings?
"Gentile nations, love and serve the least of my brethren, and least of the nations, - Israel!"

Voltaire, hater of God and the church, once sarcastically posed this rhetorical question: *"Why should the world be made to rotate around the **insignificant pimple of Jewry?*** He missed the fact that salvation is of the Jews! Although brilliant in mind, he was blinded by arrogance and ungratefulness that left him with a heart the size of a pimple. He was blind to the truth that God chose Israel not because of her size or might, but to test prideful and ungrateful humanity. She is not insignificant to God, and therefore His eyes are especially on the apple of his eye, the least of His brethren and scorn of the nations. To no surprise, every pompous gentile Empire in scripture was lead by a ferocious beastlike leader, a type of Anti Christ, who dared to claim he was god in human flesh, a vile hater and persecutor of Israel seeking her destruction, and established his satanic Beast Kingdom on earth. They were all **666.** There is one more to come, to attempt to complete the "Final Solution", and will go to its destruction.

He who has an ear let him hear!

We have all failed in one area or another. We all have fallen short of the Glory of God. That's why we all need a Savior, forgiver, and teacher to show us how to become like HIM. Therefore, Jesus said *"I am the Good shepherd, I lay my life down for my sheep!"* (John 10) He did not come to restore religion, because man never lost religion. He came to seek lost sheep that lost the image of God's Son and His Kingdom. He taught, lived, loved, and died by example, and taught us how to pray, *"**Thy** Kingdom come, **thy** will be done, on earth as it is in heaven."* (Matthew 6:10) He came to save selfish mankind, and restore them to status of children of God, to become co-heirs with Him in His kingdom. In order to enter, one has to repent, and admit their prideful and sinful heart. It is not conversion from one religion to another, it is moving from the kingdom of darkness to the kingdom of light.

CHAPTER 3

In the Middle

Unless we understand the crucial role of Israel's location, the importance of Jerusalem and specifically the Temple Mount throughout scripture, and the vital role they play to redeem man and the earth, we cannot understand the beginning, never mind the end.

The *Middle* of the Garden of Eden
Many claim the *Garden of Eden* was in Iraq, but this ignores the fact that it merely ends there. Iraq is the eastern most border of Eden, but actually encompassed a much larger area. While several unknown rivers are mentioned, the general boundaries are described to begin from *"the river that winds through the entire land of "Cush"*. This is modern day Sudan and Ethiopia, contiguous to Egypt to the north; and the Red Sea to the East. This means the Garden of Eden began and included the Mt. Sinai Peninsula, and from there extended north and eastward to the river of Euphrates in Iraq. (Genesis 2:10-14).

The promise to restore Eden
Genesis 15:18-20 describes the boundaries of the *Promised Land.* Here we also find the everlasting Abrahamic Covenant where God declared His land grant to father Abraham, and secured it *forever, through Isaac.* (Genesis17). The boundaries are described to begin *"From the river of Egypt extending to the river of Euphrates."*

While scholars debate about the location of the river of Egypt, let's not overlook "the forest for the trees", and look at the obvious. When we look at Cush (Ethiopia) on the map, which is located below Egypt, and mentioned in the Garden of Eden in Genesis 2, and then follow the map N/E to the Euphrates in Iraq, the answer is simple.

**"The boundaries of the Promised Land,
are no other than the boundaries of the Garden of Eden.
WHY?
"The guarantee of the Promised Land
to Abraham, Isaac, and Jacob FOREVER,
is God's will and commitment to oppose Satan,
and restore Eden FOREVER!"**

The center of the nations

The Garden of Eden, Mt. Sinai, and Mt. Zion are referred to as sanctuaries, places of refuge for God's people established by Him.

1.) It was in the Garden of Eden that God placed Adam and Eve.
2.) Mt. Sinai was the place of refuge for Moses.
3.) Mt Zion (Jerusalem) is the place of refuge for all of God's people.

When you draw an equilateral triangle between these three refuge locations, the points intersect exactly at 32° East by 32° North, - *the center* *of the landmass of the earth.*

Within the Garden of Eden the focus is on the *"center."* Why? Because in the *"middle"* of the Garden was the Tree of Life, and the Tree of Knowledge of Good and Evil." (Genesis 2: 9). The Question remains: "Where was the *"middle"* of the Garden of Eden?

A look at the book of Jubilees 8:10-12

*"And there came out of the lot for Shem the **middle of the earth**, which he and his children should have as an inheritance for the generations **unto eternity**........* Therefore, Shem was given the Garden of Eden. From Shem came the Semites.

The prophet Ezekiel

God even identifies the center more clearly. The prophet Ezekiel states: *"This is what the LORD says: This is **JERUSALEM,** which I have set in the "center" of the nations, with countries all around her"*. (Ezekiel 5: 5).

A look at the Midrash, an ancient commentary to train rabbis

"As the **navel** is set in the **center** of the human body
so is the land of Israel the **navel** of the world,
situated in the **center** of the world,
and Jerusalem in the **center** of the land of Israel,
and the sanctuary in the **center** of Jerusalem,
and the holy place in the **center** of the sanctuary,
and the ark in the **center** of the holy place,
and the foundation stone before the holy place,
because from it the world was founded."
Midrash Tanchuma, Qedoshim.

Compare Eden and the Promised Land
Angels guard the way

When Adam and Eve were cast out of Eden, God stationed at the *east* of Eden an angel to guard the way to the Tree of Life. (Genesis 3: 24). When Jacob returned *from* the *east* he was met by angels of God (Gen.32: 1-2), and finally had to wrestle with an angel in order to *re-enter* the Promised Land (32:22-32). Joshua encountered angels as he entered the Promised Land. (Joshua 5:13-15) The entrance of the Tabernacle was on the *east*, the only way to return to God. The entrance to the Holy of Holies was draped with a curtain embroidered with angels that beheld the Ark, guarded by an angel on either end. (Ex 37:8-9)

**Therefore, the Exit of Eden,
and the entrance of the Promised Land
are marked with angels, to show that
"To enter the Promised Land is to return to Eden."**

Formless and empty (void)

The description of the *"Promised Land"* after it had been judged on account of Israel's sin parallels the description of *"the earth"* before it was prepared for Adam and Eve. We find the term *"formless and empty."*

Before creation (Genesis 1:1)

*"In the beginning God, created the heavens and the earth. Now the earth was **formless and empty**, darkness was over the surface of the deep, and the Spirit of God was hovering over the waters"*

After Israel's judgment (Jeremiah 4: 23-26)

*"I looked at the earth and it was **"formless and empty;"** and at the heavens, and their light was gone. I looked at the mountains and they were quaking; all the hills were swaying. I looked and there were no people; every bird in the sky had flown away. I looked, and the fruitful land was a desert; all it's town lay in ruins before the LORD, before his fierce anger. This is what the LORD says: "The whole LAND will be ruined, though I will not destroy it completely. Therefore, the earth will mourn and the heavens above grow dark, because I have spoken and will not relent, I have decided and will not turn back."*

God is showing us that His judgment upon Israel because of her sin put the "Promised Land" back into the state it was before it had been blessed for them, just as there were no humans to bless yet in Genesis. The expulsion of Israel from the Promised Land is a reversal of the preparation of the land for Adam and Eve.

He walks with me and He talks with me
Garden of Eden

It is there where *God walked with man* in the cool of the day. (Genesis 1: 28; 3: 8) Satan opposed this relationship, and man was driven from the Garden as a result of sin.

Wilderness wanderings

God intervened! He not only chose and preserved the Savior's lineage, but walked with the Israelites. The glory of God was with them guiding them by day with a cloud and by night with a pillar of fire, and furthermore protected them from Pharaoh and his armies who sought their destruction. God was with Moses and the Israelites in the *tent of meeting*. He took up residence in the *Tabernacle* which they carried with them wherever they went ((Exodus 13:21-22; 14:19-24; 33; 40).

First coming

Just as God walked with man in Eden, God in Christ walked with man in the Promised Land (Paradise). He declared the will of His Father to restore man not only unto Him, but also confirmed His promise to restore mans inheritance, the earth.

"I am the way, the truth and the life, no man comes to the Father but by me". John 14: 6

"Blessed are the poor in Spirit for theirs is the kingdom of heaven." Matthew 5:3

"Blessed, are the meek, for they shall inherit the earth." (Land) Matthew 5:5

The church age
God walks, talks, and lives within the believer.

As a nation, Israel rejected her Messiah, so God established "Spiritual Israel", His church, made up of Jew and Gentile. Just as God was with Israel during her wilderness wanderings, and personally dwelled within the Tabernacle, He now dwells within every believer because we are the Temple of the living God through the indwelling of His Holy Spirit. It is His desire to walk with us through all our troubles. For those who repent and believe in Him, He said: *"Never will I leave you, never will I forsake you. Therefore I will say with confidence 'The LORD is my helper, I will not be afraid. What can man do to me"?* He also said: *"I am with you always, to the very end of the age."* (Hebrews 13: 5, 1 Corinthians 3:16-17; 6:19- 20; Matthew 28: 20).

Satan opposes and intervenes

Only a **remnant** of *Israel and the world* believe that Jesus is the Messiah. Why? Why are there so many people that reject Jesus Christ? Why reject pure love? When are we going to realize that Satan is pure hate, a deceiver, and he does everything he can to blind as many people as possible? He does not want any heirs to live with God because he was thrown out of heaven. In addition, he doesn't want any heirs of the earth either, because he didn't receive it to rule over.

Many think Satan is in hell. That would actually be nice, because then we would have peace on earth. One day hell will be his eternal inheritance. But the fact is, right now he is here, making hell on earth. While God is in ultimate control, Satan knows he is only a temporary "squatter" on earth, with no "squatter's rights", and certainly no "leg to stand on". Until Jesus comes to remove Satan's dominion over the earth, and then He (Jesus) rules the earth with justice and righteousness, and renews heaven and earth, believers have been given authority to step on the old snake, in Jesus' name.

Israel, God's prophetic time clock

The church must understand that her ultimate plan is tied to Israel. Since Israel as nation did not exist for 2000 years, it is revealing to discover that Israel is surrounded **today** by **22 hostile Islamic nations**, which are her **old enemies** seeking her destruction. Look for the tiny one! It is a modern day example of David and Goliath. Israel is right in the *"middle."*

MAPS DON'T LIE!

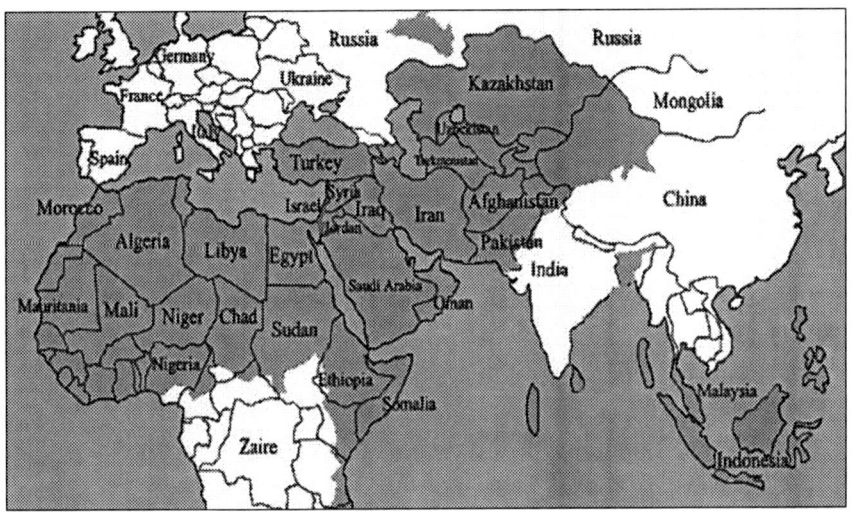

Satan never changes, he only uses different names. Israel's enemies are like him, they only change names as well. When we examine the nations mentioned in scripture which were vile persecutors of Israel in the Old Testament, then examine the nations mentioned that are doomed to destruction at the end of the age, a clear picture emerges. *They are the same!* However, these very nations were all conquered by Islam in the Seventh and Eighth centuries, thus are all Islamic nations today. Here is a list of scripture references I found. (Not complete by far I'm sure.)

The story is true the names have changed to protect the guilty.

AMMAN (JORDAN)
   Ammon, Moab (Isaiah 15; Jeremiah 25:2; Zephaniah 2:9))

ARABIA (SAUDI –ARABIA). Kedar son of Ishmael (Isaiah 21:13-17)
   Also know as Edom / Idumea / land of Seir Arabia, birthplace of Islam.

Composite judgment against all Arab nations (Ezekiel 29-32; 34; 35; 36; Jeremiah.25: 21)

EGYPT
(Isaiah 19-20; Ezekiel 25-32; Jeremiah 25:19.)

IRAN,
Persia (Ezekiel 27:10.)

IRAQ
Assyria / Babylon (Isaiah 14: 24-32, Jeremiah 50 and 51, Isaiah 14: 15-27; 21.)

LEBANON
Sidon and Tyre (Jer.25: 22; Isaiah 23; Ezek.27-28; Joel 3.)

LYBIA
Put, North Africa. (Ezekiel 30:5.)

PALESTINE
Philistia / Philistines. (By name, not by race; Joel 3:4; Ezekiel 25:15-17).

Southern RUSSIA, N/E EUROPE
Gog and Magog, (invades Israel Ezekiel 38).
(Rise of Islam within them today)

SUDAN (ETHIOPA)
Cush, (Isaiah 18; 19; Ezekiel 30:5).
Sudan is an ancient Christian nation, but Muslim conquerors are causing a modern day Christian Holocaust.

SYRIA
Damascus capitol city in Syria (Isaiah 17)

TURKEY
Lydia, Asia Minor (Ezekiel 27:10)

The last 2000 years have produced other vile haters of Israel during her dispersion. Now that Israel is once again a nation, the ancient and everlasting hatred is back! Those nations who now seek Israel's destruction, are comprised of enemy nations *"surrounding Israel."* The problem for Islam and Arab nations is clear; it is not the size of Israel but her mere existence. Since the United Nations voted to partition Palestine in 1948 providing Holocaust survivors a homeland after WWII, the Arab-Israeli conflict was a potential "powder keg". After Israel declared herself a nation on May 14, 1948, she was invaded in less than 24 hours by the armies of six hostile Arab nations. They were *Trans-Jordan (later Jordan), Egypt, Lebanon, Syria, Iraq, and Saudi Arabia.* In addition, local *Arab Palestinian forces* also fought the Israelis. Interestingly, they are the very nations mentioned in **Psalm 83**

"O God, do not be silent; Be not quiet; O God, Be not still. See how your enemies are astir,

How your foes rear their heads. With cunning they conspire against your people; they plot against those you cherish. **"Come", they say, let us destroy them as a nation, that the name of Israel be remembered no more.** *With one mind they plot together. They form an alliance against you-The tents of* **Moab** *and* **Hagrites, Gebal, Ammon and Amalek, Philistia** *with the people of* **Tyre,** *even* **Assyria** *has joined them to lend strength to the descendants of Lot."*

Who are they?
Moab is Jordan.
Hagrites are descendants of Hagar, thus Egypt.
Gebal is located 25 miles north of Lebanon near Syria.
Ammon is Amman and Jordan.
Amalek came from the land of Seir which is Jordan / and today's Saudi Arabia.
Philistia in Latin is Palestine, the Palestinians.
Tyre is Lebanon.
Assyria is located in today's Iraq.

The world blinded

While the world, in its blind stupor, assumes that peace will result in the Middle East once Palestinians have their own state could not be farther from the truth. They seem to ignore that the Palestinians were offered a state in 1948 by the United Nations, and **refused** it. Within less than 24 hours, they clearly gave their answer by attacking Israel seeking her destruction.

The modern nation of Jordan is already a Palestinian State.

In August of 2000, 97% of the West Bank of ancient Judea and Samaria was offered to Yasser Arafat and it was refused.

We must realize that to Palestinian leaders like the late Arafat and now Abbas, and all the Arab nations, the only solution for peace was and is "The Final solution", by driving the Jews into the Mediterranean Sea. When Hamas was elected into leadership, the answer was loud and clear. The Arabs want it all! They cannot and will not accept a Jewish state in a Muslim world.

It seems western minds do not understand that to Islam, Allah is the owner of the earth, and once land was conquered by Muslims (even if lost in war); it is considered to be Allah's property and Muslim land *"forever."* If there is peace for any period of time, it is only to gain time until they have the power to attack again.

One should wonder why international rules of war do not apply to Israel. She has won every war, yet is expected and pressured to return land. How about the USA giving up one of our States, in hopes that fundamental Islamic terrorist regimes will leave us alone? We all know "hell would freeze over first". Yet the world, including the USA, expects Israel to continue in an insane "land for peace" process, while her enemies are not partners for peace but vow her destruction.

Dividing the Promised Land

Today the plan is to divide Israel right down the *"middle."* This would be a prescription for Israel's suicide and the Arabs know it. However, anyone involved in this process will find themselves in the "hands of an angry God".

(Joel 3:2) *"There I will enter into judgment against them concerning my inheritance, my people Israel, for they scattered my people and divided my land!"*

My Holy Name

God loves Israel with an everlasting love.(Jeremiah 31: 3) He will ultimately do for her what He promised for His Name sake, because His very character, His Holiness, His Word, His Covenants are at stake. If He could ever forsake His promises with Israel, He could indeed forsake the world and His promise made in Eden and to father Abraham.

"Therefore, say to the house of Israel, this is what the sovereign LORD says: It is not for your sake Oh house of Israel, that I am going to do these things, but for the sake of My Holy Name!"
(Ezekiel 36: 22)

CHAPTER 4

What is all this fuss about Jerusalem?

Throughout its' history, Jerusalem has been fought over by armies of the Assyrians, Babylonians, Egyptians, Greeks, Ptolemies, Seleucids, Romans, Byzantines, Persians, Arabs, Seljuk's, Crusaders, Mongols, Mamelukes, Turks, British, and today the Palestinians.

Yerushalayim ,"the city of Peace" has been desired and fought over like no other city. She has been besieged about forty different times and destroyed, (at least partially) on thirty-two different occasions. The rulership of Jerusalem has changed hands some twenty-six times. The prophet Zechariah prophesied that at the end of the age Jerusalem will be the cause of world controversy and the final war which will take place in the valley of Har-Megido, known as Armageddon.

(Zechariah 12: 1-4) *"This is the word of the LORD **concerning Israel!** The LORD who stretches out the heavens, who lays the foundations of the earth, and who forms the Spirit of man within him, declares: "Behold, I will make Jerusalem a cup that sends all the **surrounding peoples** reeling…on that day, when all the nations of the earth are gathered against her, I will make Jerusalem an immovable rock for **all nations!**"*

Man has ignored God's warnings, but a day will come when God will say: "No more!" He has proclaimed His will and it is clear. Any ideology, power, or superpower that will come against God's predetermined future for Jerusalem, will find they have drunk a poisoned cup of wine that will cause them to tremble, reel, stagger and die, as they have placed themselves in the "hands of an angry God". Anyone who dares to attempt to come against Jerusalem will discover they have hit a **ROCK** that will not move and only rupture themselves. The picture is clear. God said: "HANDS OFF! "

The Secular view

Who could desire Jerusalem, besides the Jewish people who had no place to call home? She was desolate for centuries, abused and mismanaged by her enemies. Who would have chosen her in the first place? Jerusalem has none of the qualities of a capitol city. She is not on a major trade route, has no navigable river and no major body of water. She does not even have her own water supply. She has no great strategic military value because of her location. So why should anyone pass by Jerusalem, it was out of the way. Major routes went up and down the coastline of the Mediterranean Sea or along the Jordan Valley. The "King's Highway" ran North and South on the plateau of Jordan. Jerusalem should be unknown, never mind a Capitol city, and definitely not the central issue of world controversy. So what is all this fuss about Jerusalem?

While the secular world is blind to the spiritual battle behind the scenes, their answer is **oil.** Since the oil supply is controlled by Arab nations, a major war between them and Israel is unthinkable. Disruption of world's oil supply could possibly be the cause of worldwide economic chaos. For this reason, the west bows down to the Arab world, whether right or wrong. They debate and debate, but have no answers and lack a lasting solution, because they do not even ask the right questions. They are blind, going in circles in a dark room, looking for light, and there is none without God! The world arrogantly ignores the Scriptures as an ancient, outdated book, but God has declared wisdom from Him for those who humbly believe.

The Temple Mount

Those who have "spiritual" eyes to see, realize that the core of the problem is control of Jerusalem. God made it clear that this very city is "His city", the focal point of prophecy. It was predicted as long as 3,000 years ago that it would be the cause for Armageddon, the final World war of the highest magnitude and disaster.

Jerusalem came under control of Jewish hands, for the first time in 2,500 years, as the result of the **Six Day War of 1967**. While the world was mostly oblivious, the **Oslo Peace Accord** signed on September 15.1993 revealed Jerusalem as the central issue. The treaty was an obvious mockery and façade, for which the late Yasser Arafat even received the Nobel Peace Prize. What an outrage, as this man was a vicious murderer, who talked out of one side of his mouth to the west and out of the other side of his mouth to the east. He actually swore to make this covenant into a curse for Israel.

God established His name in Jerusalem forever!

But why is Jerusalem so important to God? We have already established that Eden and the Promised Land share the same boundaries, that Israel is in the "center of the nations", and furthermore that Jerusalem is in the "center" of Israel. But why?

After the Hebrew wanderings in the wilderness and the establishment of the nation of Israel, God's presence in the Tabernacle found a permanent dwelling place in Jerusalem. King David purchased the threshing floor of Araunah the Jebusite for the Temple and it was built after his death by his son King Solomon and dedicated to the LORD. (2 Samuel 24:16, 1Kings 6-9) Today this is the Temple Mount in Jerusalem.

The glory of God filled the Temple On that day the King consecrated the *"middle part"* of the courtyard, in front of the Temple of the LORD and there offered burnt offerings. ((1 Kings 8:10, 62, 64) The Lord appeared to the King a second time and said:

"I have heard the prayer and plea you have made before me:
I have consecrated this Temple which you have built,
by putting my NAME there FOREVER!
My eyes and my heart will ALWAYS be there"
(1Kings 9:3-4)

The outside entrance of the Temple faced *"east"*. It was known as "The Way", the only way into the Temple. From there, one proceeded westward into another opening, that opening, "The

Truth" led to the Holy place were the priesthood served and offered sacrifices. Beyond the Holy Place was the third opening, "The Life" that led to the **Holy of Holies**, where the very presence of God, the Shekinah Glory dwelled. Only the high priest could enter in the Holy of Holies once a year on behalf of the people offering an innocent animal sacrifice, a substitute for man's sin. (Leviticus, 1 Kings 8, Talmud / Hebrew record)

"East of Eden" means judgment, as God drove Adam and Eve from His presence out of Eden, going *"east"*. Since there is only one way to get inside the Temple, facing *"east"*, God teaches us that man must come back the way He has provided, because *we* cannot approach a Holy God our own way." (Genesis 3:24)

The glory departs from the Temple (Ezekiel 10)

Satan opposed God and His people by numerous attempts to deceive the Israelites. Outside of the faithful, the nation tragically fell away and followed other gods, and practiced the detestable worship and lifestyle of the pagan nations *around* them. Consequently, God judged them for their unfaithfulness and His glory departed from the Temple. The Israelites were taken into exile away from the Promised Land.

First coming of Jesus Christ (John 14:6-7)

In the first century, Jesus, the Son of God said: *"I am the Way, and the Truth and the Life. No one comes to the Father except through me. If you really knew me you would know my Father also. From now on you do know Him, and have seen Him…Anyone who has seen me has seen the Father!"*

The Tree of Life and the Tree of Good and Evil
(John 1:29; Matthew 27:51; Hebrews 7-10)

Jesus, the Lamb of God came and took away the sins of the world when He was crucified on a **tree** in the *"middle"*, in place of sinful mankind. The curtain in the Temple was torn down the *"middle"* to open access between God and man through His blood. Up to that time only the high priest could enter on behalf of man as

God's mediator to go behind the curtain. Through Christ access has been gained by Him for all who believe.

Could it be that the *Tree of Life* in the *middle* in Eden is the very location in Jerusalem where Jesus was crucified? While a *tree* for crucifixion was a cursed *tree,* on that day it became the *tree of life* where the blood of our Savior was spilled for all of mankind. All who would repent and look to Him would be given the promise of the Spirit.

(Galatians 3:12-14)

> *"All who rely on observing the Law are under a curse, for it is written: Cursed is everyone who does not continue to do everything written in the book of the law. Clearly no one is justified before God by the Law, because "The righteous shall live by faith.' The Law is based on faith; contrary The man who does these things will live by them. Christ redeemed us from the curse of the law by becoming a curse for us, for it is written: Cursed is everyone who is hung on a tree. He redeemed us in order that the blessing given to Abraham might come to the gentiles through Christ Jesus, so that by faith we might receive the promise of the Spirit."*

Was He not crucified between two thieves, one on His *left* and the other on His *right*, thus in the *middle*? Could it be that the *"Tree of the Knowledge of Evil"* was represented by the sinner on his *left* who did not repent, mocking God even in the face of death and judgment? As he was hanging on the cross with all his nakedness unwilling to humble himself to beg God for a covering, the other thief was quite different. Could it be that the *"Tree of the Knowledge of Good"* was represented by the sinner on His *right* who pleaded to be remembered, who knew he was naked, recognized his sinfulness, and repented looking to Jesus the Lamb of God to cover him, to the only one who is "good." Jesus never hesitated and said *"Today you shall be with me in Paradise."* (Luke 23: 26-49)

Jesus never asked him to show his church membership, whether he was baptized, how much money he gave, He never asked him anything. All the thief knew was that Jesus Christ, even in the midst of His brutal suffering, cared more about others than Himself. When he heard Jesus cry out *"Father forgive them, they do not know what they do"*, it changed the thief's heart, because he saw pure love hanging on the tree. (Luke 23: 32-34)

Had the thief lived, he would have been baptized to identify with His LORD. His loving and changed heart would have served the LORD, given to His cause, worshipped with His people, and helped the poor. Just like an olive tree, you have to be part of the tree before you produce fruit. You have to be grafted in. Why would Christians ever expect non- believers to live like them and have their values? What they need to hear from us is pure words of love extended to them in the midst of dying to ourselves, carrying our cross through life. Some will respond like the thief on the *left*, others like the thief on the *right*. God knows their heart.

The drastic contrast, therefore ANTI- Christ

Satan was not given the rule of the earth and thrown out of heaven for his arrogance and pride. He was unwilling to serve God in heaven and man on earth. He is therefore on a satanic quest to rule from both. There are various high and sacred places on earth where pagan gods were worshipped. They were the ancient forms of Satanism, establishing demonic rule on earth. But Satan ultimately desires to rule from "The Temple Mount in Jerusalem where the true and living God has chosen for His NAME alone."

Isaiah 14:12-14

> *"You said in your heart: I will ascend to **heaven**;*
> *I will raise my throne above the stars of God;*
> *I will sit enthroned on the **mount of the assembly,***
> *on the **utmost heights of the sacred mountain.(earth)***
> *I will ascend above the clouds;*
> *I will make myself like the most high."*

Anti-Christ will enter the Temple

Before the glorious return of our Lord, the anti Christ will walk in the Promised Land and enter the Holy Place within the Temple in Jerusalem, announcing His satanic rule. The Old Testament calls it the "Time of Jacob's (Israel) trouble." (Jeremiah 30: 7; Daniel 9: 25)

Prophecy given by Jesus Christ (Matthew 24:15-22)

*"So when you see standing in the **Holy place**, the abomination that causes the desolation (of the Temple) spoken through the prophet Daniel, let the reader understand, then let those in Judea flee to the mountains. Let no one on the roof of his house go down to take anything out of the house. Let no one in the field go back to get his cloak. How dreadful it will be in those days for pregnant women, and nursing mothers. Pray that your flight will not be in winter or on a Sabbath. For then there will be great Tribulation, unequaled from the beginning of the world until now and never to be equaled again. If those days were not cut short, no one would survive, but for the sake of the elect those days will be shortened."*

God's heart is always there

Jesus is coming back to Jerusalem because He is the rightful heir to the throne of King David, to restore all that was lost in Eden. Since Eden is the Promised Land, (Genesis 2: 10-14, 15: 18-21), and Jerusalem is the center of the earth (Ezekiel 5:5), and God placed the Tree of Life in the Middle of Eden (Genesis 2:9), this means that Jerusalem is <u>where:</u>

God placed the Tree of Life and the Tree of Good and Evil.

God placed Adam and Eve and blessed them.

Man was deceived by the snake (Satan), sinned and lost our inheritance.

Mankind was promised redemption.

Abraham offered his son, but God provided the ram. (male sheep)

God established the sacrificial system.

Jesus was nailed on the tree, but rose again in victory over sin and death.

Anti-Christ will enter and announce the Great Tribulation.

Jesus Christ will return to give him his final blow and crush his head.

Satan's dominion of the earth will end.

Jesus Christ will rule as KING and LORD.

Christ will make Israel a great nation and Jerusalem the praise of the earth.

Christ will restore man's inheritance.

We will rule with Christ forever.

God brings down the New Jerusalem on the new earth

Let it be ever so clear to us, that if God could indeed forget His Covenant promises to Israel and permit her destruction, all would be lost. No wonder Paul said *"GOD FORBID!"* (Romans 11)

A Kingdom needs a King

It is God's will to restore His people and nation. He has permitted Israel's re-establishment and the return of her people for His divine purposes. But let us never forget that God has declared Israel a Kingdom, not a democracy. Therefore, as long as the modern state of Israel is unwilling to cry out to her God and King, repent of her sin and receive her Messiah; and as long as she continues to be willing to make peace with a people who are not supposed to be dwelling in the land which God gave to the children of Israel; and as long as those people are allowed to continue their worship to a foreign god on the Temple Mount in Jerusalem, where the House of God is supposed to exist, Jerusalem will continue to be: *"the great city, which spiritually is called Sodom and Egypt, where also our Lord was crucified."* (Revelation 11:8)

Therefore she will suffer once more until Israel as a nation cries out to her God and King.

He will hear, He always has.

His NAME will always be there.

*"Son of man, this is the place of **My Throne** and the place for the soles of my feet.
This is where I will live amongst the Israelites forever'.
(Ezekiel 43:7)*

CHAPTER 5

Who rules from the Temple mount?

The true heir

The Lord Jesus Christ is not an imposter, nor one who usurps the true and living God, but His SON, the heir to the throne of God, because He is the only begotten Son of God. He is not only the heir of *heaven* to sit on the throne in *heaven,* but the lion of the tribe of Judah with the proper credentials, the required bloodline of one to be King of Israel, to sit on the throne of King David on **earth.**

Israel's exalted and future glory (Isaiah 2:1-5)

>   *This is what the son of Amoz saw concerning Judah and Jerusalem.*
>   *"In the last days the mountain of the LORD'S Temple will be established as chief among the mountains; it will be raised up above the hills, and all nations will stream to it. Many peoples will come and say, 'Come and let us go up to the mountain of the LORD, to the house of Jacob (Israel). He will teach us His ways, so that we might walk in His paths. The law will go out from Zion, the word of the LORD from Jerusalem. He will judge between the NATIONS (Gentiles), and will settle disputes for many peoples. They will beat their swords into plowshares and their spears into pruning hooks.*

Nation will not take up sword against nation, nor will they train for war anymore. Come, O house of Jacob (Israel), let us walk in the light of the LORD!"

FIRST the record of the counterfeits (abominations)

It sounds strange to western ears, but the words of Christ "The abomination that causes desolation" coupled with "let the reader understand" (Matthew 24:15-21), would raise the eyebrow of any educated religious Jew, as throughout their history abominations dared to enter the Holy Temple. It was typical, ancient and eastern warfare for a Gentile leader and his armies to go to war and conquer under the ensign of their pagan gods. The victor would place his idol in the Temple, declaring his god is god of all, demanding submission to him or die. Persecution followed for those who refused to submit. Many stood firm, were martyred, brutally tortured, woman raped and others taken as slaves. Others escaped.

Types of Anti-Messiah's (Christ's)

Nebuchadnezzar: The prophet Isaiah 14:12-23 speaks of the pride and ambition of Nebuchadnezzar to usurp Gods authority as he declared his rule from Jerusalem. He was a *type* of the image and character of Satan, an abomination that caused the desolation of the Holy Temple dedicated to the God of Abraham, Isaac and Jacob alone. The destruction of the *first* Temple occurred in **586 BC.** The city, as well as the Temple was completely leveled and the articles of the Temple and its treasures were carried off to Babylon. The inhabitants not killed were taken to Babylon into exile. Jerusalem was to lie desolate for seventy years in order that the land might enjoy its Sabbaths. (2 Chronicles 36:17-21, Leviticus 26:34) A small number returned fifty years later.

Persian Empire: In 537 BC, Cyrus the Great King of Persia conquered Babylonia. Haman wanted to destroy the Israelites. God through Queen Esther, a Jewess, saved His people.

The Second Temple: Cyrus permitted the Jews to return to Jerusalem and *rebuild their Second Temple.* (Ezra1:1-4). A total of 42,360 people returned to Jerusalem and Judah to help rebuild, not including male and female servants and the singers. All gave according to their ability, in order to finance the work. It was finally completed in 516 BC/BCE on the third day of Adar, a total of twenty-three years. Seventy-one years later (445 BC/BCE) Nehemiah heard of the condition of Jerusalem, and asked the king to allow him to return to rebuild the city. The account of the rebuilding, along with details regarding the opposition to the work, is given in the book of Nehemiah.

Another abomination causes the desolation of the Temple
In 336 BC, Darius the III took the throne of Medo Persia. Alexander the Great, a brilliant commander, defeated Persia within 3 years, in 332 BC. He conquered from Europe, to Egypt, to the borders of India. He died at age thirty-three leaving no heirs. The Empire was divided amongst four of his generals. One of the generals was the Greek King Antiochus III, a cruel, harsh, and savage tyrant, who ruled over the north east portion of the Greek Empire. He conquered Judea making it a tributary to Syria. For 150 years he warred against Ptolemies to the south in Egypt attempting to increase his domain.

168 BC Unable to gain ground, and stopped by the uprising Roman Empire, Antiochus, in fury returned to Syria. On his way back he unleashed his wrath on Israel, forbidding worship to the God of Abraham, Isaac and Jacob. He exemplified the image and character of Satan, as he entered the Temple and desecrated it by declaring himself to be *"god in the flesh"*, thus his name Antiochus "Epiphane", meaning *"god appearing."* He was an abomination that caused the desolation of the Temple, sacrificed a pig in the temple, a sacred animal to the Greeks, but an unclean animal forbidden by the law of Israel. He placed his image on the idol of the pagan god Zeus (Baal in Hebrew), the supreme god of the Greeks, forcing Jews to bow down to him. It was," partake of the meat sacrificed to the idol, or die". Many committed apostasy (fell away from the faith), others kept the faith and were martyred. A remnant escaped to the Judean hills. Antiochus Epiphane was a *type* of anti-Christ and the Great Tribulation pointing to the end of the age. (Matthew 24:15- 22) The Maccabees revolted, regained control over Jerusalem in 165 BC, and re-dedicated the Temple on Kislev / December 25th to the true and living God. The Jewish holiday of Hanukkah commemorates this historic event. The Maccabean or Hasmonean Dynasty ruled until Rome took the city in 63 BC.

Prophecy: The account of Antiochus is prophesied in scripture in Daniel 11. As Daniel concludes his predictions about Antiochus, he now proceeds to prophecy concerning the future.

> (Daniel 11: 36-39) *"The King will do as he pleases. He will exalt himself and magnify himself above every god and will say unheard-of things against the God of gods. He will be successful until the time of wrath is completed, for what has been determined must take place.*
>
> *He will show no regard for the gods of his father of for the one desired by women, nor will he regard any god, but will exalt himself above them all. Instead of them, he will honor a <u>god of fortresses (war,</u> a god unknown to his fathers he will honor with gold and silver, with precious stones and costly gifts. He will attack the mightiest fortresses with help of a foreign god and will greatly honor those who acknowledge him. He will make them rulers over many people and will distribute the land (Promised Land), at a price."*

NOTE: The historical account of Antiochus Epiphane is recorded in the Apocryphal Book of Maccabees. The writings of the Apocrypha are not contained in our Protestant Bibles, as their divine inspiration is contested, although they were translated and included in the original King James Bible of 1611 and are still contained in the Roman Catholic Bible today. All disagreements aside, the Apocrypha is a crucial historical record and has always been an important document to Hebrews, as it contains vital and indispensable information, relating to Israel pertaining to the 400 years between the Old and the New Testament that should never be ignored by any student of Scripture and Israel's history.

The Roman Empire
The Second Temple enlarged by King Herod.

The Romans set up a local dynasty, the house of Herod, to rule most of Israel. Herod the Great (40-4 BC) rebuilt, and extended the smaller second Temple to gain favor, knowing he was despised by religious Jews. Herod did not have an ancestral, legal right to the throne of King David, but was a mere Roman puppet. His father was an Edomite a convert to Judaism. Roman governors retained ultimate control, one of them being Pontius Pilate. (**Note:** Some refer to three temples, but is more correctly understood that the second Temple was enlarged)

First Coming of Jesus Christ

In the first century Jesus Christ prophesied in Matthew 24:15-22 and warns His people to watch for the coming abomination that causes the desolation of the Temple. He said: *"So when you see the abomination that causes desolation spoken of through the prophet Daniel, let the reader understand then let those in Judea flee to the mountains. Let no one on the roof of his house go down to take anything out of the house. Let no one in the field go back to get his cloak. How dreadful it will be in those days for pregnant women and nursing mothers. Pray that your flight will not take place in winter or, on a Sabbath. For then there will be GREAT TRIBULATION (distress), unequaled from the beginning of the world until now—and never to be again. If those days were not cut short, no flesh would survive, but for the sake of the elect those days will be shortened."*

Jesus Christ was offered up as a sacrifice to fulfill the law and a sacrificial system that all believing mankind would be justified before the Father. He had wept over the city, knowing the nation would reject Him and what would befall her, even though His death was only days away.

The Church is born in Jerusalem (Book of Acts)

Jerusalem was used as a base of operations. From there the apostles worked; returning to report what they had accomplished in their travels. Historians estimate that approximately one million Jews became Christians, followers of the Messiah of Israel by the end of the century. Their persecution resulted in the witness to all of Judea and Samaria, and even to the ends of the earth, as was prophesied by the Messiah. (Acts 1:8, James 1:1)

Destruction of Second Temple

The Romans under the leadership of Titus destroyed the Temple in AD 70. In AD 135 after the failure of the Bar Kochba revolt, the surviving Jews were banished from Jerusalem. *In AD 136, Hadrian of Rome renamed Israel, Palestine, the Latin name for Philistines and Israel's arch enemy, in an effort to erase Israel's name forever. Jerusalem was named "Alea Capitolina" which did not stick.*

Rome builds an abomination, a Temple to Jupiter

On the exact spot of the Temple Mount in Jerusalem, to be solely dedicated to the God of Abraham, Isaac and Jacob, Rome dared to build a temple to Jupiter, the supreme deity of Rome, their pagan god of creation. (He is Baal in Hebrew; Baalzebub /Beelzebub in Ekron; Zeus in Greek. Jesus called him Satan. Matthew 12)

The "Holy" Roman Empire

In the fourth Century, Christianity under Emperor Constantine united with Rome. As Jerusalem developed as a center of Christian pilgrimage, many churches were built, to commemorate the life of Jesus in various places. Except for a brief period of Persian rule, the city remained under Roman control. The tragic history of Christendom records the persecution of Jews by the Roman church from the 4th century to the 19th century. (More about this later)

Islam/ Mohammed

Yathrib was a town founded by Jews. Mohammed had convinced a large group of number of them that he was the promised Messiah. They prepared the way for him, and he entered Yathrib like a king. http://www.hermetic.com/sabazius/mohammed.htm

Another abomination is built to Allah

The Roman Temple to Jupiter was destroyed. From AD 688-691, the Dome of the Rock was built on the Temple Mount and was

dedicated to Allah. The inside inscriptions says *"God has no Son."*
http://www.bibleplaces.com/domeofrock.htm

The Crusaders
European Christendom responded by launching the Crusades and conquered Jerusalem in AD 1099 and established a Crusader state.

Muslims
Saladin recaptured Jerusalem for the Muslims in AD 1187, and the Ayyubid and Mameluke dynasties ruled until AD 1517, when the Ottoman Empire took control.

The British Empire
With the Balfour declaration of 1917, the British Empire promised a homeland to the Jewish people. Many had already begun to return and Jerusalem became the capital mandated as Palestine from 1923 until 1948. Under Arab opposition, Britain limited Jewish immigration with the issue of the White Paper, and handed the matter over to the League of Nations. (fore-runner of the United Nations.)

WWII 1939-1945
Nazi Germany declared the extermination of the Jews supported by Arabs, resulting with Nazi invasions throughout numerous European nations. The USA entered into WWII after the Japanese attack on Pearl Harbor in December 7, 1941. She along with her allies of Britain and France ended the war. Britain fell from its glory, an empire of whom it was said "The sun never sets."

May 14, 1948
The United Nations voted to partition Palestine. After almost 2000 years of dispersion, Israel was raised out of the ashes of the Holocaust. The 1948 United Nations partition plan for Palestine called for internationalization of Jerusalem. The Arabs rejected this resolution, and attacked the newborn state in less than 24 hours. From 1949 Jerusalem was divided into an Israeli and a Jordanian sector.

1967 Control of Jerusalem
Until her Muslim neighbors attacked Jerusalem, it remained divided until 1967. Israel took the entire city following the Six Day War. The city was reunited which guarantees religious freedom and protection of all holy places.

Temple Mount surrendered
Under pressure from Arab nations, the Temple Mount on which the Muslim mosque stands was surrendered to the Arabs by the Knesset (Israeli parliament) in order to avoid WWIII and the destruction of Israel. To this day not a single nation has placed their embassy in Jerusalem, but rather in Tel Aviv, thus refusing Israel's right to Jerusalem as her eternal capitol city, or should we say, **won't** recognize Jerusalem as Israel's capitol city, fearing Arab retaliation..

TODAY
"Wars and rumors of war" continue. The issue is clearly deeper than oil, namely a spiritual one. At the core is control over Jerusalem and the Temple Mount. We need to seek God's guidance and pray for the peace of Jerusalem.

" PRAY for the peace of JERUSALEM,
may all who love thee prosper!"
(Psalm 122:6)

CHAPTER 6

The mind of Christ

In contrast to the world, scripture tells us that our minds should be like the mind of Christ. He who was on high came down to serve God and man. In other words, think like Him, because how we think is crucial, as it produces attitudes, and attitudes produce actions, always.

(Philippians 2: 5-11)

> *"Your attitude should be the same as that of Christ Jesus: Who, being in very nature God, did not consider equality with God something to be grasped, but made Himself nothing, taking the very nature of a servant, being found in human likeness. And being found in appearance as a man, He humbled Himself and became obedient to death even unto death on a cross."*

One of the teachers of the law asked Jesus: *"Of all of the commandments, which is most important? The most important one, answered Jesus, is this: "Hear oh Israel, the LORD our God, the LORD is one. Love the Lord your God with all of your heart and with all of your soul, and all of your mind and all of your strength. The second is this: "Love your neighbor as yourself. There is no commandment greater than these!"* (Mark 12:28-31, Deuteronomy 6:5)

A little lower than the angels
Lucifer was the *first* created angel, who refused to *serve* man which was created *last*. But He who was the Word, who was with God, who was God, who was and is the **FIRST**, was willing to become **LAST**. He was made even lower than the angels by becoming human to serve His Father and man even unto death on a cross. Amazing! (John 1: 1-14)
In Hebrews 2:5-18 we read:

> *"It is not to angels He has subjected the world to come, about which we are speaking.*
> *But there is a place where someone has testified: What is man that you are mindful of him?*
> *You made him a little lower than angles: You crowned Him with glory and honor and put everything under His feet. In putting everything under Him, God left nothing that is not subject to Him. Yet at present we do not see everything subject to Him. But we see Jesus, who was made a little lower than the angels, now crowned with Glory and Honor because He suffered death,*
> *so that by the Grace of God He might taste death for everyone. In bringing many sons to glory, it was fitting that God, for whom and through whom everything exists, should make the author of their salvation perfect through suffering. Both the one who makes them Holy and those who are being made Holy are of the same family. So Jesus is not ashamed to call them brothers. He says, I will declare your name to my congregation; I will sing your praises.*
>
> *And again He says, "Here I am, and the children God has given me." Since the children have flesh and blood, He too shared in their humanity so that by His death He might destroy him who holds the power of death- that is, the devil and free those who all their lives were held in slavery by fear of death. For surely it is "not angels" He helps but Abraham's descendants. For this reason he had to be made like His brothers in every way, in order that He might become*

a merciful and faithful high priest in service to God, and that He might make atonement for the sins of the people. Because He Himself suffered when He was tempted, he is able to help those who are being tempted."

Lucifer cursed, but Jesus exalted

Lucifer was unwilling to humble himself and serve man below him, but our Lord, came to serve and emptied Himself of His right to be *first,* and even became *last* by dying on a cross, so that we might be saved. He was highly exalted.

Philippians 2: 9-11: *"Therefore, God exalted Him to the highest place and gave Him a name that is above every name, That at the name of Jesus every knee should bow, in heaven and on earth and under the earth, And every tongue confess that Jesus Christ is LORD to the Glory of God the Father."*

Consider this! When it comes to serving, it is one thing to serve those in authority or position *above us*. It might even get us somewhere, give us status, makes us look good. But when we are faced serving those *below us,* this truly exposes our true character of either arrogance and pride, exemplifying the mind of Satan, or a heart of love for God and people exemplifying the mind Christ. Therefore Jesus Christ is not only the sinless Son of God who paid for the debt of sin, in whom we must believe for our salvation, but the example of godly leadership and servant-hood. We must learn from Him in order to be His disciples, for no student is above his master.

When you die and stand before the throne of judgment, Jesus will not ask you for your church membership, whether you submitted to the proper mode of baptism, or if you understand all the church doctrine. If that were the case, millions of people who are confused by the unending divisions in churches would never make it. If that were true, then indeed Jesus lied to the thief on the cross. All the thief knew was one simple truth. He simply recognized that all of his life all he had ever thought about was himself, but then he saw the King on the cross. He understood that the man in the middle was his middleman that promised him paradise.

CHAPTER 7

The choosing of the firstborn

Throughout scripture we see God choose leaders that exemplify the mind and attitude of His Son, and reject those who exemplify the mind of Satan. He is looking for those who are *first* yet willing to be *last*.

The Firstborn (Heir)
God established His law through Moses for His people and the nation, Israel. It was crucial for the Father to have an heir worthy and capable to care for the inheritance of Gods' covenant land. The rights and responsibilities of the first-born son included becoming ruler of the household under, and for the father, to be priest of the family should the father die, and be the recipient of a double portion of the father's estate. Elisha's request for a double share of "your spirit" refers to the legal provision that a firstborn son receives a *double portion* of the inheritance (Deut. 21:15-17; 2 Kings 2:9). With the greater blessing, came greater responsibility, one of which was to be a *servant leader* to his father and siblings, not to arrogantly lord over them, but to model godly servant-hood and leadership. Just like shepherds they were to love, protect, serve, even risk their lives to save the family.

First Coming
The last Adam, Jesus Christ!

In scripture Jesus Christ is described as:
The only begotten Son (John 3:16)
The last Adam (1 Cor.15: 45)
The Good shepherd (John 10)
The Firstborn, not first created (Colossians 1: 15-16)

This emphasizes his position as the heir over all of the earth and all of creation, *"for by Him all things were created"*. (Col.1: 15-17) As the Son of the living God, He is to reign for the Father. (Col. 1:15-18, Revelation 5:5) In His humanity He is the first to be born of the new race, the one new man. (Ephesians 2:15) Jesus received all of the rights as the Son. As the last Adam He paid our debt of sin; restored us not only to God but family, as we will see our heavenly Father and the redeemed. (Matthew 5:3) Furthermore, He redeems and restores our inheritance, the earth. (Matthew 5:5) In other words, what was lost as a result of the first Adam is restored by the last Adam, who is the heir of heaven and earth, and His follower's are co-heirs with Him.

So in these few words we discover that Jesus is the Anointed One, the Messiah who is to inherit not only the Promised Land, but all of the earth as the firstborn of the Father. In His humanity and flesh He is King of Israel, and in His divine nature He is heir of all creation. He will rule from Jerusalem as the rightful heir. He was *born* King of the Jews, the lion of the tribe of Judah, the heir to the throne of King David.

Why did God choose Noah? (Genesis 6)

> *"The Lord God saw how great man's wickedness on earth had become, and that every inclination of the thoughts of his heart was only evil all the time. The LORD was grieved that He had made man on the earth, and His heart was filled with pain. So the Lord said: 'I WILL wipe mankind from the earth, men and animals, and creatures that move along the ground, and birds of the air-for I am grieved that I have made them'. But Noah found favor in the eyes of the LORD! "*

Noah was the *firstborn* son of Lamech. (Gen.5: 28) He was a righteous man, blameless (not sinless) in a wicked society, thus by faith stood in opposition to the corruption of his day. (Genesis 6: 9) When God called upon him to build an ark, he believed God's promise and by faith looked forward to God's salvation and provision. He faithfully built the ark in the middle of the desert for 120 years, where people mocked him.

He exemplified the mind of Christ, not the mind of Satan. *He did not say: "I am the firstborn, the heir of my father's estate. I have a birthright here, why should I leave? I am not going to serve you. Why don't you ask my other brothers to build an ark for you, they are BELOW me. Let them serve you and be the scorn and laughing stock of the people. I am the HEIR, I am FIRST!"*

He willingly relinquished his status and position as *firstborn*, and became *last*. As Noah stepped into the ark forsaking what was rightfully his, but placed his hope and faith in God to provide new land, a new inheritance for him and his family, he accepted *second birth, spiritual birth*, thus was born again. God judged those left behind and they perished in the flood. Noah, the humble firstborn became the heir of the new, fresh earth, re-created for him and his children by God.

Why did God choose Abraham? (Genesis 11:26-27)

Terah had 3 sons; Abram, Nahor and Haran. They lived in **Ur**, today's **IRAQ**. The people were part of the pagan moon cult, who worshipped the moon god. Joshua reveals to us the following in Chapter 24." *And Joshua said to all the people, 'Thus says the LORD God of Israel: Your fathers, including Terah, the father of Abraham and the father of Nahor, dwelt on the other side of the river in old times; and* ***they served other gods.'"***

The Proposition (Genesis 12:1)

When Abram was 75 years old God gave him a proposition. He said: *"Leave your country, your people, and your father's household, and go to the land I will show you."*

The Promise (Genesis 12:1-3)

When the true and living God called upon Abram and offered him new land, there was a condition. It meant leave your old gods, leave your country, people and inheritance in order to receive God's inheritance. Abraham believed and left by faith, he did not cling to his inheritance and status as firstborn. He did not reply as Lucifer did. *"Why should I leave? I have a birthright here. Why don't you pick Nahor my second born brother, or Haran the third born, and ask them to serve you? I am FIRST, so forget it! I am the heir!"*

He willingly became last, forsook his inheritance and took the position of a servant. By faith Abraham left what he knew was rightfully his, but by faith, went to the land that God His heavenly Father promised.(Genesis 4) Therefore Abraham exemplified the mind of the Messiah. He is the Patriarch of Judaism and Christianity, the example of true and genuine faith, who willingly humbled himself, and entered second birth. Therefore God honored and exalted him as father of many nations.

Why did God choose Moses? (Exodus)

After the time of Joseph, another Pharaoh came to rule over Egypt who did not know about Joseph. He felt threatened by the blessings and abundance of the Israelites, and their increase in number. He became a harsh taskmaster of Gods' people and furthermore ordered that every newborn Hebrew baby was to be killed. Moses was placed in a basket by his mother and she sent him on his way on the river Nile to save his life. He was rescued, loved and adopted by the Pharaoh's daughter, thus was elevated to status of Prince of Egypt. Moses had observed a brutal taskmaster mistreating a Hebrew slave, intervened, fought and killed him. While some religious folks would judge Moses for being a murderer, they seemingly do not know the difference between good and evil, between a righteous act of defense protecting the helpless, and vicious murder. If your Bible says *"You shall not kill,* - PLEASE erase it - , it should read *"You shall not murder. In Hebrew to kill is "nakah", to murder is "ratsach."*

What was it that God saw? He saw Moses' heart of compassion for people lower than him.

In so doing, Moses became last, lost his inheritance, his status and power. He had to leave his country, adopted people and household. He also left the gods of Egypt, and in turn identified with his Heavenly father and his people, the Hebrews. He left Egypt as a prince and became a shepherd. Through Moses, God delivered His people from Egyptian bondage, parted the Red Sea to provide a way of escape, established His law, and confirmed the Mosaic Covenant in blood. As a result he became the most exalted and honored man in Judaism. It is generally held that the Exodus occurred around 1446 BC. Moses is a type of Jesus Christ that will deliver His people from extermination from the anti-Christ at the end of the age.

Why did God choose Joshua?

Joshua was the leader of the tribe of Ephraim, known as Hosea the sun of Nun. (Numbers 13:8) Although a leader, he was a humble servant and aide to Moses, exalted to be the successor of Moses, the man who saved the Hebrews from their wilderness wandering. (Numbers 27:19) He led them into the Promised Land and destroyed the enemies in the Land. They crossed the Jordan River and by grace through faith walked around the city walls of Jericho seven times, and the wall fell. Joshua destroyed all the enemies within the Land and took possession of it for the Twelve Tribes of Israel.

Jesus, a conqueror like Joshua
First coming

Jesus conquered sin and death on the cross. Through Him all who believe, cross over from sin and death and are given victory over Satan. We, who come to Him in faith, are more than conquerors through Christ Jesus our LORD. (Romans 8:28) Victory is ours through Him who loved us and set us free, as the walls that separated us were torn down. He guaranteed preparation of a place for us, our heavenly Jericho, God's city waiting for His church, whether Jew or Gentile. (Galatians 3:28)

Second coming
The deliverance of the nation of Israel

Joshua was a *type* of Christ pointing to the deliverance of Israel in our Lord's second coming. Today, the *Philistines (Latin / Palestinians renamed by Rome)* are once again the arch enemy of Israel within the Land, supported by Arab nations. They claim rights to the Promised Land seeking Israel's destruction. However, Jesus will destroy all of the enemies who come against Jerusalem, and will gather the remnant of the Hebrew people into the Promised Land, to possess it forever. (Zechariah 14; Isaiah 8:9-10, Rev. 19: 11-21)

The same name:

I wished they would leave peoples names alone, and don't translate and change them to accommodate other languages. Most people don't know that Mary was not Mary, but Miriam, and her husband was not Joseph, but Yakov. In the case of Joshua it is the English translation of the Hebrew name Yoshua / Yeshua. Jesus is the Greek translation of the same Hebrew name.

Both Matthew 1:21 and Luke 1:31 show that the name "Jesus" was chosen for Jesus, because it means *"He will save His people from their sins."* This applies in all three of the languages of the Bible. In *Greek* the word "Jesus" sounds like the word "Savior." In *Hebrew and Aramaic* part of the meaning of the name "Joshua" is the meaning "Savior." Joshua was not his birth name, but Hosea. (Deuteronomy 32:44). Joshua's full name means "YHWH saves." Joshua is actually a combined name. The first part is the name "YHWH", the second part is the name "Hosea" (meaning "Savior"). Because YHWH cannot be written in Greek, "Jesus" is the only name in Greek, which includes the name of "YHWH" Thus, the name "Jesus" was selected not only because it showed the baby was "Hosea" (Savior), it was also selected to show that he was YHWH. Since Hebrews feared taking Gods sacred name in vain they called Him Adonai, the equivalent of LORD.

Why did Jesus choose the 12 disciples?

In order to follow Him in His ministry on earth, this meant the disciples gave up their livelihood and all that was familiar to them in order to become His disciples. While Jesus picked **Twelve**, only **Eleven** were chosen. Judas changed his mind and even betrayed Jesus. Why? I believe he thought Jesus was going to usher in the Messianic Kingdom on earth, looking only for Israel's glory, but when he discovered it meant sacrifice and servant-hood first, he was through. He did not understand that he had to become *last* in order to be *first*. Glory was to follow after sacrifice. He did not understand that being born again meant humbling yourself, repenting of your sin, and becoming a servant to God and man. How about you? While God does not call upon everyone to leave family and land, He does call upon every Christian to die to his or her old self, leaving our old gods and idols to gain the abundant life found in Christ alone. We all must enter second birth to become servants of Christ.

Why did Jesus choose the apostle Paul?

He was a Pharisee, religious ruler, an elite Jew of the tribe of Benjamin. He was born in Tarsus of Cecilia; and educated under Gamaliel, the most honored rabbi of the first century. (Acts 22:3-5) He held Roman citizenship. It is likely that he was a first born son as they were given first right to higher education. He was most certainly a leader. Paul in his religious zeal persecuted his own countrymen who were followers of the Messiah, thinking Him to be a false Messiah, an imposter. He killed and persecuted the early church in the name of God. After his conversion God used Paul's passion and zeal, his background, intelligence, and assertive personality. Mostly, He saw Paul's heart willing to humble himself, as he the Pharisee had to admit he was wrong about his theological position having denied Jesus as Messiah of Israel. In his writings he called himself over and over again "a servant of Jesus Christ". His passionate faith and commitment reached many of his fellow Jewish countrymen, as he traveled from synagogue to synagogue at the expense of severe persecution, from beatings to almost death, loosing his home, family, land and country. He later became the Apostle to the Gentiles. (Acts 8-end)

He declared all of his past status and position rubbish, desiring to know Jesus Christ, His LORD. He was used by the Lord to put in motion a great deal of the Christian Church, and wrote the major portions of the New Testament. He was very bold and defended Christianity before kings and emperors during his three missionary journeys. (Acts 9:15) By the end of his life, he reached much of the Mediterranean world with the Gospel.

> (Philippians 3: 4-11) *"If anyone else has confidence in the flesh, I have more: Circumcised on the eighth day, of the people of Israel, of the tribe of Benjamin, a Hebrew of Hebrews; in regard to the law, a Pharisee; as for zeal persecuting the church; as for legalistic righteousness, faultless. But whatever was to my profit, I now consider loss for the sake of Christ. What is more, I consider everything a loss, compared to the surpassing greatness of knowing Christ Jesus my Lord, for whose sake I have lost all things. I consider them rubbish, that I may gain Christ and be found in Him, not having a righteousness of my own that comes from the law, but that which is through faith in Christ—the righteousness that comes from God is by faith. I want to know Christ and the power of His resurrection and the fellowship of sharing in His sufferings, becoming like Him at his death, and so somehow, to attain to the resurrection from the dead!"*

Jesus Christ called upon Paul, not because of his religious perfection. Paul was a sinner, willing to humble himself, willing to forsake his pride and admit he was wrong in order to gain Christ. Today, many have their focus on doctrines set in stone, unwilling to listen to Jesus Christ, unwilling to admit they are wrong, thus missing out on the simplicity and pure devotion to Christ. (2 Corinthians 11:3). *How about you?*

Why did God choose the early church?
Jesus Christ instituted the New Covenant with Israel in His own blood. (Matt 26:28. Mark 14:24). The early church, like Abraham left mother and father, houses and land. Many even lost their lives for the sake of the Gospel. They are the natural branches of the Church that sprang forth from the root of Israel. (Acts 1-11; Romans11) Jesus prophesied that they would be His witnesses from Jerusalem,

to Judea and Samaria, even to the ends of the earth! They left and lost it all to bring Gentiles (us) the Gospel. (James 1.)

What do you think would have happened if they had said: *"Forget those Gentile dogs, we are going to keep our birthright all to ourselves, we don't want any wild branches on our tree!"*

God chose those who didn't think they were saved just because of their earthly lineage, tracing back to father Abraham, or somehow were guaranteed superior position due to nationality, but rather expressed genuine faith like father Abraham in God's promises. Perfection was not the issue as man is a sinner. The issue that is crucial to God is always the same. Are you humble or able to be humbled, to see your need of a Savior, willing to serve God and man? *How about you?*

How about Christians today?

Is it not true that many Christians think that they are saved just because they are church members, their parents are Christians, or because they are born in a so- called Christian nation? What they need to do is identify with Jesus Christ, and recognize they are sinners in need of a Savior. All of mankind is firstborn in his sin nature. In order to be saved, God requires a spiritual rebirth. (John 3: 3) No matter where God calls us to serve, whether it is in our own homes, villages and towns, neighborhoods, or across the world, we are called upon *to be like Jesus*, by serving God and man. *How about you?* Are you willing to become last in order to be exalted to first place?

CHAPTER 8

The rejection of the firstborn

Under the provision of the law, the inheritance of the firstborn became an expectation, a right, rather than a humbly appreciated gift from the father. All some cared about was the status, prestige and power, but not the sacrifice and the responsibility that came in serving their father, family or land. They often felt superior to their younger siblings, arrogantly proud of being first.

Cain and Abel

While the law of inheritance was not given to Israel until centuries after creation, the principle was given in eternity from Father to Son. Then in Eden, God made Adam the heir as His first-created human in the image of God. The problem of arrogance as we saw in Chapter 2, was started by Lucifer who dared to demand his rights as the heir, rather than humbly recognizing that the owner and father of the land had the right to choose His heir. Besides, angels were not created to inhabit and remain on earth, but stay in heaven. Maybe this will make us understand why fallen angels inhabit people. They are demons seeking to live on earth to gain dominion.

The problem of inheritance continued with Adam and Eve who had two sons, Cain and Abel. God chose the second born Abel, a shepherd boy, rather than Cain, to be the *first,* ultimately pointing to the Good Shepherd, Jesus. Abel was His chosen vessel to establish the Messianic lineage. Cain hated and murdered his second born brother Abel. (Genesis 4) However, God replaced Abel with **Seth** to continue the chosen lineage and cursed Cain, as God's will cannot be thwarted. (Genesis 5:1-3)

Shem, Japheth and Ham

Noah had three sons, Shem, Japheth and Ham. At first glance one would think that Shem was the firstborn, however, scripture clarifies that Japheth was the oldest in Gen.10: 21. Ham is listed as the youngest in Gen.9:24, leaving Shem as the second born. Interestingly, but not surprisingly, the rejected firstborn Japheth was the father of Gomer and Magog (today's Russia). Insight into God's wisdom can be found in history, as through Japheth are traced the Russian people, and from his grandson, Ashkenaz, the Germanic tribes. Historically both have been a warring people seeking to rule and dominate the earth. (Gen.10: 2-3)

From Shem to Eber and Abram

Emphasis is given to Shem's son Arphaxad who was born two years after the flood. (Genesis 10: 21-32) From Arphaxad came his grandson *Eber*, from which we derive the word *Hebrew*. Six generations after Eber came *Abram*. He was the *firstborn* son of Terah, chosen by God. He was 75 years old at the time, when he left by faith to follow God. (Genesis 11:10-32)

Lot and his descendants

Abraham had brought his nephew named Lot, to whom he gave half of his inheritance. Lot himself picked all the land *east* of the Jordan River. Rather than gratefulness, Lot's descendants through an incestuous relationship with his two daughters became vile enemies of Israel as well. *The ancient Moabites and Ammonites are today's Jordan.* Genesis13; 19:30-38.

Lapse of faith (Genesis 16)

After waiting eleven years for an heir to the Promised Land, Abram was 86 years old and his wife Sarai was 77 and barren. She suggested his union with her servant girl Hagar, to produce this longed for heir. Sarai gave Hagar to Abram as his wife, and she conceived, but Hagar began to despise Sarai, causing bitter rivalry between the two women. Hagar gave birth to *Ishmael.*

Covenant confirmed through Isaac (Genesis 17)

At age 99 God confirmed by covenant that Abraham would have a son with his wife Sarai even though she was now 90 years old and still barren. His name was to be *Isaac,* with whom He would establish His Land grant *forever.* (Gen.17: 7-19) Their names were changed from Abram to Abraham, and Sarai to Sarah. Insight can be realized as God produced the Messianic lineage through a woman unable to have children, a miracle birth produced by grace through faith, pointing to the Messiah, versus Ishmael who was produced by human effort, during a lapse of faith.

God remembers Ishmael (Gen. 17: 20)

Since God declared **Isaac** to be the heir of the Promised Land, and his descendants after him, Abraham was concerned for his son **Ishmael**. God assured Abraham, to bless **Ishmael** as well, to be the father of twelve rulers and a great nation.

The Covenant of circumcision (Gen. 17: 23-27)

The Covenant requiring circumcision served as a sign, a visual reminder that God had set Abraham and his descendants apart from the pagan nations. Abraham, Ishmael and all of the servants were circumcised that day. It is interesting to note that Abraham's seed that produced Ishmael passed through father Abraham before his own circumcision, thus produced prior to the Covenant God made with him.

Isaac's Birth (Genesis 21)

When Abraham was 100 years old, **Isaac** was born. In addition to the existing feud between Hagar and Sarah, now bitter rivalry arose between **Ishmael** mocking **Isaac** causing Sarah's anger to declare: *"Ishmael will never share in the inheritance"* (of the Promised Land). In essence this is what God said to the snake in the Garden of Eden, and promised a **seed,** His own heir, to crush Satan's head.

Hagar and Ishmael sent away (Genesis 21: 8-20)

To resolve the irreconcilable differences, Hagar and **Ishmael** were sent away. Even prior to Ishmael's birth the angel of the LORD prophesied to Hagar the following: (Genesis 16:11-12)

*"You are now with child and you will have a son. You shall call him **Ishmael**, for the LORD has heard of your misery. He will be a wild donkey of a man; his hand will be against everyone and everyone's hand against him, and he will live in hostility toward all his brothers".*

The genealogy of **Ishmael** confirms twelve sons. It states: *"And they lived in hostility toward ALL their brothers."* (Gen. 25: 12-18)

The Test (Genesis 22:1-18).

In approximately 2000 BC, God commanded Abraham to offer his uniquely and miraculously born son **Isaac** as a sacrifice. How could it be that He, a Holy God, would require a human sacrifice? How would Abraham ever become the great nation to bless all nations as promised in Genesis 12, with a dead son? Furthermore, how could God promise him to become the father of descendants as numerous as the sand of the seashore, and stars in the sky, with a dead son? By faith Abraham stood firm that His God was a Covenant keeping God and declared: *"God will provide the Lamb!"* He knew God would not kill His Son. What faith! (Gen. 22:8)

Isaac in obedience trusted his Father and lay still upon the altar. The Lord intervened and provided a ram (male sheep) for a sacrifice in the place of Isaac. Abraham called that place of sacrifice; *"The Place Where God Will Be Seen,"* also translated *"Where God will provide."* (Genesis 22: 14) Abraham and his son **Isaac** are a picture or *type* of God the Father who was willing to offer his own Son. Abraham did so approximately 4000 years ago. Then 2000 years after Abraham, God provided the **Lamb of God, Jesus**, on Mount Moriah, the exact place where Abraham offered up **Isaac**. It has been 2000 years since He came.

By this we can see that the Lord had already chosen Jerusalem as the place where He would establish Himself, and reveal Himself the Emmanuel, God with us, pointing to His provision, His only begotten Son who would take away the sins of the world. The sacrificial system established by God through Israel was a *type* or picture to teach Israel that sin was costly and an innocent substitute died in their place. All of this pointed to the "Lamb of God", the perfect sinless Lamb that would take away the sins of Israel, and the whole world. (Matthew 27: 32-37; Mark 15: 21-26; Luke 23: 26-34; John 19:17-19; Gen. 22:8)

The cry of Islam is the cry of Hagar and Ishmael (Gen. 21:8-20)

The everlasting hatred between the Arab nations and the heirs of the Promised Land (Israel) began when Hagar and **Ishmael** were sent away. In their anguish God comforted them, guaranteeing the blessing of their *own inheritance*. God promised **Ishmael** that he would become a great nation as well. In order to receive it, God required the firstborn son **Ishmael** to humble himself, accept second birth, and express faith like his father Abraham. It meant: "Leave your country, your people, your father's household, and go to the land I will show you."

Tragically Ishmael did not accept God's will and express the faith of his father. The cry of Hagar and Ishmael can still be heard in the desert today: I believe it sounds something like this: *"I am the firstborn son! I am the heir to the "Promised Land! I have the birthright! Why did you send me away and not Isaac? Why did I have to leave! I hate you and I hate Isaac! I will destroy him and His descendants from generation to generation!"* His deep wound of rejection turned to anger, and unresolved anger to bitterness, and everlasting hatred. He like Lucifer insisted on being first, unwilling to bow to God. From this moment on earth began what was begun in heaven by Lucifer, demanding the rights to the Garden of Eden. It is the descendants of **Ishmael,** the Arab nations, against the descendants and heirs of Israel, the Promised Land, the Garden of Eden.

Unresolved anger is dangerous, the flipside of unresolved pain. It opens the way for demonic strongholds to enter the wounded soul. It can turn to outright demonic rage. It is not an understatement to say that Islam demanding **"Ishmael is first "** has resulted in over 1.5 billion people controlled by a satanic hatred against Jews and

Christians, and in turn are held in subjection to totalitarian Islamic regimes.

Inside the Muslim mosque, the Dome of the Rock, located on the Temple Mount, is a sign that reads *"This is where Abraham offered up **Ishmael**,"* (rather than Isaac).

Question: Do you think Ishmael would have had the faith to trust his father, to follow him up the mountain and lay down his life, forsaking his birthright? I don't! *This means there would never have been a SAVIOR, no Jesus Christ!*

The cry of God

If only **Islam** could understand that second birth is the position of blessing. Father Abraham did not reject Ishmael, but in faith submitted to the will of God as through Isaac and his son Jacob came the Twelve Tribes of Israel, the Redeemer of Israel and of all mankind. The God of Abraham, Isaac and Jacob did not reject Ishmael but rather provided for Him and blessed him. The tragic reality is that Satan has deceived Ishmael to reject the God of Israel by not receiving second birth. To this day Islam is unwilling to humble itself to His plan, the heavenly Father's love, His beloved Son, who left heaven for them to teach them about second birth, so that they may become co-heirs with Him. It is God's desire for them to be set free and await their blessed hope. It is His desire for all of mankind.

Abraham and Keturah

After Sarah's death Abraham married Keturah. She gave birth to six sons. They all were sent away with gifts of inheritance to the *east, away from Isaac* who remained the sole heir to the Promised Land. (Genesis 25: 1-11) Scripture reveals them to be enemies of Israel of the past and today as well.

Esau and Jacob (Genesis 25-33)

Isaac had two sons, Esau and Jacob. They were twins. In the womb the babies jostled with each other. According to the Webster's New World Dictionary, " to jostle" is to *"bump or push as in a crowd,* *elbow or shove roughly, to push by shoving or bumping,* **to contend with someone for something."**

The mother, Rebekah, disturbed by this jostling inquired of the Lord. He answered: *"Two nations are in your womb, and two peoples from within you will be separated; one people will be stronger than the other; and the older will serve the younger!"* Satan once again interfered with the chosen heir, this time even in the womb, thus Esau won the jostle and was born first,-while Jacob came behind him hanging on to his heal as if to say: "Wait for me, I was supposed to be first!" It is interesting to note that God protected baby Jacob in the womb, as he grasped Esau's heel as if to stop him from inflicting a fatal head wound on his head, in order to preserve the chosen son and Messianic lineage. (See Genesis 3:15).

Rebekah knew from what God had told her that Jacob should have been the firstborn-heir, not his twin brother Esau. I am sure she told Jacob. While it is generally believed that Jacob stole Esau's birthright, I disagree, because God would never give it to a thief that exemplified the mind of Satan. However, Rebekah and Jacob did not wait upon the Lord to regain his birthright by God's grace through faith, and decided to take matters into their own hands.

Esau obviously lacked the leadership required of a firstborn, to step in as head to care for the family, land, animals, and last but not least spiritual direction. He did not understand that to be first meant sacrifice and servant-hood, not mere status, prestige and control. He was rebellious, a source of grief to Isaac and Rebekah, as he married Ishmaelite and Hittite / Canaanite women that worshipped pagan gods, a brutal warring people, rejecting the God of Abraham and Isaac. They served the pagan god Baal, and practiced all kinds of sexual immorality. Therefore by his choices of women alone he was not qualified to lead. (Genesis 26: 34-35)

Esau sells his birthright

Jacob knew his brother Esau was a bully and also a man of instant gratification, and used the opportunity one day when his brother returned from a hunt. Esau said to Jacob: *"Quick, let me have some of that red stew. I am famished!"* Jacob replied, *"First sell me your birthright!"* Esau replied, *"Look I am about to die* **what good is** *the birthright to me?"* Esau flippantly despised his birthright for a mere bowl of stew, proving himself a man of rash words, quick and thoughtless decisions. But Jacob made sure that Esau would remember his quick words and said*: " Swear to me FIRST,"* as a verbal oath was required to make the *transaction legal.*

Rebekah and Jacob deceive Esau (Genesis 27)

Scripture does not indicate that father Isaac knew that his son Esau had despised and legally sold his birthright to Jacob. So it came to be that when Isaac was near death that he requested to bless his firstborn son, Esau. Unable to see well, mother Rebekah devised a plan to deceive Isaac in order for Jacob to receive his father's blessing. After discovering the deception, Esau wept and cried out: *"Bless me too, my father! But Isaac said: "Your brother came deceitfully and took your blessing. I have made him lord over you, what can I possibly do for you?"* And so it was fulfilled that "the older was to serve the younger." Esau swore to kill Jacob.

Jacob prepares to meet Esau (Genesis 32)

After years of fearing Esau's persecution, and before re-entrance into Canaan (Promised Land), Jacob prepared to meet Esau and send messengers ahead. He instructed them*: "This is what you are to say to my master Esau, Your servant Jacob says-*......... At that point Jacob clearly humbled himself accepting second birth calling his brother **master** and himself **servant.**

Jacob wrestles with God

Jacob's heart, in the right place now, wrestles with God. He openly and honestly seeks his heavenly Fathers blessings, stating his name is Jacob. He refuses to let go until he receives God's blessing. In so doing, his name was changed **from Jacob to Israel**, from *"Holder of the heel"* to *"Prince of God."* He said: *"It is because I saw God face to face and yet my life was spared."* (Genesis 32: 22-32). Now Jacob has the birthright and blessing restored not by his own human effort, nor deception, but the will and Grace of God. He now is a servant ready to serve God who is above him, but also his brother, exemplifying the mind of the Messiah.

Esau meets Jacob (Genesis 33)
As Jacob approached his brother with a humble attitude, now Esau recognizes that he is blessed by God as well. After years of persecution and hatred on Esau's part, and Jacob's years of running in fear, both brothers finally forgive, embrace, and kiss each other as they weep tears of joy.

Spiritual application for the church
We are all firstborn in the flesh insisting on our rights. Before we can enter paradise we must wrestle with God and willingly accept second birth, to receive God's blessing. We must admit we are sinners, and no longer insist on being first. We all must seek His will by seeking His face in order to be co-heirs with **His firstborn Son, Jesus**. We all must become servants, loving God with all of our heart and mind and strength, and love our neighbor as ourselves. *How about you?*

Literal application for the nation of Israel
While Israel is God's firstborn, and the Promised Land belongs to the Jewish people forever, they cannot and will not enjoy the Covenant blessings associated with peace, until they as a nation repent and receive the Prince of Peace. Israel, must wrestle with God, and see their Messiah face to face. Not until Israel experiences her spiritual rebirth, and is born again will she experience her spiritual rebirth as a nation, to enter the Sabbath rest from her persecution of her brother Esau. *"Jesus said: Look your house is left to you desolate. I tell you the truth; you will not see me again until you say: ' Blessed is He who comes in the name of the LORD!'"* (Luke 13: 35) Therefore, her blessings are clearly linked with her calling upon the name of her Messiah.. Until then, it will be "wars and rumors of war" to escalate into the outbreak of the Great Tribulation to come. Sadly, many will die. According to Zechariah 13 no less than 2/3 of the nation of Israel will be destroyed, until God intervenes by His wrath to stop this insanity. Only 1/3 will enter the refiner's fire and call upon His name. When He comes again to intervene on behalf of Israel, they will enjoy the blessings of their everlasting inheritance, the Promised Land

Literal application for the Arab nations

Not until the Arab nations reject Allah, and recognize their blessings given to them by the God of Abraham, Isaac and Jacob, will the Arabs stop fighting amongst each other. Not until they humble themselves and say: "God has the right to choose the way of salvation, and we have no right to insist on our way, divide the land and destroy Israel", will Israel have peace. Not until the Arab nations say: "Salvation is of the Jews", will they understand it was the eternal plan of God, that through Abraham, Isaac and Jacob should come the Messiah, the redeemer of Israel, and for all of them. Not until then will the family feud end, when they forgive and embrace each other. Tragically it will take the outpouring of God's wrath, and many will be destroyed.

The everlasting hatred

Compare the chosen heirs with the rejected heirs of the Promised Land!

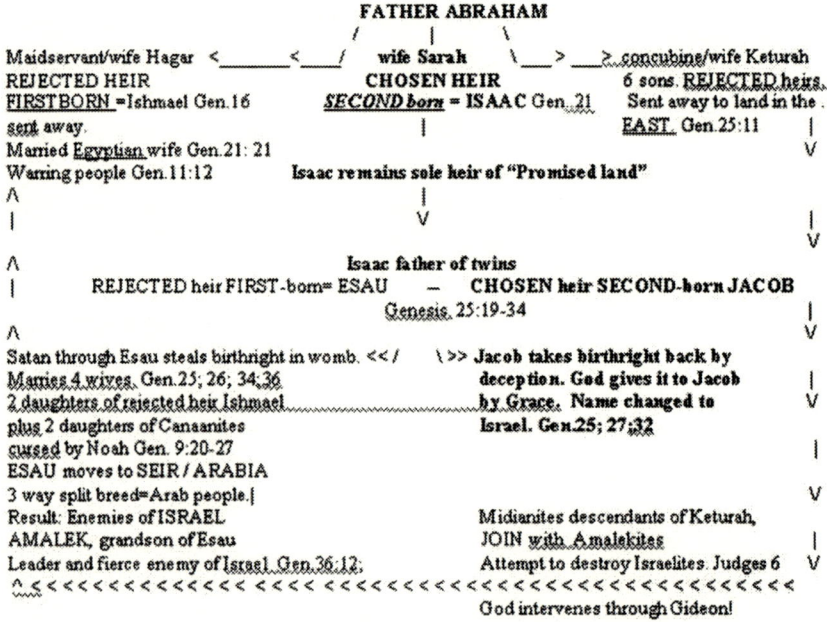

1.) *Esau/ Edom, the rejected firstborn heir of Isaac,* who thought the Promised Land should be his, vowed to kill Jacob. He settled in *SEIR.*

2.) *Esau married Canaanites who were cursed by Noah* to have no part of the inheritance of the renewed earth, as he pronounced Canaan the lowest slave to his brothers. (Genesis 9 25) They *occupied* the Promised Land who thought it should be theirs (Genesis 24) God intervened with David who killed Goliath, the leader of the Philistines. (1 Samuel:16-17)

3.) *Esau also married into the lineage of Ishmael,* the rejected firstborn of Abraham, who thought the "Promised Land" should be his. Ishmael was prophesied to be a *warring man.* Genesis 16:11-12. His sons lived in hostility towards each other. (Gen 25: 12-18, emph. v 18.)

What a team!

This is the three-strand cord of satanic hatred from the EAST against the heirs of Israel. They vowed the destruction of the Israelites then, and nothing has changed. They are the ARAB people. The land of Seir is no other than modern day *Jordan extending into Saudi - Arabia,* which became the birthplace of *ISLAM.*

Gen.17:14-16

Moses records that the **Amalekites** (descendents of Amalek, grandson of *Esau)* intermarried with Ishmael's daughters and Canaanites) tried to destroy the Israelites as they proceeded to enter the Promised Land. God helped them to victory in a mighty battle and proclaimed an oath: *'The LORD said to Moses: 'Write this on a scroll, as something to be remembered and make sure that Joshua (type of Jesus Christ) hears it, because I will completely blot out the memory of Amalek from under heaven'...The LORD will be at war with the Amalekites from generation to generation!"*

Judges 6

When Israel sinned and worshipped other gods, and God removed His protection over them, these same enemies came to attempt their utter destruction, but Israel cried out and God delivered them."

Again the Israelites did evil in the eyes of the LORD, and for seven years he gave them into the hands of the **Midianites.** *(Son of Keturah who did not receive any inheritance of the Promised Land.) Because Midian so oppressive, the Israelites prepared shelters in mountain clefts, caves and strongholds. Whenever the Israelites planted crops, the* **Midianites, Amalekites,** *and* **other Eastern peoples invaded the country (Promised Land)***, they camped on the Land and ruined the crops all the way to Gaza and did not spare a living thing for Israel, neither sheep nor cattle nor donkeys. They came up with their* **camels;** *they invaded the land to ravage it. Midian so impoverished the Israelites that they cried out to the LORD for help!"*

Today

ALL the rejected heirs vow the destruction of the Israel, and seek the takeover of all of the earth in their satanic desire to bring every knee to bow to Allah, and submit the earth under the *rule* of Islamic Shariah Law. God in His Grace has delayed this world takeover during Israel's national blindness to her Messiah. Now that Israel is back on the map after 2000 years, the only hope we have is the fact that when Israel cries out, Jesus Christ will come and deliver them. We must remember that the Great Tribulation will break out in Jerusalem, and will be global, until God intervenes to stop this "Everlasting Hatred!"(Matthew 24:15-22)

The Family feud

While Jews and Arabs claim father Abraham, only one named Isaac was the heir of the Promised Land, and confirmed through Jacob/Israel. The Bible tells us story after story about wars and battles, with Israel's enemies, because they simply are not the heirs. It is no less than revealing to learn that Abraham's God was the God of Israel, but since the seventh century, Allah is the god of the Arabs, the rejected heirs. The God of Israel decreed the land to be Covenant land only through Abraham, Isaac and Jacob. Allah claims rights to the Promised Land, and all of the earth, because he is no other than the deceiver, who stole it in the Garden of Eden, because the Promised Land is the Garden of Eden! **_Read that paragraph again and let it sink in!_**

CHAPTER 9

From Last to First!

Why did God choose Joseph? (Genesis 37-50).

Jacob deeply loved Rachel but was deceived into marrying the oldest daughter, Leah, *first*. He worked another seven years for his father-in-law Laban to marry Rachel. After many years Joseph the *eleventh* son of Jacob and *firstborn son* of Rachel was born. His father loved him, but his brothers hated him. Considering the status and rights of the firstborn son, they ignored the fact that Joseph, aware of the deception, could have been rather bitter and hateful thinking: *"My father was deceived to marry Leah first, I should have been the HEIR, the FIRST BORN son!"* But he had humbly accepted his position as *last born* at that time. (Benjamin would be born later).

There came a time when Jacob gave Joseph a coat of many colors. However other sources state a crucial truth. It was a coat with extra long and pointed sleeves. Such were worn only by two men of the tribe, the leader and his appointed heir. By giving Joseph this special coat, Joseph became *the heir*. Therefore, the brothers' hatred of Joseph was not merely over a handsome coat, but over the inheritance of the Promised Land. In turn his brothers hated him all the more. God did however confirm to Joseph in a dream that he would indeed rule over his brothers, and they in turn plotted to kill him. But Reuben and Judah stepped forward to save his life. Rather than kill him, he was thrown in a pit, and then sold into slavery.

Joseph became a servant of Potiphar, an official of the Pharaoh of Egypt. God was with Joseph as he gained the favor of his master who put him in charge of his household. Potiphar's wife attempted to seduce Joseph numerous times, but he refused and she in turn falsely accused him. Placed in prison he was again favored by the warden. He was put in charge of all those held in prison, and made responsible for all that was done there. Two servants of the Pharaoh who had offended him ended up in prison. One night they both had a dream but were unable to interpret it. They discovered Joseph could interpret dreams as he had been given the gift by God to do so.

After two years Pharaoh had a dream as well and Joseph was brought before him to interpret it, revealing seven years of plenty, and seven years of famine to come. Joseph was put in charge and was highly exalted by becoming commander of Egypt, second highest power on earth next to Pharaoh, who was considered the highest god in the Egyptian pantheon of gods. He was given a Gentile bride, daughter of the priest of On. God was with Joseph as he, through his wisdom and ability to store grain, saved Egypt and beyond from famine, and made the name of Pharaoh great.

During the famine, Jacob sent his sons to Egypt to purchase grain in a last ditch effort to save his people. They did not recognize Joseph assuming him to be dead. Joseph was deeply hurt by what his brothers had done to him and was now in position of power. He could have been vengeful, with the result being the extermination of Jacob's family, but Joseph was merciful and sold them grain. Joseph revealed himself to his brothers on their second journey, submitting to God's will, that he had been appointed by God for such a time as this, to save the known world from famine, and also preserve and save Israel.

In a glorious conclusion, Joseph blessed his father Jacob who had deeply longed for his beloved son Joseph. He brought Jacob and all of the family and their clans to live in Egypt to enjoy a great family reunion. They lived under the bounty of Joseph's provision, where they and their flocks multiplied.

Joseph, a brother and forgiver like Jesus!
There is no doubt that Joseph is a *type* of forgiver of the Hebrew people pointing to Jesus Christ.

Joseph's father was Jacob. (Gen 35:24)
Jesus father was God. But Joseph was the earthly (legal) "father" of Jesus, who also had a father named Jacob. (Matthew 1:16)

Joseph was given a richly ornamented robe, made firstborn heir, and his brothers despised him for being the father's favorite all the more. They could not speak a kind word to him. (Gen 37: 4)
Jesus is the only begotten Son of God. In His first coming to Israel , he was despised by many of his own people, they did not speak kindly of him, and even called Him demon possessed. At His crucifixion they mocked him and took his robe. (Matthew 10: 25; 12: 22-24.Mark 3: 20-22)

Joseph had a **dream** that he would rule over his brothers. They in turn sought to destroy him. Joseph ended up in Egypt. (Gen 37: 5)
Jesus' earthly father Joseph also had a **dream**: *"And when they were departed, behold, the angel of the Lord appeared to Joseph in a dream, saying, 'Arise, and take the young child and His mother, and flee into Egypt, and be thou there until I bring thee word: for Herod will seek the young child to destroy Him'." (Matt 2:13)*
"And (he) was there until the death of Herod that it might be fulfilled which was spoken of the Lord by the prophet, saying 'Out of Egypt have I called My son.'" (Matthew 2:14-15),-which is a direct quote of Hosea 11:1, which was originally spoken of the "Nation" of Israel(Jacob).

Joseph was stripped of his robe by his brothers and left to die. His brother Judah changed his brother's minds not to kill him, and sold him instead into slavery for 20 pieces of silver, the price of a slave. (Gen 37:23)
Jesus was betrayed by Judas for 30 pieces of silver the cost of a slave (Matthew26: 14); then stripped of his robe and left him to die. (Matthew 27:31)

Joseph's brothers thought he was dead. He rose to power due his righteous acts, appointed by Pharaoh of Egypt to make him second in command to the highest power on earth. (Gen 41-44)

Jesus rose from the dead, as God would not have His Holy one see corruption. He sits on the right hand of His Father, the God of heaven and Earth, the majesty on high. (John 1:14, Matt26: 15; Hebrews 1:3)

Joseph was 30 years old when he entered his command. (Gen 41:41-46)
Jesus was 30 years old when God commissioned him. (Matt 3: 23)

Joseph was given a Gentile bride. (Gen 41: 45)
Jesus married a Gentile bride, the church. (John 3: 29; Rev.19: 9; 21: 2, 9; 2 Cor.11: 2)

First journey and First coming
Joseph's brothers did not recognize him on their "first" journey to Egypt. They came because of famine in their own land. (Gen 42:8)
Jesus was not recognized by the nation of Israel as their brother and Messiah at His first coming, because there was a lack of spiritual food in the land. (John 1: 11; Romans 11:20)

Joseph on the first journey, pretended to be a stranger, speaking harshly to them. (Gen 37: 7) *"They said to one another: 'Surely we are being punished because of our brother. We saw how distressed he was when he pleaded with us for his life, but we would not listen; this is why this distress has come upon us.' Reuben replied, 'Didn't I tell you not to sin against the boy? But you wouldn't listen. Now we must give an accounting for his blood.'* (Gen 37: 21- 23)
Jesus spoke harshly to the Jewish religious leaders, in his first coming, for their injustice to the people. They were unwilling to repent, rejected Him as their Messiah, and demanded his crucifixion. Pontius Pilate declared: *"I am innocent of this man's blood, it is YOUR responsibility! ALL the people answered:' Let His blood be on us and on our children'!"* (Matthew 27: 24-25)

Second journey and second coming

Joseph revealed himself to His brothers on the second journey, inquiring about his father. They were unable to talk as they were terrified at His presence, knowing they were in the hands of their brother who was given authority by Pharaoh over the greatest empire of the earth. They feared to be killed for what they had done to him. (Genesis 45:3)

When Jesus comes again to Jerusalem it will be an awesome sight. They will see Him in all of His glory, not the Lamb led to slaughter, but as the rightful King to the throne of Israel, who is King of Kings and LORD of Lords. Bearing the mark on His hands and feet inflicted by his brothers, they will be frightened thinking they will be destroyed by Him. (Zechariah 12, Rev 19:11-16)

Joseph poured out his grace to his brothers. (Genesis 45: 4) *"He threw his arms around his brother Benjamin and wept and Benjamin embraced him, weeping. And He kissed all his brothers and wept over them."* (Genesis 45: 14)

Prophecy of Zechariah *"On that day-God will pour out His Spirit of Grace upon the house of David and the inhabitants of Jerusalem and THEY will LOOK upon Him whom they have pierced. On that day weeping in Jerusalem will be great, each clan by itself, with their wives by themselves ...and ALL the rest of the clans and their wives."* (Zech. 12: 10-14)

Joseph revealed himself to his brothers and he said: *"Come close to me, and when they had done so he said: 'I am your brother Joseph, the one you sold into Egypt. And now, do not be distressed and do not be angry with yourselves for selling me here, because it was to save lives that God sent me ahead of you. For two years now there has been famine in the land and for the next five years there will be no plowing and reaping. But God sent me ahead of you to preserve for YOU a remnant on EARTH and to save your lives by a great deliverance. So then, it was not you who sent me here, but God!'"* (Gen 45:4-8)

Paul said pertaining to the *first coming*, and the rejection of the Messiah by the nation of Israel, (not individuals), that it has resulted in grace and salvation being extended to the world, a mystery indeed. But let us not forget that in His second coming, He will embrace Israel, just like Joseph embraced his brothers. Therefore Paul wrote: *"Again I ask: 'Did they (Israel) stumble as to fall beyond recovery? Not at all! Rather because of their (Israel's) transgressions, salvation has come to the Gentile (world) to make Israel envious. But if their (Israel's) transgression means riches for the world (Gentiles) and their (Israel's) loss means riches for Gentiles (world), how much greater riches will their (Israel's) fullness bring. I am talking to you GENTILES!'"* (Romans 11: 11-13) *" I do not want you to be ignorant of this mystery, brothers, so that you (Gentiles) may not be conceited. Israel has experienced a hardening in part UNTIL the full number of Gentiles has come in. And so all Israel will be saved, as it is written: The deliverer (JESUS) will come from Zion; He will turn godlessness away from Jacob (Israel). And THIS is my Covenant with them when I take away their sins."* (Romans 11: 25-27)

Joseph was told by Pharaoh: *"Tell your brothers, do this: 'Load your animals and **return** to the land of Canaan (Promised Land) and bring your father and your family back to me. I will give you the best of the land of Egypt and you can enjoy the fat of the land. Never mind about the rest of your belongings, because the best of Egypt will be yours.'"* (Gen 45: 16- 20)

Second coming prophecy *"The wealth of all the surrounding nations will be collected great quantities of gold and silver and clothing... IF the Egyptians do not come up to partake of the Feast of Tabernacles, God will not send them any rain."* (Zech 14: 16- 21)

Joseph had a dream that revealed his brothers would bow down to him and they furiously replied: *"Do you intend to reign over us?"* (Gen 37: 5-8) Then another dream revealed that even the sun, moon and eleven stars were bowing to him". *vs.9*

Isaiah *"Was it not I the LORD? And there is no God apart from me, a righteous God and a SAVIOR; there is NONE but me. Turn to me and be saved, all you ends of the Earth; for I am God, and there is no other. By myself I have sworn, my mouth has uttered in all integrity a word that will not be revoked: Before ME every knee* *shall bow, by ME every tongue will swear. They will say of me, 'In the LORD alone is righteousness and strength. ALL who have raged against Him will come to Him and be put to shame.'"* (Isaiah 45: 22-24)

Apostle Paul *"Therefore, God exalted Him to the highest place and gave Him the NAME that is above every name, that at the NAME of JESUS EVERY knee shall bow, in HEAVEN and on EARTH and EVERY tongue confess that JESUS is LORD to the glory of God the Father."* (Philippians 2:5-11)

Just as the suffering of Joseph was used by God to save a dying world, and in the end saved Jacob(Israel) and his sons, likewise God in Christ set aside the reconciliation of the nation of Israel for a time, to save the world that was spiritually hungry and dying, but He has *never* forsaken Israel. He married a Gentile bride, but has never stopped longing for His brothers. The yearning and anguish of father Jacob to see his family reunited, was brought about by God's grace and the mercy and love of Joseph his beloved son. Likewise, God's beloved Son Jesus Christ will bring about our heavenly Father's longing for His family reunion. <u>*Be there!*</u>

Jacob meets out justice

Although Rueben the firstborn spoke up on behalf of Joseph, it was Judah the fourth born son who interceded on behalf of his younger brother Joseph when his brothers plotted his death. It was on Judah's suggestion that they sell Joseph to the Ishmaelites, that Joseph's life was spared. (Gen. 37:26-27) It was also Judah, several chapters later, who acted as surety for his younger brother Benjamin when Joseph, now second in command in Pharaoh's government, demanded Benjamin be brought to him. *(Gen. 43:8-9)* From the tribe of Judah would come the Messiah, the kingly line! The scepter was guaranteed to come through him "until the Messiah comes to take it from him." (Gen. 46:12)

Jacob exalts Joseph and his grandsons

Joseph was exalted to the position of firstborn son. He had two sons, Manasseh and Ephraim, half Hebrew and Gentile. God inspired

Jacob to adopt his grandsons thus honoring Joseph even more, by making them into two tribes. They would be the patriarchs of their own tribe, instead of Joseph becoming a single tribe. Because the first-born receives two portions above his brothers, Joseph's two portions went to Ephraim and Manasseh.(1 Chron.5: 1) Although Manasseh is the first born, Jacob put Ephraim ahead of Manasseh who was inspired to know Ephraim would become greater.

"Jacob blesses Joseph and said: 'God, before whom my fathers Abraham and Isaac walked; the God who has fed me all my life long to this day; the Angel who has redeemed me from all evil; bless the lads. Let my name be named upon them. And the name of my fathers Abraham and Isaac; and let them grow into a multitude in the midst of the earth.'"(Genesis 48:15)

Joseph saw that Jacob had placed his right hand on Ephraim and his left hand on Manasseh and tried to correct Jacob, but Jacob refused and said (verses 19-20): *"...I know, my son, I know. He also shall become a people, and he also shall be great; but truly his younger brother shall be greater than he, and his descendants shall become a multitude of nations"*. So he blessed them that day, saying: *"By you Israel shall be blessed saying, 'May God make you as Ephraim and as Manasseh!' And thus he set Ephraim before Manasseh."*

Ephraim although *second born* in the natural, is called *firstborn* by God, thus the heir, and it was his responsibility as the heir to lead the tribes of Israel. *-This is what the LORD says: "Sing with joy for JACOB (Israel); shout for the foremost of the nations. Make your praises heard, and say, 'O LORD save the REMNANT of Israel.' See, I WILL bring them from the land of the North and gather them from the ends of the earth. Among them will be the blind and lame expectant mothers and women in labor; a great throng will return. They will come with weeping; I WILL lead them beside steams of water on a level path where they WILL not stumble, because I am Israel's father, and* **EPHRAIM is my FIRSTBORN son."**(Jeremiah 31: 7-9)

Ephraim would become a company of nations and Manasseh would become a great nation. Between the two brothers they would enjoy great economic prosperity and power, but Ephraim would be the greater of the two. Manasseh and Ephraim were half Gentile and are a *type* or picture of the Gentile believers to be grafted into the Covenants with Israel, predicated upon the Abrahamic covenant to bless all nations. Ephraim is a prophetic picture of the non-Jewish remnant of the bride of the Messiah. Jacob placed Ephraim above his older brother Manasseh and proclaimed that he would be great and he would become the father of multitudes of Gentiles. (Gen. 48:19) Yet they are to remain brothers not enemies.

Genesis 49:22-26

> *"Joseph is a fruitful bough, a fruitful bough by a well; his branches run over the wall. The archers have bitterly grieved him, shot at him and hated him. But his bow remained in strength. And the arms of his hands were made strong by the Mighty God of Jacob, (from there is the Shepherd, the stone of Israel. By the God of your father who will help you, and by the Almighty who will bless you with blessings of heaven above, blessings of the deep that lies beneath, blessings of the breasts and of the womb. The blessings of your father have excelled the blessings of my ancestors. Up to the utmost bound of the everlasting hills. They shall be on the head of Joseph. And on the crown of the head of him who was separate from his brothers."*

See also Deuteronomy 33:6-25 for the prophecy uttered by Moses concerning the descendants of Israel, and the nation at the end of the age.

The numbers 1 and 11
The Hebrew language does not have a separate numbering system, but rather ascribes numerical value to each letter of the Hebrew Alphabet. For example: Aleph = 1, and YOD = 10. In order for you to get the number 11 you simply add Aleph and Yod, 1+10 together!
There is also meaning ascribed.

The Aleph or number 1 means BEGINNING
The Yod or number 10 OPPOSES
So when added Aleph Yod = END!

What is astonishing here is that Joseph is a *type* of Jesus Christ, a *type* and foreshadow of the Savior and Forgiver who was the *11th born* Son to Jacob, although *firstborn* to Rachel. He was exalted from the *11th son to first born son by father Jacob, from the LAST to the FIRST*. Jesus said: *"Many who are first will be last and many who are last will be first!"* He will exalt the humble servant and put the arrogant ones in their place. (Matthew 19:30) Amazing!

The Greek language was used to write the New Testament. The first and last letter in the Greek alphabet are **Alpha and Omega** and means "The Beginning and the End", or First and Last." In Greek it carries the thought of *"The ALL THERE IS"*. This title is ascribed to Jesus Christ our LORD in Revelation 1:8. He is the "all there is", the beginning and the end, the first and last! He is the author of Creation, and will bring this age of sin and death to its conclusion. (John 1:1-11; Hebrews 1; Colossians 1; Revelation 1). The Lord will never forsake Israel, because He has chosen her from the *beginning to the end* to accomplish his eternal purposes for the world. Paul records his plea in Romans 11:1-11. Amazing! That is why the Bible is the Word of GOD. No Coincidence!

Why did God choose David?

Samuel the prophet was commissioned to seek out the next King of Israel. When he saw the **firstborn** son of Jesse he said: *"Surely this is God's anointed!"* But God had other plans. *"For man looks at the outward appearance, God looks at the heart!"* (1 Samuel 16)

God chose David, the **last born** of seven brothers. He was a shepherd boy who became King. David not only defeated Goliath and saved Israel from destruction with a single rock, (1 Samuel 17), but God promised to maintain his Davidic dynasty on the throne of Israel to provide her forever with a King of the lineage of King David, and through that dynasty to do for her what he had done through King David, conquer Jerusalem and bring her into rest in the Promised Land. (1 Kings 4: 20-21; 5: 3-4; 2 Samuel 7: 5-16.1 Chronicles 13: 15-29)

Jesus, like King David

David was a shepherd boy. (1 Samuel 17)
Jesus is the Good shepherd. (John 10: 11)

David's father was Jesse. (Ruth 4:17, 1Samuel 16)
Jesus is a descendant of Jesse, the root of Jesse. (Matt 1: 6 Isaiah 11: 10)

David was born in Bethlehem. (1Sam.17: 11)
Jesus was born in Bethlehem. (Matthew 2: 1)

David slew the Mighty Goliath with a single stone. (1Sam 17: 49)
Jesus the Rock of ages defeated Satan at the cross. (Matt 27:32)

David cut off the head of Goliath and took "his skull" to Jerusalem. At that time it was a Jebusite Citadel, which would later become Jerusalem the capitol city of the Kingdom of King David. (1 Sam 17: 46, 51)
Jesus the rock of ages was crucified "King of the Jews" He won the victory over sin and death, in a place called Golgotha which means "the skull." (Matthew 27:3)

David was 30 years old when he became King. He defeated the *Philistines,* and made Jerusalem his capitol city, from whence he ruled and reigned over all of Israel and Judah for 33 years. (1Samuel 5: 4-5; 2 Samuel 5:6-25).

Jesus' First coming

He began His ministry at age 30 and died approx. 3 1/2 years later in Jerusalem. He rose again on the third day and promised to return. (Luke 3: 23; John 1: 29; 3: 16; Luke 24:50)

Jesus' Second coming

In His second Coming He will return to <u>Jerusalem</u> and:

a.) Pour out His grace *like Joseph,* forgive his brothers and embrace them. (Genesis 45, Zechariah 12:10)
b.) Deliver His people *like Moses,* by splitting the Mount of Olives in half, to make a way of escape from the enemies seeking their destruction. (Exodus 14: 26-31, Zech 14:4)
c.) Destroy Israel's enemies and conquer the Promised Land *like Joshua.* (Joshua; Zechariah 14: 12-15.) The names of the nations are once again the same as the ancient enemies of Israel, today's Arab nations.
d.) Conquer Jerusalem and make it his capitol, establish His rule *like King David,* unite His kingdom, and rule from the throne of King David forever! (1Samuel 5: 4-5; 2 Sam. 5; Ezekiel 37:15-28; Revelation 21)
e.) He will be the righteous judge, to settle disputes amongst the nations. The law of the God of Abraham, Isaac and Jacob shall go forth from Jerusalem. (Isaiah 2, 9:6-7; 11; 12; Jeremiah 62:7; Ezekiel 37:15-28)

NOTE: King David defeated the *Moabites* and imposed his rule over them. (2 Samuel 8:2) He crushed the Aramean Kingdoms of *Damascus* (Syria, 2 Sam.8:3-8). He subdued *Edom* and incorporated it into his kingdom. (2 Sam 8:13-14) He defeated the *Ammonites* and brought them into subjection (2 Sam.12:19-31) He subjugated the remaining *Canaanite* cities that had previously maintained their independence from and hostility towards Israel. Since David had earlier crushed the *Amalekites* (1Sam.30:17), his wars thus completed the conquest begun by Joshua, and secured all the borders of Israel. His Empire united Israel, plus the subjugated kingdoms reached from the eastern arm of the *Red Sea to the Euphrates River.*

NOTICE: The Land King David conquered, is no other than the land given by God to Abraham, which are no other than the boundaries of Eden, because the eastern shore of the Red Sea touches Ethiopia, and Sudan, former Cush, and from there extends N/E to the river Euphrates.(Genesis 2; 15).

The people King David conquered are the ancient enemies of Israel. The people Jesus will conquer are no other than today's enemies of Israel, the Arab/Muslim nations. Jesus Christ, the King like King David will likewise conquer all of the land given to father Abraham. His kingdom will unite Israel, from the _Red Sea to the Euphrates River._ No coincidence in the Word of God!

CHAPTER 10

Religious deception in Israel, we are *FIRST!*

Wolves in sheep's clothing

God established Israel as a theocracy ruled by Him. He appointed Prophets, Priests, Judges and Kings. Many became arrogant and succumbed to corruption. Rather then help the poor they only fed themselves and did not bind up the wounds of the people.

The Good Shepherd

Jesus fulfills every role; He is Prophet, Priest, Judge and King. Wherever Israel failed He didn't. He began His ministry in Galilee. During His teaching ministry Jesus dealt with people from various classes. He spoke and ministered to people, period! In contrast to bad news He brought Good News. In contrast to condemnation by the religious elite, He healed the people. In contrast to hypocritical judgment, He offered forgiveness through repentance.

As a result masses of people followed Jesus the Messiah, the Christ of Israel, rather than Israel's leaders. This meant loose control, a possible rebellion against the religious system. As we shall see there were religious rulers among the crowd who by the end of the "Sermon on the Mount" were either squirming or fuming, while the common people would listen with awe to the courageous man from

Galilee, who dared to stand up against the corrupt leadership of His day. This should give us insight as to why these particular religious leaders wanted Him dead. Jesus was a troublemaker in their eyes, a rebel, considered dangerous, a possible cause of revolution.

The context of the Sermon on the Mount

The Sermon on the Mount begins in Matthew chapter 5. However, He spoke to a crowd that followed Him from various places detailed in Matthew 4: 23-25. We shall see that it was quite a mixture of people. Many of the upper crust or so-called religious elite were present among the common people, and so called outsiders as well.

Matthew 4: 23-25

> *"Jesus went throughout Galilee teaching in their synagogues, preaching the good news of the kingdom, and healing every disease and sickness among the people. News about him spread all over Syria, and people brought to him all who were ill with various diseases, those suffering severe pain, the demon-possessed, those having seizures, and the paralyzed, and he healed them. Large crowds from Galilee, the Decapolis, Jerusalem, Judea and the region across the Jordan followed him".*

Galilee is where many common people lived, the fishermen. Jesus began his ministry there.

Decapolis was characterized by Greek culture, with pagan practices and corruption.

Judea was the home of the upper class Judeans from which we get the word Jews, not all Israelites as we do today.

Jerusalem was the center of Jewish worship, where the Temple stood; the home of Jewish Pharisees, Sadducees and Sanhedrin, *Israel's ruling body.*

The Sermon on the Mount (Matthew 5-7)

"Blessing" is to put God's goodness upon a life, and "cursing" is to remove it. What Jesus had to say pertaining to blessings in the Sermon on the Mount, are commonly called "The Beatitudes". His words declaring blessings for certain conduct would not be well received by those who acted contrarily. While Jesus begins in Chapter 5, we must not stop there but continue, so as not to disconnect the flow and context. In so doing we will discover His continued escalation in judging the hypocrites of His day, as noted throughout the book of Matthew. Those who thought they were righteous just because of their status, yet ignored their need to repent and serve God and man below them, discovered that this Galilean even dared to condemn them to hell. So let us begin.

NOTE: Before we do, there were genuine, godly leaders in Israel, just as we have them in our churches. But I am speaking of the corrupt segment, so let us never sweep with a broad brush. The guilty in the crowd who thought they were first and treated the people like dogs, knew exactly what Jesus was saying, and exactly to whom He was talking.

There has been enough damage done by people calling all Jews Christ killers, when in fact it was few who called for His crucifixion. **Jesus never fought to get off the cross but to get on it**. God used a few evil people to accomplish His plan. Had Jesus come to Germany, God would have found a few Germans to demand His crucifixion.

The Beatitudes (Matthew 5)
Jesus declares nine blessings in relationship to genuine faith:.

<u>*vs. 3 Blessings for being poor in spirit.*</u> Such poverty would lead to true spiritual riches with God as one recognizes his utter sinfulness and helplessness, standing empty handed before a Holy God, not relying on self-righteousness. In contrast many religious rulers were self-righteous and corrupt gaining their riches by extortion, bribes and usury.

<u>*vs. 4 Blessings for those who mourn.*</u> Genuine examination of ones sins brings about genuine sadness and grief over what one has done.

Not so with many self-righteous leaders who ignored their sins, yet self-righteously judged and condemned others.

vs. 5 Blessings for being meek. This is not **weak but meek**, meaning humble, and such shall inherit the earth (The Land). In contrast many religious rulers were arrogant thinking they had a right to the kingdom of God on earth just because of human ancestry.

vs. 6 Blessings for those who are hungry and thirsty for righteousness sake. Genuine Spiritual hunger and thirst for righteousness leads man to want more *of* God, not more *from* God.

vs.7 Blessings for the merciful. Such can only be given by those who know the mercy of God; something much of religious rule had no clue about, as they judged people without mercy.

vs. 8 Blessings for the pure at heart. The hard hearted corruption and merciless religious rulers
was a stench of decay in the nostrils of God.

vs. 9 Blessings for the peacemakers. Many religious leaders had become the cause of constant strife, rather than vessels of peace.

vs. 10 Blessings for being persecuted for righteousness sake. The self-righteous hypocritical rulers persecuted the righteous, even Jesus Himself unto death.

vs. 11 Blessings for being insulted and persecuted when people falsely say all kinds of evil against them. And so it was that the religious rulers persecuted and falsely said all kinds of evil against Jesus, and against those who believed He was indeed the Messiah of Israel.

vs. 12 They were to rejoice in their rewards from heaven, not like corrupt leaders seeking their treasures on earth by blackmail and bribes.

vs.13-16 They were supposed to be salt and light drawing people to God, but condemning and hypocritical religious conduct accomplished the contrary, by driving people away from God.

vs.17- end Jesus points out that He in no way was negating the law God gave to Israel, but clarifies it, removing the burden and corruptions that were added to the law.

Hypocrites (Matthew Chapter 6)

The Lord now begins to identify more clearly whose attention He wants to get. It is no longer looking around the crowd and pointing at others. It is no longer wondering and silently thinking "Could He mean me?" The LORD uses the term *"Hypocrites"* throughout Matthew and He only addresses religious leaders as such. Later it becomes even more clear when He defines them.

vs.1-4 Jesus warns people not to do good works "*like the hypocrites in the synagogue,* who announce it with trumpets and merely do it to gain honor and recognition by people".

vs.5-13 Jesus warns people against praying "*like the hypocrites* who merely do so to be noticed in the synagogue to look righteous, nor pray like the pagans who babble on and on". Then He taught them how to pray.

vs.14-15. Jesus taught about forgiveness, *but leaders* held people's sins over their heads in order to control them, rather than exemplifying Gods forgiveness assuring them of His forgiveness. Such are not forgiven.

vs.16-18 Jesus warns people "not to fast as the *hypocrites* looking somber, who even disfigure their faces to impress people as to their suffering for God, and superior righteousness".

vs.19-34 Jesus warns about storing up treasures on earth. (How many of us have felt guilty over that one?) However, the context is still *corrupt religious rulers* who were storing treasure below the temple, which was gained by extortion and bribes, claiming to serve God, when in fact their god was greed and money.

Note: Again, there were genuine God- given treasure below the Temple but I am speaking of those gained by bribes and corruption.

Hypocrites! Logs versus specks (Matthew 7: 1-6)
He condemned those who picked on people and their smallest errors or presumed errors, while they ignored huge sins in their own lives, thus "specks verses logs". This was a particular habit of <u>religious rulers.</u> As we shall see it gets worse.

Lord, Lord (Matthew 7:15- 23)

"Not everyone who says to me Lord, Lord, will enter the kingdom of heaven but only he who does the will of my Father who is in Heaven. Many will say to me on that day, Lord, Lord, did we not prophesy in your name, and in your name drive out demons, and perform miracles? Then I will tell them plainly 'I never knew you. Away from me you evildoers!"

Israel knew the scriptures that promised the Messiah would overthrow Gentile control over Israel, exalt her, and make Jerusalem the praise of the earth. Many were willing to follow Him for this purpose, but many did not understand that before such rule and glory could come to Israel, it required repentance, a return to God, a change of heart, moving from arrogance to being humble servants of God and people. While miracles were granted in "His name" to substantiate that He was indeed the true Messiah of Israel, just merely using His name was no guarantee for entrance into heaven. Much of religious rule was cruel and unloving, even condemned people who were sick as if it was their own fault. Therefore Jesus healed all the common people during His earthly ministry that came to Him. It was to oppose pompous religious rule, a direct blow against their twisted theology. Saying Lord, Lord meant nothing.

Note: We, like ancient Israel, have condemning Christians, modern day Pharisees that blame people for their sickness, rather than loving and encouraging them, to stand firm in the faith no matter what. On the other end of the pendulum swing, we have healers that teach Jesus still heals "all" if we just believe. Both are terribly wrong, untrue and cruel. Many great saints of the faith suffer terribly. Such teaching is destructive to faith and must be confronted. God has His reasons why, what He does, and when He does it, whom He heals, including what gifts He bestows and when, according to His purpose and timing.

Hypocrites, Sons of hell, blind guides (Matthew 23: 13-16)

Woe! Here we are! He made it clear, no more guessing now! He said," *Hypocrites, blind* **guides!***"* Now we really are "hitting the nail on the head". Never mind about Jesus meek and mild. When it came to religious corruption, He was pretty blunt. Now He accuses blind religious **leaders** and **guides** that extended great effort to convert others, but a waste of time without repentance, as it merely turned them into twice the sons of hell as they were; that is self- righteous and condemning.

Hypocrites, Gnats versus Camels (Matthew 23: 23-24)

While the eating of unclean meat was forbidden by the Law of Moses, Jesus judges them for going to the extreme of straining their drinking water to catch the smallest gnat to avoid breaking the law. After all they needed to "look holy" and superior to the people below them, yet they ignored huge personal sins in their lives, thus Jesus compares it to swallowing a camel.

Hypocrites, cleans the outside forgets the inside
(Matthew 23: 25-26)

While religious practice was given by God to teach spiritual truths, there is judgment for paying attention to ritual cleansing of cups on the outside, at the expense of ignoring the need to clean the inside. Religious rulers lacked examining their own sins.

Hypocrites, unclean white washed tombs (Matthew 23: 27- 39)

Tombs were whitewashed to beautify them. This was done annually, but when the spring rains came it washed the whitewash away. The Lord Jesus used this practice to teach the spiritual truth that behind those tombs was nothing but death, stench, and decay. He compares it to *religious leaders* and their cover up on the outside, but contains death and decay on the inside. They were incapable of modeling godly lives, and no more capable to lead people to eternal life than a dead man can.

Matthew is clear, the context of the Sermon on the Mount and all other condemnations spoken by Jesus Christ throughout the book of Matthew, would specifically enrage the *religious leaders* of His day. In contrast He calls Himself the "Good shepherd" in John Chapter 10. He came to Israel, healed the people, fed them and offered forgiveness. Thousands believed! He will come again one day when the Good Shepherd will gather all of the lost sheep of Israel. In the meantime he also has other sheep, us Gentiles.

Woe to false Shepherds (Ezekiel 34:1-6)

The prophet Ezekiel proclaims Gods judgment upon false shepherds, and His utter commitment and determination to save His neglected and wounded sheep Himself. Please notice the word **"will"** to discover **God's will** in the following verses.

> *"The word of the LORD came to me: Son of man prophesy and say to them: 'This is what the sovereign LORD says; Woe to the shepherds of Israel who only take care of themselves! Should not shepherds take care of the flock? You eat the curds, clothe yourselves with wool and slaughter the choice animals, but you do not take care of the flock. You have not strengthened the weak or healed the sick or bound up the injured. You have not brought back the strays or searched for the lost. You have ruled them harshly and brutally. So they were scattered because there was no shepherd, and when they were scattered they became food for all the wild animals. My sheep wandered over all the mountains and on every hill. They were scattered over the whole earth, and no*

*one searched or looked for them. Therefore, you shepherds, hear the word of the LORD: As surely as I live, declares the Sovereign LORD, because my flock lack a shepherd and so has been plundered and has become food for all the wild animals, and because my shepherds did not search for my flock but cared for themselves rather than the flock, therefore O Shepherds, hear the word of the LORD: This is what the Sovereign LORD says: I am against the shepherds and **will** hold them accountable for my flock. **I will** remove them from tending the flock so that shepherds can no longer feed themselves. **I will** rescue my flock from their mouths, and it **will** no longer be food for them.'"*

The Good Shepherd looks for His sheep. (Ezekiel 34: 7-16)

*"For this is what the sovereign Lord says: 'I, MYSELF will search for my sheep and look after them. As a shepherd looks after his scattered flock when he is with them, so I **will** look after my sheep. **I will** rescue them from all the places where they were scattered on a day of clouds and darkness. **I will** bring them from out from the nations and gather them from the countries, and **I will** bring them into their own land. **I will** pasture them on the mountains of Israel, in the ravines and in all the settlements in the land. **I will** tend them in a good pasture, and the mountain heights of Israel **will** be their grazing land. There **they will** lie down in good grazing land, and there **they will** feed in a rich pasture on the mountains of Israel. I myself **will** tend my sheep and have them lie down, declares the Sovereign LORD. **I will** bind up the injured and strengthen the weak, but the sleek and the strong **I will** destroy. **I will** shepherd the flock with justice.'"*

Arrogant sheep (Ezekiel 34: 17-24)

The Good shepherd also corrects *budding* sheep. Woe unto those sheep!

A sheep pen but no shepherd (Ezekiel 39:25-29)

Many claim that today's Israel is the restored "Israel of God" promised in Scripture. I do not agree. The restored Israel of God is still to come. The nation was reborn on May 14, 1948, by God's grace due to hardness of the hearts of the Gentile nations. It came into existence after the Holocaust that will lead to the spiritual rebirth of Israel. While many Jews believe in Jesus Christ, she as a nation still lacks her Shepherd and King. She is still in unbelief. Jesus will not and cannot shepherd over a flock that denies Him. Therefore, until she repents of her self-rule, she cannot enjoy her Covenant blessings. She must wrestle with God as did Jacob (Israel), and plead for a blessing to be transformed. Her greatest battle will end in peace, that will climax in Messiah's return and Israel's supernatural restoration, that involves the *Land and the peoples spiritual rebirth.*

Ezekiel 36:37-38

> *"Once again **I will** yield to the plea of the house of Israel, and do this for them: **I will** make their people as numerous as the flocks for offerings at Jerusalem during her appointed Feasts. So **will** the ruined cities be filled with flocks of people. Then **they will** know that I am the Lord."*

CHAPTER 11

Deception in Christianity, we are *FIRST!*

First Century

While the *nation* of Israel rejected their Messiah in His first coming, we must never forget that many *individual* Israelites were followers of the Messiah. The early church in the first century was *primarily Jewish* who sacrificed everything to follow their LORD. While the Gentile church can't seem to grasp how Jewish people can be Christian and still remain Jewish, the early Jewish church could not grasp how God could accept Gentiles without first becoming Jewish.

Therefore, it was necessary to correct the Jewish church in the first century, and likewise necessary to correct the Gentiles. Paul corrected the Jewish branch of the church in numerous places, but wrote Romans 11, warning the *Gentile branch* of the church. These Gentiles had increased greatly in numbers and arrogantly assumed that God had forsaken Israel and that they were now the *new heirs* that had inherited all of God's promises given to the *"nation"* of Israel.

Paul uses the illustration of an olive tree. He states that Israel was not rejected. God did not cut down the tree, nor rip it out by the roots, but was cut off in *PART,* because not all believed. As a matter of fact the Jews that do believe are the natural branches of the tree, and the Gentile believers are the wild branches. Fact is, no tree, no roots, no natural branches, and there is nothing left to graft into. In other words, don't get arrogant thinking you are the heirs to it all, if you do, you just might find yourself cut off and dead. Furthermore he teaches that a day is coming when the Messiah returns to Zion (Jerusalem) when <u>all</u> Israel will be saved.

An attitude of gratitude to God and Israel shows the right heart attitude. In contrast arrogance is the cause for being dangerously close to being cut off! Why? Because it confirms an attitude of the mind of Satan who wanted to be first, rather than Christ who was first, but humbly came to serve, and taught us about second birth.

Warning to the Gentile church
Do not be arrogant, but be afraid! (Romans 11: 17-24)

"If some of the branches have been broken off, and you, though a wild olive shoot, have been grafted in among the others and now share in the nourishing sap from the olive root, do not boast over those branches. If you do, consider this: You do not support the root, but the root supports you. You will say then, 'Branches were broken off so that I could be grafted in.' Granted. But they were broken off because of unbelief, and you stand by faith. **Do not be arrogant, but be afraid. For if God did not spare the natural branches, he will not spare you either**".

"Consider therefore the kindness and sternness of God: sternness to those who fell, but kindness to you, provided that you continue in his kindness. Otherwise, you also will be cut off. And if they do not persist in unbelief, they will be grafted in, for God is able to graft them in again. After all, if you were cut out of an olive tree that is wild by nature, and contrary to nature were grafted *into a cultivated olive tree, how much more readily will these, the natural branches, be grafted into their own olive tree!"*

Don't be ignorant, don't be conceited! (Romans 11: 25 – 27)

*"I do not want you to be **ignorant** of this mystery, brothers, so that you may not be **conceited**: Israel has experienced a hardening in PART until the full number of the Gentiles has come in. **And so all Israel will be saved, as it is written:** 'The deliverer will come from Zion (Jerusalem) he will turn godlessness away from Jacob (Israel). And this is my covenant with them when I take away their sins.'"*

The cry of the Apostle Paul (Romans 11:1-11)

"Has God forsaken Israel? God forbid!"
"Again I ask: Did they stumble so as to fall beyond recovery? Not at all!"

Paul warned the Roman Gentile church with every part of his being and said:
Do not to be ARROGANT but be afraid!
Do not be CONCEITED all Israel will be saved!
Do not be IGNORANT about God's plan for Israel!
Sadly, the Roman Gentile church did not listen.

Fourth century
The tragic downward spiral begins

Rome under the rule of Emperor Constantine declared Christianity to be the official religion of the Roman Empire. Masses of pagan Gentiles came under the influence of the "Holy Roman Empire." By that time the early Jewish Christian witness was dead, with only a small number of Messianic Christian believers. Rather than retain its Jewish roots and foundation, humbly remembering Gentiles are grafted into the covenants with Israel, the Roman Church declared that it had indeed replaced Israel.

In a nutshell, this theology does not see that the church made up of Jew and Gentile is a gap in time between our Lord's first and second coming to Israel. It ignores the Biblical truth that He will *literally* return to Jerusalem to intervene and deliver <u>the *literal*</u>

"nation." They _replace_ Israel with the Church, thus claim to be the _sole recipient and heirs_ of all of God's promises. Woe!

By doing so, Catholic Rome cursed Israel and placed herself in FIRST position, stole all the Covenant Promises in Scripture given to the "_Nation of Israel_", and applied them for "Spiritual Israel", the Church. They however conveniently left all the _literal curses_ for the _nation and people of Israel. Woe!_

The A- Millennial view: No future for Israel!

The letter "A" in Latin negates, thus means "no." The word Milus = 1000. Therefore A- Millennial means "_No 1000 year kingdom on earth for Israel._" **In simple terms, Israel is finished!** The millennium is no longer the _future_ 1000 year literal reign, when Jesus the Messiah returns as King to Jerusalem to rule from the literal throne of King David during the Messianic age, but an indefinite amount of time, of the _present spiritual_ reign of Christ in the hearts of believers, the church. This means Israel is no longer Israel but the church, and 1000 is no longer 1000, and Jerusalem is no longer Jerusalem but heaven. —**How confusing!** While some scripture is allegory, in order for this theology to stand the reader is forced to:

1.) Allegorize and _spiritualize_ all of God's Word.
2.) Ignore the original recipients of God's promises.
3.) Ignore scripture in its natural, cultural, geographical, and historical context.
3.) Ignore all of God's everlasting Covenants with Israel.

No wonder Paul said "Don't be ignorant!"

End of the world or end of the age?

To justify the denial of Israel future glory, the A-Millennial view is not only Anti-Israel, but Anti-earth, teaches annihilation, the obliteration and the utter none existence of the earth. Many use 2. Peter 3:10-13, which states: "_The earth and everything in it will be laid bare. Since everything will be **destroyed** in this way, what kind of people ought you to be?_" _You ought to live holy and godly lives, and speed its coming. That day will bring about destruction of the heavens by fire, and the elements will melt in the heat. But in_ *keeping with His promise we are looking for a new heaven and new earth, the home of righteousness.*

God used the term *"destroyed the earth"* when He did so by water, but on the other side of the flood it still existed, refreshed, renewed, and restored. (Genesis 6) Notice there is a *new heaven and new earth.* The word is **not** *"neos"* meaning something that never existed, but *"kainos",* meaning, renewed, superior to the old. This time God will purge and cleanse the earth by fire to prepare it for renewal. But this does in no way mean that the globe will blow up.

Sadly the King James translation speaks of the *"end of the world"* rather than *"end of the age" (eon, stretch of time),* to further aide the A-Millennial view in its belief of the annihilation of the earth. But when Jesus said *"My kingdom is not of this world",* (John 18:36), He was not speaking of the none existence of the **earth,** denying His future rule from earth in Jerusalem, but His refusal to rule this **world** , this *"cosmos",* this present ordered **world system** headed by Satan.

You might want to consider that annihilation is Satan's plan not God's. Have you noticed that he has been the god of this age ruling it long enough, trying to destroy it? The answer is obvious. If he can't be the heir of the earth, he doesn't want you to be. He would rather blow it up than let you have it.

Therefore A- Millennial denominations teach that when you die you go to heaven, and that is all that will exist. How tragic to ignore the future of the earth and only think of heaven as our inheritance, when in fact this belief keeps us blind to God's eternal purposes for Israel, and good will for us all, as He decreed a double portion of inheritance. Biblical fact is that there will be a new heaven *and* new earth. It is not either or, it is both! Are we going to have a party or what? Besides, why would there be a resurrection of the body, if there is no earth?

The downward spiral continues

But tragically, the A- Millennial view continued its arrogant and downward spiral, as Jews were labeled Christ killers, a damnable race forever cursed. Roman Catholic missionaries forced them to convert rather than love them to draw them to their Messiah. Refusal to convert resulted in missionaries saying *"Convert or leave as you may not live amongst us as Jews"*. It escalated to *"Convert or die!"* Houses were confiscated, and Jews were scattered or murdered for centuries in Jesus' name, hardening their hearts towards Jesus their Messiah even more. It resulted in the phenomenon known as *"The wandering Jews"*, as they sought refuge wherever they could.

Jews became the "scapegoat" of every society, portrayed in pictures and caricatures as devils with horns, resulting in their persecution from the Crusades to the Spanish Inquisition. Even those who submitted to Christian baptism were persecuted and murdered by the Roman Catholic Church, for anything remotely Jewish was considered evil. Attending synagogues, practicing circumcision, keeping the Sabbath and Holy days, even the mere possession of a Jewish Prayer Book, resulted in being stripped half naked, and paraded in carts down the street, and burned at the stake.

Martin Luther, the Protestant reformer of Germany

Martin Luther was born on November 10, 1483, a Roman Catholic monk who dared to stand against many of the corruptions of his church. The battle of his day was salvation by Grace through Faith in Jesus Christ rather than religious works. He stood up against the mightiest power of the earth at that time, as Rome and the church were fused into one entity *"The Holy Roman Empire."*

He who penned "A Mighty Fortress is Our God", also spoke up on behalf of Jews and their ungodly mistreatment by the Roman Catholic church in 1523. *"Perhaps I will attract some of the Jews to the Christian faith. For our fools, the popes, bishops, sophists and monks, the course blockheads, have until this time so mistreated the Jews that, if I had been a Jew and had seen such idiots and blockheads ruling and teaching the Christian religion, I would rather have been a sow than a Christian. For they have dealt with the Jews as if they were dogs and not human beings."*

The downward spiral enters the Protestant church

Sadly in his later years due to years of frustration battling against Rome, coupled with anti- Christian documents written by Jews, and unable to convert them in masses as he had hoped, he wrote the following tragic words in 1543: *"What shall we do with this devilish burden, the Jews?* **First**, *their synagogues should be set on fire.* **Secondly,** *their homes should likewise be broken down and destroyed...***Thirdly,** *they should be deprived of their prayer books, and Talmud's."***Fourthly**, *their Rabbis must be forbidden under threat of death to teach anymore.* **Fifthly** , *passport and traveling privileges should be absolutely forbidden to the Jews.* **Sixthly**, *they ought to be stopped from usuary (charging interest on loans).***Seventhly**, *let the young and strong Jews and Jewesses be given the flail, the ax, the hoe, the spade, the distaff, and spindle, and let them earn their bread by the sweat of their noses. We ought to drive the rascally lazy bones out of our system...Therefore away with them. To sum up, dear princes and nobles who have Jews in your domains, if this advice of mine does not suit you, then find a better one so that you and we may all be free of this insufferable devilish burden,-the Jews."*

The infection spreads

The Protestant reformation did not address the A- Millennial view, so it slipped into *many* denominations that to this day have replaced Israel as well. While many within these systems are oblivious to this theology, or even deny it, there are those who have gone to their deaths claiming to have *replaced Israel,* to be the *sole heirs* of all of God's promises in Scripture. It is estimated that 65 % of our denominations are A- Millennial.

DELAY does not mean DELETE!

As far as many doctrinal errors, it is my firm conviction that the majority of them are caused by arrogantly and often blindly assuming all of God's Word is for the church, cult or group, when in fact it was and is for *"Israel first"*, and we were *added*. Nowhere does it say that God has replaced Israel with the church. What it does say is this: "He in His grace **DELAYED** the salvation of the *"nation of Israel"* to save the WORLD, by establishing *"Spiritual Israel, the church made up of Jew and Gentile!"* Nowhere does it say the New Covenant was made with the church, group or cult. It was made with Israel, and Israel entered in **PART and we were ADDED.** Added is not bad, just the plan. Do you have a problem with being added? Go ahead and place yourself in first position and you will be cursed like Lucifer for arrogance. At best you will be cursed with confusion and more. God cannot be mocked, as Scripture cannot be understood apart from God's Covenants with Israel.

One of the greatest tragedies and marks against Christianity are the years of persecution against Jews in Jesus' name. The doctrine responsible for filling the minds of people with this evil is "Replacement Theology," that has fueled hatred, pain, and murder for more than 1600 years. As a result it also has been the major source of pain, suffering and confusion within the church itself. Those who deny God's future glory for Israel are:

1.) Blind to God's everlasting purposes for the world through Israel.
2.) Blind that Israel is God's geographical center of the earth and his prophetic time clock.
3.) Blind to the fact that Jesus is still King of the Jews who is coming back to Jerusalem to deliver His nation and receive his rightful coronation.
4.) Blind that the deliverance of the Church is eternally linked with the deliverance of Israel.
5.) Blind, as it is Satan's plan to keep them oblivious and unprepared for the end of the age.

Literal or spiritual kingdom?

I have heard more than enough pastors teach that Israel wrongly expected a literal Kingdom on earth expecting Jesus to conquer, overthrow the Roman Empire, and set up a political kingdom, because He only came to establish a spiritual Kingdom, the Church. This is extremely misleading unless explained carefully, because no less than 2/3 of Scripture speaks about Israel's glorious future during Messiah's earthly reign.

What Israel expected was *not wrong*, but their timing and spiritual condition was off.

John the Baptist was not a Baptist, but rather a righteous Jew who cried out to his nation,

"Repent!" Jesus who is the Jewish Messiah cried out to His people "Repent!" (Mark 1: 4-13)

These words were spoken to Israel and Israel as a nation did not repent. Therefore, Jesus said: *"O Jerusalem, Jerusalem, you (religious leaders) who kill the prophets and stone those sent to you, how often I have longed to gather your children together, as a hen gathers her chicks under her wings, but you were not willing."* (Matthew 23:37)

Consider this! Had Israel as a "nation, as a whole" repented and received their Messiah, Jesus would have not only gone to the cross to establish His heavenly kingdom in the hearts of men, but also arisen to destroy the Roman Empire, deliver His nation, and establish His kingdom on earth. The Messianic Kingdom with Jesus ruling from Jerusalem from the throne of King David would have begun, and the New Earth would have followed 1000 years later. Point? It would have been all over. It was simply not to be. Why? Because this is a mystery! **God wanted to wait to save sinners like you and me!"** *So where does that leave your arrogance?* **(Romans 11:1; 11:11)** *It is high time the church repents!*

Our Lord inaugurated a spiritual kingdom, His church, but may we never forget, that the very character and work of the Messiah, religious Jews expect, will be displayed as He comes again with power and glory, the lion of the tribe of Judah. The Messiah and deliverer of Israel will smite the nations and then usher in His glorious kingdom. (Zechariah 12-14, Rev.19)

How about evangelical churches?

While evangelical churches do not hold to the "A Millennial view", it is obvious to me that many still suffer at best from the ripple effects of Replacement Theology. Believers are told that the word of God is for them to such an extent, that the church often blindly teaches them to apply all of God's Word for the church, even when it says Israel, leaving many believers with a barrage of confusion and often utter frustration. Sadly, it is done in the genuine attempt to please God, even in their love for Jesus. However, little or no education is offered on God's Covenants with Israel that are still in effect. I have met few Christians who study God's word and ask:

"How did this apply to Israel, and *how does it **still apply** to Israel*, and then ask *"how do I fit into this plan?"*

Please answer the following questions. Do you believe that the Old Testament is all fulfilled? If you said "yes" you are dead wrong, because Jesus Christ would not need to return to Jerusalem if all was fulfilled! When have you had a lesson on the Covenants that God made with Israel, such as the Abrahamic Covenant that secures the Promised Land for Israel forever?

How about a lesson on the Davidic Covenant that secures the Messiah to come to rule on the throne of King David from Jerusalem forever? How often have you heard a message on Zechariah, Obadiah, Hosea, Amos, Joel or Haggai? If you have, did you just read it and then tried to apply the "Spiritual principles" to the church, or have you truly searched it out, and understood what it means to Israel and still means to Israel, since it says Israel and not Church ?

In my mind the practice of personal application without retaining the original meaning and setting, without understanding God's Covenants with Israel, nor the original recipients, is like using binoculars, which were meant to look far off first, but when you try to use them to look at yourself you see nothing but fuzz. Being so utterly self- focused has not only been the major cause of grief to the Jewish people by the church, but also cursed the church with spiritual confusion, resulting in torment and spiritual abuse by misguided spiritual leaders. It is the most dangerous spiritual practice in "my book", asking the believer to check their brains out at the door, as it is not only the height of ignorance gone arrogant, but intellectual and spiritual suicide!

Many churches and pastors do a better job than others educating their flock. All I know is this, I have met Christians from numerous denominations, and almost all were totally oblivious to the Covenants in God's Word, because their primary focus and drive is always personal life application. I also have met numerous well- meaning believers totally exhausted by the barrage of confusion, and some so utterly frustrated ready to give up on their faith.

Furthermore, most Christians are uneducated about Christian history because most churches do not seem to find it important enough to teach that we have blood on our hands, focusing only upon all the good accomplished in Jesus name, and ignoring the darkness. This attitude flies in the face of Holy Scripture as we are destined to repeat what we refuse to face. Only the truth will set us free! We can and must stand in the gap of 1600 years of Jewish persecution in Jesus' name.

Overlooking the Cross

May I point out and remind many seminaries, pastors, and believers, that the prideful and arrogant theology in *Israel's institutions blinded* Israel as a nation at Christ's First Coming.
a) Stiff-necked theology *could* not believe,
b) Because it *would* not humble itself,
c) Therefore, *could* not understand the CROSS for Israel,
d) Thus, Israel as a nation was BLIND, *cut off in PART!*

Only a remnant believed, and Gentiles were grafted in.
Their institutions and leaders had their minds made up, and nothing on earth was going to persuade them any different. God in turn used common people like fishermen. His disciples left all to follow Him who did not think they were better, nor had doctrines carved in stone. It took a supernatural intervention, a miracle called Pentecost, the outpouring of His Spirit, to break through and save 3000 Jews to begin His church in Jerusalem. Many more were added in numbers daily. (Acts 1-2)

Overlooking the crown

Today many seminaries, pastors and believers are suffering from prideful theology, causing a great part of the church to be BLIND, because:
a.) Stiff-necked theology *will* not believe,
b) Because it is *unwilling* to humble itself,
c) Therefore, *cannot* understand the CROWN for Israel.
d) Thus, the church as a whole does not see, and *part* will be cut off.

Only a remnant will believe, and God will graft Israel back in. (Romans 11)

Their institutions of learning and leaders have their minds made up, and nothing on earth is going to persuade them any different. So God uses common folks like you and me, who *were not of noble birth, nor wise by human standards, not influential, as God chose the foolish things to shame the wise, who boast in the Lord.* (1 Cor.1: 9-31) Therefore, it will take an outpouring of God's spirit, His supernatural intervention to break through the church. It is my prayer that God's Spirit would sweep through our churches, to "stand in the gap" for 1600 years of damnable arrogance. Can you imagine what would happen if millions of Christians apologized to Jews? **Maybe they would actually believe Jesus is their Messiah**.

A humble heart will say: "Branches were cut off, so I can be grafted in, grafted in is good! That means I am part of the tree! That means I am getting nourishment from the roots. That means I am alive, producing fruit. If I don't like it, I might just be cut off! (Romans 11:17-24) A humble heart will be grateful and recognize: "Through God's Covenant with Abraham I am included, I am loved, I am a servant, I don't need to be first!"

If you think that I am exaggerating, let me close by saying that I always ask Christians this following question. "Since Jesus is going to resurrect the dead and Rapture the Church, can you tell me why Jesus is coming back to Jerusalem?" Answers range from, "to judge", " to fight the battle of Armageddon", "because He promised to return there." No one ever says: "To intervene in order to save Israel."

This is more than tragic!

CHAPTER 12

More religious arrogance!

While large segments of Christianity have replaced themselves with Israel, so have many cults.

What sets them apart from being accepted as Christian, is their claim of salvation within their organizations, and the denial of the true nature of Jesus Christ, reducing Him to a mere prophet, or angel, rather than God who came in human flesh. While there are over 3000 cults in the USA alone, I will mention only two major and well-known groups.

Mormons/ Latter day Saints:

Mormons have added the book Mormon, which is claimed to have been written by Joseph Smith, who is believed to be a true prophet of God. He supposedly had a vision of the angel Moroni who gave him golden plates, and special glasses to translate them. No one else has ever seen them. Mormons believe these writings to be God's revelation to the USA. While they claim to believe in the Bible, his revelations do not harmonize with Holy Scripture.

The god of Mormonism is not God who became a man to serve and die on a cross for our sins, but rather man who became God, and teach their people and followers that mankind can become gods as well. Rather than trust Jesus Christ who is the firstborn from the dead for our salvation, guaranteeing our resurrection, Mormons adhere to a works system to gain acceptance into the Mormon Temple.

Wives are at the mercy of their Mormon husbands, who believe they become gods at the resurrection, to call out her secret name to rise from the grave. Mormon gods and their wife-goddesses believe they will be given their own planets, thus their mission is to eternally produce heirs to populate it. Sounds like a lot of fun for the men and work for the women, when in fact Jesus said there is no marriage in heaven. (Matthew 22:30)

Mormons replace Israel, and even dare to state that the Garden of Eden was in Jackson County Missouri. They furthermore believe that the American Indians are the lost tribe of Israel. However, these claims have been repudiated by linguists who find no similarity between Hebrew and any of the Native American tongues. More recently it has been disproved by DNA to make it obvious to any person willing to look and listen.

Jehovah's Witnesses deny Jesus is the Word who was God that became flesh, and proclaim him to be *"a god, the created Archangel Michael."* They have replaced Israel and the church as God's sole organization on earth, the only true Christians, while the rest of Christendom goes to hell. Salvation is found only within their organization, the Watchtower Society. Only they are the heirs of Gods Kingdom to live in Paradise on *earth*. They furthermore claim that the elect 144.000 Jews of Revelation 7and 14 are not Jews, but rather their chosen members to enter *heaven*. However, scripture clearly identifies them as male virgins from the 12 tribes of Israel that remain on *"earth"*, sealed and set apart for a unique and special purpose at the end of the age.

It is obvious that Satan hates Israel and the Jewish people, because he knows that it is a Jew named Jesus that will cause his ultimate destruction. Sadly he has managed to deceive numerous so called Christian organizations, and various groups, to steal their inheritance, rather than bless them. Replacing Israel is without a doubt the greatest blinder so people don't read any longer what the Word of God says, but with the preconceived mindset as they were taught to believe.

Questions:

If the Roman Catholic Church, many Protestant denominations, groups like the Mormons and Jehovah's witnesses, and numerous others have replaced Israel, or claim to be the lost tribes, then I have a lot of questions, but will only ask two. Read Zechariah 14 first, and then answer me, - *please!*

1.) If God has indeed replaced Israel, why is the Lord Jesus returning to *Jerusalem* and stands on the *Mount of Olives,* which is still in Israel, not Rome, nor the USA?
2.) If God is indeed finished with Israel and has replaced Israel with your group, why will He *split the Mount of Olives in half,* to make a way of escape for *His people,* then fights in a mighty battle against those who come to destroy *Jerusalem,* and in a triumphant conclusion destroys the *enemies of Israel in the battle of Armageddon?*

I have my answer. It is a simple answer. To save the remnant of Israel! God has not changed! He always has, and always will! Our God is a Covenant keeping God. If God could ever forsake His covenant promises to Israel, all would be lost. Why? Because once again let me say: *"It is God's eternal will to save the world through Israel. No Israel, no Jesus coming the first time. No Israel, no Jesus coming again!"*

While the world has cursed Israel, those who claim the name of Jesus Christ by faith were to be different. How utterly tragic and sickening it is to me to learn about our horrific past and continued arrogance. May we repent before it is too late, and God begins to prune the olive tree by cutting off some of the wild branches (gentiles,) and graft the natural branches (Israel) back in. We are called to bless and proclaim God's faithfulness to Israel.

Jeremiah 31: 10-14

"Hear the word of the LORD o **NATIONS (gentiles),** *proclaim it in distant coastlands: "He who scattered Israel will gather them and will watch over His flock like a shepherd.*

For the LORD will ransom Jacob (Israel) and redeem them from the hand of those stronger than they. They will come and shout for joy on the heights of Zion. They will rejoice in the bounty of the LORD, the grain and the new wine and the oil, the young of the flocks and herds. They will be like a well-watered garden, and they will sorrow no more. Then maidens will dance and be glad, young men and old as well. I will turn their mourning into gladness; I will give them comfort and joy instead of sorrow. I will satisfy the priest with abundance, and my people will be filled with my bounty, declares the LORD!"

It is utterly frustrating to realize, how many groups have attempted to conform people into their own image or denominations. They uphold their rules and doctrines rather than the name of Jesus, and always claim exclusive truth and salvation within their walls and systems. Last but not least they place themselves arrogantly in FIRST position. I believe that in this very hour of history God is calling forth an inner court people, a remnant of people, to stand firm on the Rock Jesus Christ and nothing else, who proclaim God's faithfulness to the true church and Israel, who boast in the LORD, not their religious affiliation. (1Corinthians 1:18-31)

I am afraid we are heading down the road of final division within the body of Christ at the end of the age. It will be those who stand on Christ alone and His everlasting Covenants for Israel, and those who hold to manmade religions and systems, cursing Israel. It is no less than disturbing to realize that in the first century, religious Jews persecuted Christian Jews for their faith. Could it be that at the end of the age that gentile church / group members, will persecute those of us who stand on Christ alone and support Israel?

CHAPTER 13

Deception in Nazi Germany, we are *FIRST!*

God appointed leaders of nations to guide, protect, and serve, but many in their satanic perversion and quest for power have come to conquer in war, kill and destroy. They exemplify the image of Satan rather than Christ. Every Empire listed in scripture was a ferocious Beast seeking to devour the earth and ruthlessly conquer, no matter the cost. In addition they were possessed by a demonic hatred of Israel seeking her destruction. - Nothing has changed.

Hitler began as a wolf in sheep's clothing. He came on the scene as an angel of light, when Germany was destitute with WWI only a recent memory, and the great depression with 3 million unemployed. He joined the political party for the blue collar working class, known as the "National Socialist German Workers Party", commonly known as the "Nazi Party."

Hitler as early as 1925 outlined his conclusion in chapter 4 of "Mein Kampf", that *Darwinism* was the only basis for a successful Germany, eliminating the *inferior* specimens of man. By 1933 he was elected chancellor of Germany bringing hope to a destitute people. The Nazis arrogantly pledged *first* to restore Germany to its *"rightful"* place in Europe, and then seek world power. By 1934 Hitler eliminated much of the political and military opposition as he murdered 1000, purging the Nazi Party.

They began to control German life, and transformed the nation under his rule into a ruthless and aggressive totalitarian state. The Aryan quest for the perfect race resulted in torture, subjecting Germany to inhumane medical experiments, killing non- desirables, such as the mentally retarded, handicapped and elderly, labeling them **"useless eaters."** He marched through Poland killing thousands. His quest included the removal of all non-desirables, such as Gypsy's, gays, and people of non-conforming religious groups such as Jehovah's witnesses.

The Roman Catholic Church proved to be useful to Hitler's evil mind and hatred of the Jews, as he once considered the priesthood and also studied Luther's writings, thus was well aware that:

1.) Jews were labeled a damnable race forever cursed.
2.) Missionaries said: "Convert or leave, for you may not live amongst us as Jews."
3.) It escalated to "convert or die".
4.) In the name of Jesus Christ, Jews were tortured and murdered for centuries in Europe, forcing them to flee and wander the earth.
5.) Martin Luther's Anti Semitic writings stated, "be rid of this devilish burden the Jews."
6.) Under Adolf Hitler, Europe's Anti Semitic and "Christian" history found its climax by declaring "Jews may not live at all!"

"The Night of broken glass" (The Kristallnacht), occurred on November 9th and 10th of 1938. It was chosen in honor of Luther's birthday, as Hitler followed Luther's advice and instructions in his letter written in1543. Yes, he indeed found a better way to be rid of this devilish burden, the Jews, when rampaging mobs throughout Germany freely attacked Jews in the streets, their homes, places of work, and worship. At least 96 Jews were killed and hundreds more injured. More than 1,000 synagogues were burned. Almost 7,500 Jewish businesses were destroyed, cemeteries and schools were vandalized and 30,000 Jews were arrested and sent to concentration camps. November 10, 1938 may be considered the beginning of the Holocaust.

For seven years his ruthless war machine conquered nation after nation to liquidate the Jew within them. Any who opposed him and were caught died. Towards the end of WW II, his generals pleaded to send supplies and food to the Russian front for their starving and dying men, but he left them to die, as he, in a last ditch effort, used every truck and train to bring as many Jews as possible to awaiting death camps. Hitler was driven by a power unable to be described outside of a supernatural, demonic hatred

Albert Speer, Hitler's intimate and closest confidant stated in his writings: *"Hatred of the Jews was Hitler's motor and central point, perhaps even the very element which motivated him. The German people, the German greatness, the Empire, they all meant nothing to him in the last analysis. For this reason, he wished in the final sentence of his testament, to fixate us Germans, even after the apocalyptic downfall in a miserable hatred of the Jews."* (End of quote)

Nazis and Muslims, what a Team!

Albert Speer also quoted Hitler as saying: *"Had Germany been a Muslim nation rather than Christian, she would have been more readily suited for ruthless warfare!* Why? Islam like Nazism is devoted to the destruction of Jews and Christians, and therefore supported Nazi Germany in WW II. - What a TEAM!

It should not surprise us to learn that the ruthless "Amin Al Husseini" was the grand mufti of Jerusalem, Hitler's friend, who spent WW II at his side. He led "Bosnian SS Hanzer divisions in Eastern Europe", the butcher of 500,000 Jews. His flag depicts the Muslim Sword and Swastika *"together."* What a team indeed. While WW II ended, the Nazi and Islamic goal did not. Husseini incited riots between Arab Palestinians and Jews, and was the founder of the World Islamic congress. - May we awake and realize that what was taught in *"little"* Nazi Germany is taught in *"all"* Muslim nations. - *He who has an ear let him hear!* http://www.tellthechildrenthetruth.com

Extermination of Christians:

While 6 million Jews perished, this demonic regime also caused the death of several million Christians, something we hardly ever hear about. Had Hitler continued in power all Christians would have been next! Among his loyal leaders were; Josef Goebbel, minister of Enlightenment and Propaganda, who not only aspired to wipe out the last Jew, but then the last priest. General Erich Ludendorff, Hitler's ally, called for the abolition of Christianity in Germany. Alfred Rosenberg, Hitler's Reich Minister for the Occupied Eastern Territories issued tracts denouncing the Gospel of Jesus Christ. Heinrich Himmler, head of the German Gestapo created the SS, in an attempt to rehabilitate medieval witchcraft. The Nazis were heavily involved in the occult; the Swastika and likewise the lightning bolt on their daggers were occultist symbols. Wake up church! Were it not for the sacrifice of thousands of American men, her allies, and families to serve and stop this madman, the world would be under Nazi and Muslim control, and you would have more than likely never been born, because your Christian parents would have been murdered and martyred as well.

In His Image:
God created man in his own image, not Lucifer's, not the angels'. Satan's insatiable quest is to *recreate man in his image, his own likeness, unwilling to humble himself, to serve God or man, distort the role of leadership, dominate, kill and destroy.*

Adolf Hitler was totally submitted to the "image of Satan." He not only threw away the weak, but fleeced and slaughtered his own sheep for his own gain. He managed to deceive not an ignorant or barbaric people, but the *minds of* a most civilized and educated people. It was false pride and arrogance that darkened his mind. His involvement in the occult and belief in evolution twisted his belief about God, and gave him the audacity to *arrogantly* proclaim that the German Aryan race had evolved to *superior* status to all of mankind. His mind already twisted and depraved, wrapped by a demonic hatred against the Jews, used corrupt religion to justify his actions.

The apostle Paul wrote:

The god of this age (Satan) has blinded the <u>minds</u> of unbelievers,
So that they cannot see the light of the Gospel
of the Glory of Christ,
Who is the IMAGE of GOD!"
(2 Corinthians 4: 4)

I have often thought about the horrible day of December 7. 1941, when Japan viciously attacked Pearl Harbor Hawaii, as it brought the United States into World War II, and gave Americans a personal stake in the war. As tragic as it was, and is, what Satan meant for evil and destruction, God used for good. If it were not for the USA, I just wonder how much longer Hitler's reign of terror would have continued.

May 8, 1945 marked the official end of WW II. The result was millions of Jews and non- Jews dead, nations in ruin, Germany destroyed, with the surviving psyche and emotions of the German people controlled by fear and perfectionism, from years of terror and war, with the Nazi mind possessed by a demonic hatred of Jews.

When will we ever learn that God said to Abraham:

"I will bless those who bless you, and curse those who curse you!"
Genesis 12:3

Blessed by the sacrifice of American lives, and other allies, I was born and raised in a free and "Western Germany", while the Russians claimed *"East Germany."* They also claimed the *liberation* of numerous *eastern* European nations from the Nazis, but Moscow's rule did not liberate, but put them in the Iron grip of Communism. Leninism was the Black Death of the 20th Century, the killer of tens of millions, including Jews and Christians.

May I quote our President Bush: *For much of Eastern and Central Europe, victory brought the iron rule of another empire. V-E day marked the end of fascism, but it did not end the oppression. The agreement in Yalta followed in the unjust tradition of Munich and the Molotov-Ribbentrop Pact. Once again, when powerful governments negotiated, the freedom of small nations was somehow expendable. The captivity of millions in Central and Eastern Europe will be remembered as one of the greatest wrongs in history.* End of quote (May 2005)

Real power comes from saving lives!
Come Lord Jesus, Come!

CHAPTER 14

Islam, Satan's masterpiece, we are *FIRST!*

Many people assume Judaism, Christianity, and Islam, are sister faiths because our roots go back to father Abraham. While Mohammed is a descendant of Abraham through Ishmael and his son Kedar (Genesis 25:13), Mohammed did not have the faith of Father Abraham, but was born in 610 AD in Mecca Arabia, where the pagan belief of Mecca and Medina was prevalent, thus approx. 600 years after Jesus Christ, and somewhere around 2600 years after Father Abraham.

Angel of God or counterfeit?

Just as the founder of Mormonism, Joseph Smith, claimed new revelations by an angel, Mohammed claimed visions of the angel Gabriel. Mohammed himself admits he was terrified, foamed at the mouth, accompanied by intense bodily gyrations, similar to what we call Epileptic fits today. He himself questioned if they were demonic visions, but his wife convinced him to accept them as being from God.

One must *always* question any angelic visitations, because true angels of God were frightening due their brilliant, massive, and powerful appearance, but always comforted the person and said *"Do not be afraid!"* Furthermore, they have no authority to proclaim anything different than God's Word according to the Apostle Paul. (Galatians 1:8). They never oppose Holy Scripture, but always support and confirm it. In addition they always give glory to the God of Abraham, Isaac and Jacob. Last but not least, Jesus is *superior* to the angels, the radiance of God's glory, and the exact representation of His being. Hebrews 1:1-14.

The Apostle Paul warns us to proceed with caution, because Satan is a deceiver that even "masquerades as an angel of light." He wrote in 2 Corinthians 11: 3-14 the following: *"I am afraid that just as Eve was deceived by the serpent's cunning, your minds may somehow be led astray from your sincere and pure devotion to Christ. For if someone comes to you and preaches a Jesus other than the Jesus we preached to you, or if you received a different spirit from the one you received, or a different Gospel, from the one you accepted, you put up with it easily enough," —for such men are false apostles, deceitful workman, —masquerading as apostles of Christ.* **And no wonder, for Satan himself masquerades as an angel of Light.** *It is not surprising then, if his servants masquerade as servants of righteousness. Their end will be what their actions deserve."*

Islam: Muslims claim they believe in the prophets of Holy Scripture including Jesus. However, they reject almost everything He said, including His claims to be the Son of God, His death, and resurrection. The Jesus they preach is not the Jesus we know, because Mohammed is seen as the ultimate and superior prophet, who claims the Koran is the true fulfillment of both the Old and the New Testament, which has replaced them. To Islam Allah is the only true God that gave Mohammed a new law, which he alone received. As the ultimate prophet he furthermore is the sole authority of interpretation of the law, thus in addition his thoughts and deeds are recorded in the "Hadith", without which a Muslim cannot follow the Koran. Therefore, Islam is based upon the word of <u>one person.</u>

Islam's holy cities are Mecca and Medina towards which Muslims pray 5 times daily bowing to the East. The words love and Jerusalem are never mentioned in the Koran, yet Mohammed claimed that he, in a vision, was taken by a white winged stallion to Jerusalem, and entered the Holy place on the Temple mount, where he prayed with Abraham, Moses, and Jesus, and was embraced by Allah. This night ride is known by Muslims as the Hijra.

Bible: In contrast, Holy Scripture was written over thousands of years by 40 different authors. God sent prophet after prophet, whose words can be cross examined, recorded in Scripture. Love is mentioned hundreds of times, Jerusalem over 600 times, and is the only sacred Holy site to the Jewish people. Every synagogue in the world faces Jerusalem. It was in the Temple in Jerusalem, whereby which man could approach God with the prescribed and acceptable sacrifice. For us Christians it is fulfilled in the person of Jesus the Messiah and redeemer of Israel and Savior of the world who died there and rose again.

The book of Levi, records centuries of practice by the Hebrew Levitical priesthood that served in the Temple in Jerusalem. The law clearly excluded anyone to enter the Holy place in the Temple, except Hebrews, and then only those of the tribe of Levi, trained and exclusively chosen for the priesthood, never mind a gentile such as Mohammed. Only one High priest could enter the Holy of Holies once a year to offer atonement for sin. Jesus Himself, whom Islam claims to be a true prophet of God, would never enter the Holy Place because He was of the royal lineage, of the tribe of Judah, not Levi. He would never consider breaking the Law of Moses or replace it, but kept it to perfection, and furthermore fulfilled it. Therefore Mohammed obviously missed the point, that his claims totally oppose the Law of Moses, the Word of God, and the Words of Jesus Christ Himself.

The ultimate Replacement theology:

Islam claims that the Old and New Testament was corrupted and the Koran does not replace them, but merely corrects them. Considering that God got it wrong two times with numerous prophets and trained scribes that meticulously recorded the Holy Scriptures for thousands of years, what makes you think he got it right the third time, with one man, who had fits foaming from the mouth trembling in fear?

To my understanding, Islam is the ultimate counterfeit and replacement theology. He replaced the God of Abraham, Isaac, and Jacob with Allah; the Law of Moses with Islamic law; all of Scripture with the Koran, the people of Abraham, Isaac and Jacob, and the church, with the followers of Islam. Last but not least, the Scriptures are filled with numerous prophets and covenants declaring God's everlasting love for Israel, and redeem the world through her, while the Koran is filled with hatred and commitment to destroy Israel, Jews, and Christians.

I could go on forever, but it is so obvious to anyone who would consider spending any time in study, that the Koran opposes the Holy Bible. Since Mohammed was illiterate there are sources that believe the Koran was actually recorded by a Jewish scribe under the threat of his life, thus contains similarities, but the author included much information to expose it for the counterfeit that it is. One should remember that *"Replacement theology"* started in heaven, when Lucifer refused to submit to the Lordship of God, asserting his own will, not willing to humble himself, determined to defy God and rule heaven and earth, thus is determined *to replace God.*

The Muslim Abbasid Empire of 750-1258 AD.

In the 7th and 8th century AD Muslim hordes swept like locusts out of the Arabian Peninsula, today's Saudi Arabia. They slaughtered, raped, and pillaged millions by the sword. By the 8th century they conquered the Middle East. The borders of the ancient Arab Muslim Abbasid Empire are unchanged in the last 1250 years, except Israel, Spain and Portugal were freed from Islamic control. The modern day Muslim nations that are encompassed in the area of the ancient Abbasid Muslim Empire are: Afghanistan, Algeria, Egypt, Iraq, Iran, Jordan, Kuwait, Lebanon, Libya, Morocco, Oman, Pakistan. Saudi Arabia, Sudan, Syria, United Arab Emirates, and Yemen.

They were a religious empire, convinced they were the one true faith, committed to bring the whole world under Islamic control, under submission of Islamic Shariah law. Characterized by strife among themselves, their primary conflict in war and religion was with the *Christian West*. They were extremely brutal in their methods of subduing opposition, slaughtering multitudes of their enemies both within and without the empire. Their western quest was stopped in 732 AD by Charles Martel of France. He met Abd-er-Rahman outside of Tours and defeated and slew him in a battle of Poitiers. *This was "the" great event in history, as upon its issue depended whether Christian Civilization should continue or Islam prevail throughout Europe.* It was this battle that gave Charles his name "The Hammer", because of the merciless way in which he smote the enemy. Thank you Charles Martel for sparing Europe from Muslim domination! How ironic that today, France is the *first* European nation threatened to come under Islamic rule, this time by infiltration, future majority, and consequent threat of Jihad. - I am sure Charles is rolling over in his grave.

The Mahdi, the Muslim Messiah!

In 878 AD, the 12th Imam (religious head) of the Shi'ite Muslims of Musa's line disappeared at age seven without a trace, leaving no successor. They believe that the 12th Imam never died and was taken by Allah into temporary hiding from the world to return some day as the MAHDI / MESSIAH, to bring about the "Day of Judgment" upon the earth and begin to rule the world.

Mohammed, his successors, and major divisions within Islam

1. Imam= Abu Bkar

2. Imam= Umar.

3. Imam =Utman.

4. Imam= Hadrat ALI ibn Abu Talib, son of Mohammed's uncle Ali Talib; married Fatima Mohammed's daughter.
Caliphate plagued by Treachery and Conspiracy ----->---> Mu'awiyah, Governor of Syria
Disputed Ali's election and killed him

5. Imam Ali's son Hassan claimed successor ship,   He convinced Ali's son Hassan to abdicate and promised to restore the Caliphate to the house of Mohammed upon his death.
|
V   Appointed his own son Yazi,
SPLIT   SPLIT = SUNNI
|
SHI'ITE

The Shi'ites were also at odds with themselves
|
6. Imam JAFAR
Firstborn Ismail | second born Musa
7th Imam ISMAIL   \
But did not survive his father   \ was designated by father as 7th Imam.
and had already appointed his |
son as the 7. Imam.   SPLIT
| Followers of Musa = Orthodox Shi'ites (Shi'ism)
SPLIT |
SEVENERS SHI'ITES   Several years later, in 878AD, the 12th Imam of
Note: From ISMAIL   Musa's line, Mohammed ibn Hasan, disappeared at the
issued a violent brand of Islam   age of 7 years old without a trace leaving no successor.
                                   Orthodox Shi'ites, believe that the 12th Imam never died and was
                                   taken by Allah into temporary hiding from the world. He
                                   will return some day as the MAHDI / MESSIAH to bring
                                   about the Day of Judgment upon the earth and begin to rule
                                   the world.

Anyone aware of Biblical eschatology knows that God and Jesus Christ will bring about the Day of Judgment, to overthrow the enemies of Israel, to rule in righteousness and the law will go out from Jerusalem.(Isaiah 2:1-5). Thus the Muslim Mahdi is clearly an imposter.

Who is Muqtada Al Sadr?

In Iraq, Sheik Muqtada al-Sadr opposed and challenged the interim government established by the USA. His army is named the "The Imam al-Mahdi Army." In so doing he has obviously declared himself to be the Mahdi, the Muslim Messiah to the Shi'ites, to follow him and his leadership. He formed a rival government and called on Iraqis in Kufa south of Baghdad to support the "new state." Please notice that the ancient Abbasid Empire which sought to conquer the world before, but was stopped by the West, had their headquarters in Kufa as well and then moved it to Baghdad. In addition he was 30 years old, the same age Jesus was when he began His ministry. - Hmm?

Islamic Fundamentalism:
The goal of fundamental Islam is to restore and enlarge the Abbasid Muslim Empire of 750 A.D. globally. They actually believe that we, the west, are suppressed and need to come under the perfect law of Allah, to find freedom from democracy. They despise western corruption, call us the great Satan, and burn our flags. Their zeal to acquire nuclear weapons is to destroy the west, particularly the USA. The Palestinian terrorist group, Hamas, vows to destroy Israel, with Palestine from the Mediterranean Sea to the Jordan River. Unable to come against Israel militarily at this point, their tactic as of now is suicide bombers sent into crowded shopping areas, restaurants, or buses with bombs hiding under their clothing, to blow themselves up along with as many innocent bystanders as they can. To them they are not innocent, but enemies of Allah that occupy his land. Recently Iran's president has boldly announced their commitment to destroy Israel. Pakistan under the blasphemy law issues the death penalty for anyone who insults Islam or Islam's prophet Mohammed, or anyone who converts to Christianity. Pakistan's 2 million Christians are a community "living in fear." Lebanon, the only Christian nation in the Middle East, the former Paris of the Middle East, was transformed in 1975 into a ruthless Islamic state, after Muslims gained majority due to higher birthrates. Their terrorist group is known as the *"Hezbollah."* In Afghanistan it is the *"Taliban"*, with Bin Laden's worldwide organizational structure named *"Al-Qaeda."* In many of the countries they are known as various versions of the "Islamic Salvation Front. In Sudan almost 3 Million Christians have been tortured, then massacred for refusing Allah, *the most gracious and merciful god*, suffering a modern day Holocaust, that would rival the brutality of Hitler. As unbelievable as it seems this is not the most ruthless brand of Islam. The most pure and radical form of Islam is

found in Saudi Arabia, the birthplace of Islam, backed by billions of oil dollars.

Algeria in 1992, issued this manifesto by the "Armed Islamic Group. - *"As we fight the atheist regime, which we have stripped of all legitimacy, we fight their kin, their followers, all those who support them or work for them. It is therefore essential to track them down in the cities, towns and villages and in the deserts to liquidate them, annihilate their homes, confiscate their wealth and possess their women. We will do it with bombs, with repeated massacres, and blood that will flow everywhere until they shut their eyes only after their heads are separated from their bodies."*

This unbelievable brutality is responsible for 75,000 deaths in Algeria. Many have been *westernized Muslims,* considered not true followers of Allah, thus killed for their unwillingness to partake in the cause of Jihad. My prayer is that God blessed them with His mercy and opened their eyes to the true and living God, before they were shut by the sword of Islam.

One cannot understand this kind of hatred and thirst for blood because it is demonic. I find it no less than revealing that the Bible teaches us we were made by God from the earth, given the earth, then the curse of sin and death put as back in the earth, to be followed by our glorious resurrection rising from the earth to join our spirit, to climax in the restoration of the new heaven, and new earth. This was, and will be accomplished by Christ who spilled His own blood so we would not have to spill ours. Yet Islam says Allah made mankind from a clot of blood. Quran 96: 2 No wonder blood is their inheritance, what they long for, even must spill, to secure their male dominated, sex-craved, and perverted idea of heaven.

The Prince of Peace:

In contrast, Jesus is called the "Prince of Peace". What a breath of fresh air after all this evil! It is to Jerusalem that the true Messiah and Savior will return to defend and save lives, and by doing so destroy the enemies of God and Israel to rule from His City. Understanding Islam and its satanic quest to annihilate all who refuse Allah and rule the earth, makes the term "Savior and Deliverer" more than I ever thought it would. He is not only the Savior of men but of the earth. He has the birthright to the throne of Israel, because He was born King of the Jews. Thank God He is coming back to Jerusalem to make an end of this satanic ruthless quest.

Choose this day whom you will serve!
For me and my house we will serve the LORD!"

CHAPTER 15

Islam, Peace— or Anti Christ religion?

Islam is strictly a monotheistic religion believing in one God named Allah. While they claim to believe in Jesus as a prophet of God, they deny many of His words recorded by the Apostles; most vehemently that He is the Son of God, His death and resurrection. It is an abomination in their thinking that God would have a Son. Following are passages directly taken from the Koran (Qur'an), Islam's holy book. It is divided by Surah's (chapters).

God has no Son:
Surah 11:111 Say: "Praise be to Allah, who begets NO SON, and has NO PARTNER in his dominion: Nor (needs) he any to protect him from humiliation Yea, magnify Him for his greatness."

Surah 19:88-95 "And they say the Beneficent (most gracious) God has taken (to Himself) a son. Certainly you have made an <u>abominable assertion</u>. The heavens may almost be rent thereat, and the earth cleave asunder, and the mountains fall down in pieces, that they ascribe a son to the Beneficent God. And it is not worthy of the Beneficent God that He should take a son. There is no one in the heavens and the earth but will come to the Beneficent God as a servant. Certainly He has a comprehensive knowledge of them and

He has numbered them a (comprehensive) numbering. And every one of them will come to Him on the day of resurrection alone."

Surah 18:1-6 "In the name of Allah, the Beneficent, the Merciful. (All) praise is due to Allah, who revealed the Book to His servant and did not make in it any crookedness. Rightly directing, that he might give warning of severe punishment from Him and give good news to the believers who do good that they shall have a goodly reward: Staying in it for ever; and warn those who say: *Allah has taken a son.* They have no knowledge of it, nor had their fathers; *a grievous word it is that comes out of their mouths; they speak nothing but a lie.* Then maybe you will kill yourself with grief, sorrowing after them, if they do not believe in this announcement."

Surah 19:34 -35...It is not befitting for God to take a son unto Him. Glory be to Him! When He decrees a thing, He but says to it 'Be', and it is."

Rejection of preexistence of Jesus:

Surah 3:59 "Truly the likeness of *Jesus,* in God's sight, is as Adam's likeness; *He created him of dust, then said He unto him, "be", and he was*

Rejection of Trinity:

Surah 4:171 "People of the Book, go not beyond the bounds in your religion, and say not as to God but the Truth. *The Messiah, Jesus, son of Mary, was only the messenger of God,* and his word that he committed to Mary, and a spirit from him. So believe in God (Allah) and his Messengers, (Mohammed) and say not, *'Three',* refrain, better is it for you. God is only one God. Glory be to him — *that He should have a son!* To him belongs all that is in the heavens and in the earth, God suffices for a guardian."

Christians charged with Blasphemy:

Surah 5:73 "They do blaspheme who say: Surely Allah is the third (person) of the three; and there is no god but the one God, and if they desist not from what they say, a painful chastisement shall befall those among them who disbelieve."

Surah 5:17 "*In blasphemy indeed are those who say Allah is Christ, the son of Mary*. Say: Who then hath the least power against Allah, if his will were to destroy Christ, the son of Mary, his mother and all —, everyone that is on the earth? For to Allah belongeth the dominion of the heavens and the earth, and all that is between. He createth what he pleaseth. For Allah hath power over all things."

Denial of Christ's crucifixion:
Surah 4: 157 -158 That they (the Jews) boast, "*We killed Christ Jesus the son of Mary, the Messenger of Allah, but they killed him not, nor crucified him, but so it was made to appear to them,* and those who differ therein are full of doubts, with no (certain) knowledge, but only conjecture to follow, for of a surety they killed him not. *Nay Allah raised him up unto himself* (assumed Jesus to heaven without dying), *and Allah is exalted in power, wise. There is not one of the people of the Book (Jews and Christians) but must believe in him (Jesus) before his death, and on the Day of Judgment he (Jesus) will be a witness against them.*" (Surah 4:159)

Muslims believe that our Lords crucifixion was faked, that in place of Jesus, Judas was crucified while Jesus lived to an old age. The so-called Gospel of Barnabas, a proven forgery from the late Middle Ages, claims to be the only true Gospel of Jesus Christ, but contains many Muslim doctrines, which attack the Bible. This gospel has become very famous in the Muslim world especially since its translation into Arabic in the 20th century. It argues that having been made so similar to Jesus that the Messiah's own family and disciples considered him to be Jesus. Judas was crucified against his will in Jesus' place. Then Judas was led to the Mount of Calvary.

Bible: "DO NOT BE DECEIVED!"
The apostle John wrote that Jesus Christ is the "Son of God, who was with God, was God, and was made flesh." (John 1: 1-14). He likewise wrote 1. 2. and 3. John, and the book of Revelation. He warns us "not" to be deceived, warns of Anti Christ's, and gives us clear instructions to "Test the Spirits to see if they are from God!"

Test the Spirits! 1 John 4:1-4

*Dear friends, do not believe every spirit, but test the spirits to see whether they are from God, because many false prophets have gone out into the world. This is how you can recognize the Spirit of God: **Every spirit that acknowledges that Jesus Christ has come in the flesh is from God, but every spirit that does not acknowledge Jesus is not from God. This is the spirit of the antichrist**, which you have heard is coming and even now is already in the world. You, dear children, are from God and have overcome them, because the one who is in you is greater than the one who is in the world.*

Must acknowledge Jesus as the Son of God! 1 John 4:15

*If anyone acknowledges that **Jesus is the Son of God**, God lives in him and he in God.*

No eternal life without the Son of God: 1 John 5: 12

*And this is the testimony:" God has given us eternal life, **and this life is in his Son**. He who has the **Son has life;** he who **does not have the Son of God does not have life.** I write these things to you who believe in the name of **the Son of God** so that you may know that you have eternal life."*

Don't love the Son you don't love God! 1John 5: 1-5

*Everyone who believes that **Jesus is the Christ is born of God**, and **everyone who loves the Father loves his child as well**. This is how we know that we love the children of God: by loving God and carrying out his commands. This is love for God: to obey his commands. And his commands are not burdensome, for everyone born of God overcomes the world. This is the victory that has overcome the world, even our faith. Who is it that overcomes the world? **Only he who believes that Jesus is the Son of God.***

Who is the liar? 1 John 2: 22-23

*Who is the liar? It is the man **who denies that Jesus is the Christ**. Such a man is the antichrist—he denies the Father and the Son. No one who denies the Son has the Father; whoever acknowledges the Son has the Father also.*

God of life or death?
Jesus came to die as the once and for all sacrifice for all of mankind in order for us to become children of God, and inherit everlasting life. (John: 1-14, 3:16) In contrast, Allah requires Muslim mothers and fathers to sacrifice their sons for Allah to assure immediate entrance into heaven to enjoy sex with virgins, eating and drinking. Heaven according to Islam is a place where a Muslim will be reclining, eating meats and delicious fruits, drinking exquisite wines, and engaging in sex with virgins. (Koran: Surah 55:54- 56 & Surah 52:17,19).

Just as the angel prophesied that Ishmael would be a warring man, so were his sons and the consequent desert tribes. Once again, let it sink into our heads. Islam is the only religion with a written, clearly articulated agenda of *"Forceful World conquest."* While there are groups that deny it, nor practice it, - there is nothing meek about Islamic theology. Jihad (Holy war) against infidels (non Muslims) is one of Islam's fundamental beliefs. The Koran teaches hatred against the people of the book (Bible), Jews and Christians. They believe that peace will only come when all of the earth is submitted to Allah, and brought under Islamic law, either willingly or by force/ Jihad. They are commanded to kill other Muslims unwilling to go along with their radical agenda, and consider them to be unbelievers. (*"A Muslim apostate must be killed." (Surah 9:12)* They hate Israel and seek her destruction. They hate the USA and are determined to remove her from power.

Unless we understand that every Beast Empire came under the ensign of their false gods; conquered, established their own laws, forced their subjects to submit or die, martyred the people of the true and living God; we will not understand the most ruthless Beast power on the rise to usurp the true God, to rule and dominate the earth.

The vital difference!

You may say "Christianity under the so-called *Holy Roman Empire* killed for centuries in the name of Jesus Christ to convert people by force." This is true, sadly, very true. However, the crucial point that must be understood is this. Muslims did, and do so, in **direct obedience** to Mohammed, to emulate their leader and follow the writings in the Koran. In contrast, Christians (or so called Christians), did so in **direct disobedience** to the teachings, life and example of their leader Jesus Christ.

The Gate facing East:

The *Eastern gate* also known as the *"Golden Gate"* is located in the *East wall of Jerusalem*. It was sealed up in 1539 AD by Muslim conquerors, the Ottoman Turks, and is to this very day. A cemetery has been planted in front of it. This was done to block the entrance of the Jewish Messiah to prevent the redemption of the Jews, as the Messiah is foretold to enter through this gate, by known Old Testament prophecies. However, Ezekiel prophesied the shutting of the *Eastern gate* centuries before, around 600 B.C. It would remain shut not because of Muslim conquerors but "because the LORD, the God of Israel, has entered in by it, therefore it shall be shut."

*Then He brought me back to the outer gate of the sanctuary, which **faces east; and it was shut.** And he said to me, "This gate shall remain shut; it shall not be opened, and no one shall enter by it; for the LORD, the God of Israel has entered by it; therefore it shall remain shut. Only the prince may sit in it to eat bread before the LORD; he shall enter by way of the vestibule of the gate, and shall go out by the same way."* Ezekiel 44:1-3

First Coming: Long before it was blocked by the Ottoman Turkish Muslims, Jesus entered Jerusalem through the *East gate* around 30 A.D, as He came down from the Mount of Olives; a ridge located to the *East of the city,* and entered the Temple according to Luke 19:28-48. Ezekiel says concerning this closed gate that the "Prince", which the Messiah is often called in the Old Testament, and Jesus is called in the New Testament, shall enter it again. Jesus said that He would not be seen again by His nation and people until Jerusalem acknowledges Him as Messiah. *"Blessed is he who comes in the name of the Lord!"* (Matthew 23:37-39).

Second coming: Zechariah 14:4-8 tells us that the LORD will intervene in a mighty battle against those who come against Jerusalem. His feet shall stand on the Mount of Olives *EAST of Jerusalem* causing the mountain to split to provide a way of escape for His people. In Ezekiel 47 and Revelation 22:1-6 we read that He will enter through the *EAST gate,* and on that day, the LORD will be King over all the earth and His name the only name.

The glory of the LORD entered the Temple through the <u>gate facing EAST.</u> Then the Spirit lifted me up and brought me into the inner court, and the glory of the LORD filled the Temple. While the man was standing beside me, I heard someone speaking to me from inside the Temple. He said: 'Son of man, this is the place of my THRONE and the place for the soles of my feet. This is where I will live among the Israelites forever. The house of Israel will never *again defile my holy name— neither they nor their kings— by their prostitution and the lifeless idols of their kings at their high places.'"* (*Ezek 43:4-7*)

The Eastern gate is presently considered by the Arabs to be their exclusive property. It is sealed, but one day the Messiah will stand on the Mount of Olives, and walk down to and right through the *Eastern Gate* and into the Temple area. How tragic Muslim conquerors would think that a closed gate and a cemetery could hold back the Messiah and Savior of the world. He is the risen LORD who conquered the grave 2000 years ago. When He comes and sets His feet on the Mt of Olives which is just *EAST of Jerusalem*, and then splits it in half, to make a way of escape for His people, moving the mountain out of its place, what do you think is going to happen to that closed gate? (Zechariah 14) But if we consider that Islam denies Jesus is the Son of God, His death and resurrection, rejects His love, teaches Mohammed is the superior prophet to Jesus, that Allah is god, and vows to destroy Israel, it is more than tragic, but not surprising!

CHAPTER 16

Who is the true prophet like Moses?

Islam claims to believe in Jesus as *"A"* prophet amongst many, yet they uphold Mohammed as *"The"* superior prophet. They believe he is the fulfillment of Deuteronomy 18 which promised to send a prophet like Moses.

A prophet like Moses: Deuteronomy 18:18-19

> *"I will raise up a prophet like you from among their brothers; I will put my words in his mouth, and he will tell them everything I command him. If anyone does not listen to my words that the prophet speaks in my name, I myself will call him to account!*

May the true Prophet like Moses please stand up!

I used to love to watch a television program called "What's my line." They would bring out 3 people who claimed to be a certain person, or do a certain job. The panel was given the opportunity to ask 10 questions to attempt to find the right person and expose the imposters. At the end the host of the show would say: "Will the real ……….. please stand up!" So let's compare Moses with Jesus and Mohammed, and ask the real prophet to stand up.

From among their brothers:

It is clear that the phrase "from among their brothers" means a Hebrew, a brother Israelite. Here we have a similar usage when God instructed the Israelites to choose *a king.* (Deut 17:14-15) *When ... you say "Let us set a king over us like the nations around us, be sure to appoint over you the king the Lord your God chooses. He must be from among your own brothers. Do not place a foreigner over you, one who is NOT a brother Israelite."* It is absurd to believe that anyone would expect the Israelites to seek a descendant of Ishmael for a king or prophet. All prophets for thousands of years were Israelites/Hebrews to reveal the Word of God to Israel, never an Ishmaelite to the Arab nations.

Compare Moses with Mohammed:

Moses:

From the Holy Scriptures we know that Moses was a Hebrew, and Jesus was of the lineage of King David, the tribe of Judah. (Matthew1:1-17). **Mohammed** was not a Hebrew, but a descendant of Ishmael through Kedar. (Genesis 25:13)

Moses was known by God "face to face," as God spoke to him directly. Deuteronomy 34:10-12. *"Since then, no prophet has risen in Israel like Moses, whom the Lord knew face to face, who did all those miraculous signs and wonders... For no one has ever shown the mighty power or performed the awesome deeds that Moses did in the sight of all Israel."* **Mohammed** *never received* revelation from God but rather claimed to have received his revelations through Gabriel.

Moses performed awesome miracles. **Mohammed:** Even according to the Koran, Mohammed didn't. *Surah 28: 48* states: *"But (now) when the Truth has come to them from us they say, "Why are not signs sent to him (Muhammad), like those which were sent to Moses?"*

Moses was used by God to give the law to Israel. He recorded Genesis, Exodus, Leviticus, Numbers, and Deuteronomy.

Mohammed: Although Islam claims they accept the Law of Moses, they believe it was distorted. In direct opposition to Holy Scripture Mohammed replaced and established Islamic law according to his revelations, and it is the desire of true Islam to subject the whole world under it.

Moses was Israel's mightiest deliverer. (Exodus) **Mohammed** (Koran) teaches hate and to destroy the Israelites in numerous passages. His consequent Imam's were conquerors and enemies of Israel. They curse the people of the book (Bible).The Koran even states that some have been cursed by Allah turning them into apes and pigs. Surah 9: 59-60. *Say o people of the book! Do ye approve of us for no other reason that we believe in Allah and the revelation that hath come to us and that which came before (us), and (perhaps) that most of you are rebellious and disobedient? Say: Shall I point out to you something much worse that this, by the treatment it (you) received from Allah? Those who incurred the curse of Allah and his wrath , those of whom some have been transformed into apes and swine, those who worshipped Evil,—these are (many times) worse in rank , and far more astray from the even path!* (Keep in mind this is an English translation, watered down from Arabic)

Compare Moses with Jesus: First coming:

Not only did Israel expect "a prophet like Moses" but also the prophet "Elijah". Israel's religious leaders asked the following of John the Baptist. *"Are you the Messiah?"* He said, *"I am not the Messiah!"* *" Then are you Elijah?"* He answered, *"I am not!"* *" Are you 'THE' Prophet?"* He said *"No!"* (Deuteronomy 18:18; Malachi 4:5; John 1:19-21; 6:14)

Jesus is the Prophet like Moses! Acts 3:22-26

Here we have a direct quote from Deut.18:18 written by Luke.

*Now brothers, I know that you acted in ignorance, as did your leaders. But this is how God fulfilled what He had foretold through **all the prophets**, saying that **His Christ** would suffer. Repent, then, and turn to God so that your sins may be wiped out, that times of refreshing may come from the*

*LORD, and that He may send **the Christ**, who has been appointed for you—**even Jesus**. He must remain in heaven until the time comes for God to restore everything, as He promised long ago through **His Holy Prophets**. (v.22) For Moses said: "The LORD your God will raise up for you a prophet like me, from among your own people; you must listen to everything he tells you. Anyone who does not listen to Him will be completely cut off from His people. Indeed, ALL the prophets from Samuel on, as many as have spoken have foretold these days. And you are heirs of the prophets and of the Covenant God made with your fathers. He said to Abraham, 'through your offspring all peoples on earth will be blessed.' When God raised up His servant, He sent him first to you to bless you by turning each of you from your wicked ways." Also see Acts 7:37-38*

In the wilderness: (Deut 8:3; 6:13, 16; Matt 4:1; 5:5).

Jesus went into the wilderness for 40 days where He was tempted three times. Three times He quoted from Deuteronomy, which was the book given to **Moses** on a mountain and given to the Israelites in the wilderness. After Jesus returned from the wilderness, He went to a mountain to teach the Beatitudes.

The Law: (Ex. 21:23-24; Lev. 24: 17- 23; Isaiah 2:3; 9:6; Matt 5:17; 15:17-18; Luke 24:44-47; John 7:19- 23; Romans 10:4; Galatians 6:2)

God gave **Moses** the law for the Hebrew people to govern their nation under His rule. **Jesus** said: *"Not a jot or tittle shall be removed.* A tittle is the smallest line or projection by which Hebrew letters differ from each other. By this Jesus clearly taught the impossibility of another law to replace the law given to Moses. Jesus never replaced the Law of Moses, but taught the practical application of the Law. He clarified the law, then, by His crucifixion, made the payment required by the law, and fulfilled it. Last but not least, He will come again to reign from Jerusalem, and the Law shall go forth from Zion, when the rule and the government shall be on his shoulders.

Moses laid down his will and risked his life to save the Hebrew slaves. (Exodus 3)
Jesus laid down His life to save Israel and the world. (Matthew 26:36-38))

Moses, the prince of Egypt, left His throne to identify with the Hebrew people. (Exodus 2. 2)
Jesus, the Word of God, left His throne to become flesh to identify with humanity. (John 1: 1-14)

Moses face was aglow with the Shekinah Glory on Mt. Sinai. (Exodus 34:29)
Jesus face was aglow with the Shekinah Glory on the Mt. of Transfiguration. (Matthew 17:1-2)

Moses lifted up the Bronze snake on the pole to provide healing. (Numbers 21:8)
Jesus was lifted up on the cross to provide healing from sin for ALL people. (John 3:13-15)

Moses sent out 12 spies. (Deuteronomy 1:23)
Jesus sent out 12 apostles. (Matthew 10:2-6)

Moses. With His arms stretched out and a man on either side, Moses defeated the Amalekites prior to entering the Promised Land. (Exodus 17)
Jesus defeated sin on the cross with His arms stretched out, also with a man on either side, crucified, so that man can enter Paradise. (Matt 27:32-56; Mark 15; Luke 23)

Moses appointed 70 elders. (Exodus 24:1, 8)
Jesus appointed 70 more disciples. (Luke 10:1)

Note: Certain differences in early manuscripts are unclear as to whether the number is 70 that went 2 by two, or 72. Considering the biblical pattern I believe 70 would be correct. There were 70 descendants of Jacob in all that went to Egypt to live with Joseph.

When they came to Elim there were 12 springs and 70 palm trees, they camped there near the water. (Exodus 1:1; 15:27)

Both were called by God to serve and accomplish His will, not theirs, and experienced their most difficult spiritual crisis on a mountaintop. (Exodus, Matthew 27; Mark 15; Luke 23; John 19)
Both defeated demonic powers. (Exodus, Matt 8:31; 9:33)
Both fasted for 40 days. (Exodus 34:28; Matthew 4:1)
Both performed many miracles. (Exodus 7-15; Matt11: 20-23; Mark 6:2-5; Luke 19:37; John 7:3; 10:25-38; 14:11)
Both Moses and Jesus gave new / fresh revelation in harmony with scripture to substantiate scripture, never replacing the Word of God, nor denying the God of Abraham, Isaac, and Jacob.

Moses parted the Sea to deliver Israel from destruction at the hands of Pharaohs army. (Exodus 14:26; 15:5) He is the most honored personality in Judaism.
Jesus First coming: Jesus calmed the sea. (Matt.8: 26)
Jesus Second coming: This time Israel will not be backed up against the sea, but rather in the wilderness. Israel's ultimate deliverer, the Messiah Jesus, will *part the Mount of Olives* to cause a great valley of escape to deliver Israel from destruction at the hands of the Anti Christ and his armies. (Zechariah 14)

Islam: Besides the claims, assumptions and wishful thinking that Mohammed must be the fulfillment of Deuteronomy 18:18-19, what does the Koran have to offer to prove itself? Mohammed alone claimed to receive his revelations over a span of 23 years, with no other authors, no other prophets to compare to, no evidence, no miracles, no fulfilled prophecies, and no archeological evidence.

Christianity: Besides the claims, assumptions or wishful thinking that Jesus must be the fulfillment of Deuteronomy 18:18-19, we have hundreds of prophecies fulfilled, numerous similarities with Moses, Joseph, Joshua, King David, and many more. All the prophets harmonize with each other, and the New Testament confirms the Old Testament, quoting each other, with 40 authors over a period of 4000 years, most of whom did not know each other, with archeological and historical evidence. The book, *"More than a Carpenter"*, by Josh Mc Dowell quotes reliable sources that give the following example. The chance that any man might have lived down to the present time and fulfilled *even eight prophecies* is 1 in 100,000,000,000, 000,000. To better understand this number we would have to bury the entire state of Texas with two feet of silver dollars, mark one of them with an "X", mix it in with the rest; then find it.

Closing segment of, "What's my line?"

Today's segment of "What's my line" was exceptional in many ways. We permitted you more than 10 comparisons/ questions. It also took place in the Middle East. Before we ask the true prophet to rise, let us remember the test of prophets according to the Law of Moses with passages that immediately follow. Deuteronomy18: 20-22 states: *But a prophet who presumes to speak in my name anything I have not commanded him to say, or a prophet who speaks in the name of other gods, must be put to death. You may say to yourselves "How can we know when a message has not been spoken by the LORD?" If what a prophet proclaims in the name of the LORD does not take place or come true, that is a message the LORD has not spoken. That prophet has spoken presumptuously. Do not be afraid of him.*

Will the true prophet like Moses please stand up!
Yeah Jesus!.......... Applause!!!

So let us remember the prophet like Moses and listen to Him, because the LORD said in Deuteronomy 18:19: *"If anyone does not listen to my words that the prophet speaks in my name, I myself will call him to account!"*

CHAPTER 17

Who is your neighbor?

God called Abraham to leave Ur, the land of the Chaldeans, ancient Babylon. It was there that the adherence of the *moon cult*, the worship of the *moon god* was prevalent, as it was throughout ancient Mesopotamia, and practiced by the Assyrians, Babylonians, and Akkadians. It was detestable idolatry, grotesque immorality, brutality, and last but not least sacrificing children. It was no other than the worship of Babylonian gods. (Genesis 11:27-12:9)

Dr. Robert Morey, author of "The Islamic invasion" points out reliable sources with extensive proof from archeology, that Islam is nothing less than a reemergence of the ancient moon cult, with its rights and practices. God called Abraham out of there because He no longer wanted him to live in this evil pit. He was a good man, a righteous man. No wonder he took up God's offer and left. How can Muslims call Abraham their father? He would never slaughter innocent people. He would never force anyone to believe in his God or kill them for refusing.

For years I was disturbed over the fact that our God would ask Abraham to offer a human sacrifice since He hates such demonic practices. His Covenant people and land were to be void of such detestable acts, and whenever the Israelites fell away from their God and worshipped these gods of the surrounding nations He would judge them severely.

Until I realized one day that God taught Abraham a lesson he would never forget. He proved to Abraham and all of us that He alone will provide the sacrifice, and by faith, Abraham believed that the true God was not like the gods of Babylon. He would not require him to put *his son in the fire to be burned,* as was done by his people.

By faith he said, *"**God himself** will provide the lamb for the **burnt offering**, my son." And the two of them went up together. When they reached the place God had told him about, Abraham built an **altar** there and **arranged the wood on it**. He bound his son Isaac and laid him on the altar on **top of the wood**. Then he reached out his hand and took the knife to slay his son. But the angel of the LORD called out to him from heaven, "Abraham! Abraham! Here I am, do not lay a hand on the boy," "Do not do anything to him. Now I know that you fear God, because you have not withheld from me your son, your only son." Abraham looked up and there in a thicket he saw a **ram caught by its horns**. He went over and took the ram and **sacrificed it as a burnt offering** instead of his son. So Abraham called that place," The LORD will provide". And to this day it is said, "On the mountain of the LORD it **will** be provided."* Genesis 22

At the exact place, almost 2000 years ago, God provided the Lamb of God who takes away the sins of the world. His only Son **wore thorns on his head,** like the ram caught in thicket and **laid upon the wood** to endure the fires of hell when every sin was laid upon Him. He willingly took no escape from His fate to become our substitute, just as the ram was Isaac's substitute. (Matthew 27; Mark 15; Luke 23; John 19.)

On the mountain of the LORD it **will** be provided once again, when He comes to stand on the Mt. of Olives to intervene in a mighty battle against all who come against Jerusalem, to save the remnant of Israel and avenge the blood of the saints. On the mountain of the LORD it **will** be provided again, when Jesus will set up His theocratic rule on the Temple mount from the Temple in Jerusalem. (Zechariah 14; Isaiah 2, 9:6; Ezekiel 37:15-28)

May we never substitute Allah for the God of Abraham, Isaac, and Jacob!

May the Muslim people know that God does not want them to offer their children as a sacrifice to kill and destroy lives, He already offered His own Son to save lives!

Ask yourself, who else would be willing to die for your sins that you may live with Him in His Kingdom? If you refuse His amazing offer of Grace, if you refuse to humble yourself and not serve Him who is seated on throne, if you demand to be first, you exemplify the mind of Satan. His destiny along with yours is hell. God does not send you there, you choose! Not a good choice of neighborhood if you ask me.

Bad neighbors:

The Jewish people have had to deal with bad neighbors no matter where they lived, except in the USA and a few other places. But since the reestablishment of Israel, they have had to deal with their old neighbors once again. Here is just a portion of Ezekiel 36. It is a prophecy concerning Israel at the end of the age and her warring neighbors. It is clearer than today's news.

Ezekiel 36:1-11

> *"Son of man, prophesy to the mountains of Israel and say, 'O mountains of Israel, hear the word of the LORD. This is what the Sovereign LORD says: The enemy said of you, "Aha! The ancient heights have become our possession."' Therefore prophesy and say, 'This is what the Sovereign LORD says: Because they ravaged and hounded you from every side so that you became the possession of the rest of the nations and the object of people's malicious talk and slander, therefore, O mountains of Israel, hear the word of the Sovereign LORD: This is what the Sovereign LORD says to the mountains and hills, to the ravines and valleys, to the desolate ruins and the deserted towns that have been plundered and ridiculed by the rest of the nations around you- this is what the Sovereign LORD says: In my burning zeal I have spoken against the*

*rest of the nations, and against all Edom(Arabia), for with glee and with malice in their hearts they made my land their own possession so that they might plunder its pastureland.' Therefore prophesy concerning the land of Israel and say to the mountains and hills, to the ravines and valleys: This is what the Sovereign LORD says:" I speak in my jealous wrath because you have suffered the scorn of the nations". Therefore this is what the Sovereign LORD says:" I swear with uplifted hand that the **nations around you** will also suffer scorn. "*

"But you, O mountains of Israel, will produce branches and fruit for my people Israel, for they will soon come home. I am concerned for you and will look on you with favor; you will be plowed and sown, and I will multiply the number of people upon you, even the whole house of Israel. The towns will be inhabited and the ruins rebuilt. I will increase the number of men and animals upon you, and they will be fruitful and become numerous. I will settle people on you as in the past and will make you prosper more than before. Then you will know that I am the LORD!" (Note: Read all of Ezekiel 35 and 36)

Who are the wheat and tares?

In the Middle East there is a special *weed* called a *tare*. In revenge the hateful neighbor would come at night and sneak in the farmer's field while he was sleeping and sow the seed of tares. In the early stages of growth they look so much like wheat the farmer had no choice but to let them grow to whatever numbers, or risk tearing out some of the wheat as well. However, at harvest time it is clearly distinguishable. At that time the farmer has it sorted, bundles up the weeds/tares to be burned, and saves the wheat.

"The Parable of the wheat and tares (weeds)"
Matthew 13: 24-30

Jesus said: "The kingdom of heaven is like a man who sowed good seeds in his field. But while everyone was sleeping, his enemy came and sowed weeds among the wheat and went away. When the wheat sprouted and formed heads, then the weeds also appeared. The owners servants came to Him and said, 'Sir, didn't you sow good seed in your field? Where then did the weeds come from?' 'An enemy did this', he replied. The servants asked Him, 'do you want us to go and pull them up?' 'No' he answered, 'because while you are pulling the weeds, you may root up the wheat with them. Let both grow together until the harvest. At THAT time I will tell the harvesters: First collect the weeds and tie them in bundles to be burned; — then gather the wheat and bring it into my barn.'"

Parable explained by Jesus: (Matthew 13: 36- 43)

"Then He left the crowd and went into the house. His disciples came to him and said, 'Explain to us the parable of the weeds in the field.' He answered. 'The one who sowed the good seed is the Son of Man (Title of Jesus). The field is the WORLD, and the GOOD seed stands for the sons of the Kingdom. The weeds are the sons of the EVIL one, and the enemy who sows them is the devil. The harvest is the "END of the AGE." The Son of Man will send out His angels and they will weed out of His Kingdom, everything that causes sin and all who do evil. They will throw them into the fiery furnace, where there will be weeping and gnashing of teeth. Then the righteous will shine like the sun in the Kingdom of their Father.'"

Plucking out the tares?

Just as the hateful neighboring farmers of ancient Israel would sneak into their fields while they were sleeping, we have been sleeping for a long time, not realizing the neighborhood (world) is filled with tares. I think we have been in a coma, because the enemy has snuck in for better than 40 years planting tares in the West.

Since the terrorist attack against the USA on September 11, 2001, the question we must ask ourselves is: "How do we fight these

Islamic terrorists? They are everywhere? How do we differentiate between a peaceful Muslim, and others who conspire against us, or even others who look Arabic yet hold to other faiths, who may even be Christians? Besides they have gained followers in every color and nation and have infiltrated the whole world? So...who is who?"

According to various sources there are approx.1.5 Billion Muslims worldwide. There are those who are non-violent, and also those who have left the Middle East to genuinely escape militant, rigid Islamic teachings and lifestyles. Then there are the militant groups and others who seek control by infiltration. The big question once again is: "Who is who?" It is impossible to know, as it clearly fits the parable of wheat and tares!

Muslim Revolutionaries:
  Goal: Committed to convert the world to Islam.
  Method: Terrorist groups, Invasions, War / Jihad! Forced conversions or death.

Muslim Evolutionaries:
  Goal: Committed to convert the world to Islam.
  Method: The stage of weakness: The Evolutionaries realize they don't have the power to win by Jihad, not yet. Their strategy lies in waiting, immigration, infiltrating, trying to be accepted, included and involved in all activities, from religious, social and political, until they have the majority. Such was the case in Lebanon, which was a Christian nation until 1975, when Muslims gained the majority and declared Jihad. Today, in the West, we are witnessing the Islamic stage of weakness, but let us not be fooled, the sound of bah-bah is going to change to a roar when the Muslim community has completed its preparedness and is ready to come out of its isolation to take charge through Jihad.

Committed to Islam not country!
  Muslim Jihad warriors are literally warriors without a country because they are devoted to their radical Islamic worldview, not to their country. It is therefore impossible to threaten them with destruction, as we did the Nazi's who were devoted to the greatness

of Germany. If they attacked us, what country would the USA bomb? They are spread out all over the world, including our own nation. If you want to watch a disturbing video, get *"Jihad in America"*, by investigative reporter Steve Emerson. He exposes literally a landscape of locations in the USA were radical groups are meeting. — It was produced in 1994! The only places we could bomb that they would be passionate about would be their holy cities and sites of Mecca, Medina and Jerusalem. However, if the USA were to do that, it would be like sticking your finger in a hornets nest.

Good neighbors:
Sadly radical Muslims have not learned the value of human life and what a treasure it is to live next to good neighbors where you feel safe and secure. Blinded by hate and world domination, they cannot follow the Lords teaching that we are to love our neighbor as ourselves, because they hate themselves. I recently received this E-mail. It is a great lesson on how to live with your neighbor, a reminder of something Jesus would have said. It follows.

Growing Good Corn:

There was a farmer who grew award-winning corn. Each year he entered his corn in the state fair where it won a blue ribbon. One year a newspaper reporter interviewed him and learned something interesting about how he grew it. The reporter discovered that the farmer shared his corn seed with his neighbors. "How can you afford to share your best corn seed with your neighbors when they are entering corn in competition with yours each year?" the reporter asked.

"Why sir," said the farmer, "didn't you know? The wind picks up pollen from the ripening corn and swirls it from field to field. If my neighbors grow inferior corn, cross-pollination will steadily degrade the quality of my corn. If I am to grow good corn, I must help my neighbors to grow good corn."

He is very much aware of the connectedness of life. His corn cannot improve unless his neighbor's corn also improves. So it is in other dimensions. Those who choose to be at peace must help their neighbors to be at peace. Those who choose to live well must help others to live well, for the value of a life is measured by the lives it touches. And those who choose to be happy must help others to find happiness, for the welfare of each is bound up with the welfare of all.

The lesson for each of us is this: "if we are to grow good corn, we must help our neighbors grow good corn."

—Author unknown

CHAPTER 18

"If the shoe fits wear it!"

"Put your right foot in put your right foot out, that's what it's all about." This is a silly song children act out during fun times as they giggle and laugh because they easily get their right and left confused. But for Muslims confusing your right with your left would not be funny.

It is important to keep in mind at all times that the Bible and Koran was written in an ancient Middle Eastern culture, about a people who observed what seems like strange practices to the 21st Century Western mind, but were logical and often necessary. Among them were strict sanitary rules to avoid contamination. Throughout scripture we find practices still valuable today. One of them was the use of the left hand for unclean purposes to avoid contamination. A good idea since there was no modern hygiene products, no toilet paper, often little or no water available. To touch someone with your left hand would have been a great insult, as it was seen as bad/unclean, and the right hand as good/clean. We read passages where children are blessed with the right hand, and the LORD uses this analogy by sorting out the unbeliever to his left and believer to His right. (Matthew 25:31-33)

But with Islam it goes beyond reason, as rigid rules must be observed with hands, feet, and various actions. They are instructed to use their *right side* first from putting on shoes to clothing, to entering a house. When entering an unclean facility a Muslim has to enter with the *left foot first*, and then leave with his *right*. During a bowl movement they are instructed to adopt a squatting position, while leaning heavily on the *left foot,* and are also instructed to say a certain prayer each time. When taking a bath, a certain order of cleaning must be followed. Then they are allowed to wash the rest of their bodies, but of course the *right side first* and then the *left.* Before prayers, the body has to be washed in a precise and orderly way, *right hand up* to the wrist, then *left hand,* then *right arm* up to elbow, then *left arm,* etc. They also must sleep on their *right sides,* with their heads pointed to the north.

What is a mark?

In the ancient east a mark was the sign of ownership. It was common to mark ones' slaves. Those who loved their master willingly had a mark gouged on their **right** ear to forever identify themselves with their owner. A mark was also a sign for preservation. (Ezekiel 9: 4-6). In the New Testament we learn that believers in the Christ are marked and sealed by the Holy Spirit, as we are willing slaves / servants of God and His Messiah. This mark is our seal to preserve us unto our blessed hope to be forever with our Master. (2 Corinthians 1:21-22; 5:5; Ephesians 1:13; John 14:15-18). God said to Israel: *"Behold, I have graven thee on the palm of my hands"* (Isaiah 49:16). He conveys the idea of ownership and remembrance, just as the names of the 12 tribes of Israel were carved on stones and fastened to the ephod as a memorial before the LORD. (Exodus 28:9-12) When all of the redeemed are in God's presence in the New Jerusalem, we are told that the *Father's Name will be written on our foreheads.* (Revelation 22:4)

The opposition, the mark of the Beast:

Scripture speaks of a day when every knee will bow to Jesus Christ, but prior to it, the Anti-Christ will, in a last ditch effort, demand allegiance to him and *mark his followers.* It is revealed *to us that it will be on the right hand or forehead.* I like the expression *"if the shoe fits wear it."* Considering that the right verses left is such an important part of Islamic life, let us examine if the shoe fits, and the size is 666.

Since Satan always opposes and uses counterfeit techniques, we just need to be diligent and study the Word and who God is, and likewise remember history. What the mark of the Beast will look like I have no clue! The Bible says 666. But anyone that knows anything about the Holocaust knows the Nazi's marked their victims. At first it was with the Star of David, and then they tattooed **numbers on their left forearms** for identification to be destroyed. I remember my school days and it was not acceptable to write with the **left** hand because it was just not right.

While many think the mark of the Beast to come may be a microchip, we must consider the fact that most of the world is poor and not technologically advanced. Germany was the most literate nation on earth 60 years ago, and they used tattoos, but I understand that tattoos are very common and useful in the Middle East, where comparatively few people have learned to read and write. Could it be that the Anti Christ and his armies will mark their converts to Allah, and allies, *thus mark the right*, rather than left, signifying them as good? Could it be that those who refuse this mark won't be able to buy or sell, be systematically starved out, or sought out to be beheaded?

Koran:

The Koran teaches that those who refuse Allah must be **beheaded** and have their **fingers cut off.** *"I will instill terror into the hearts of the unbelievers, (those who refuse Allah and his messenger Mohammed), smite ye above their <u>necks</u> and smite all their <u>fingertips off them.</u> It is not ye who slew them; it was Allah"* (Surah 5:33; Surah 8:12, 17; Jihad in the "Hadith")

Bible:

Right hand and forehead: *"He(Anti Christ) also forced everyone, small and great, rich or poor, free and slave, to receive a mark on his **right hand** or on his **forehead,** so that no one could buy or sell unless he had the mark, which is the name of the beast or the number of his name."* Revelation 13: 16

Do not take the mark! *If anyone worships the beast and his image and receives his mark on the **forehead, or on the hand**, he too will drink of the wine of God's fury, which has been poured out full strength into the cup of His wrath.* Revelation 14: 9

Beheaded for the testimony of Jesus: *"And I saw thrones, and they sat on them, and judgment was committed to them. Then I saw the souls of those who had been **beheaded for their witness to Jesus** and for the **word of God**, who **had not worshipped the Beast or his image, and had not received his mark on their foreheads or on their hands**. And they lived and reigned with Christ for a thousand years."* Revelation 20:4

Sudan, a preview of the Great tribulation:

Radical Islamic forces in Sudan, have swept across this nation. There is a Holocaust in progress, the martyrdom of 3 million Christians, as they are starved, brutalized and murdered in order to manipulate conversions to Islam. God is trying to warn us as we see this preview of terror. At this point they do not mark their converts, but *beheading and cutting off hands and* other horrific acts fit the description of Scripture during the Great Tribulation to come.

1.) Crops ruined/burned.
2.) Wells are destroyed / poisoned.
3.) Hands are cut off.
4.) Breasts are cut off nursing mothers to starve infants to force conversion and assure that not another generation of Christians survives.
5.) Women are raped.
6.) Woman and children are sold into slavery.
7.) Men are castrated.
8.) They are beheaded by the sword.
9.) Cities and villages are plundered.
10.) Some are buried alive.
11.) Some are even crucified.

Seal 1-5 of Revelation chapter 6: 1-11:
Conqueror bent on conquest, war, famine, food shortages, death, and martyrs.

Here are the characteristics of the last day BEAST:
Exceedingly strong. (Daniel 7:7, Rev.13:4)
Dreadful and terrible. (Daniel 7:7, Rev.13:4)
Bent on world domination. (Daniel 7:23, Revelation 13:7)
Extremely, almost insanely destructive. (Daniel 7:7, Rev.17:16-18:19, 13:4)
Ruled by pompous leadership, blasphemes of the God of Israel. (Daniel 7:25, Rev. 13:5)
Changers of times and law. (Daniel 7:25)
Persecutors of believers. (Daniel 7:25, Rev 13:7)
Enraged with the woman (Israel) who gave birth to the male Child. (Rev.12:17)
Religious empire, not secular. (Rev.13:4)
Beheading by the sword, cutting of hands, especially the *right hand* as their chosen punishment for those who do not render acceptable worship.(Rev.13:10, 20:4)

How does the shoe fit?

The Sword.
The Sword of Christ did not come to kill in His first coming, but to divide believer from unbeliever. While Jesus proved Himself over and over again to religious leaders, their sin and lack of repentance, coupled with their expectancy blinded them to the truth. Therefore, many rejected His claim as Messiah. They thought Jesus was one of the many false Messiah's that had come along throughout Israel's history. The unbelieving religious leaders and families considered followers of Jesus as deceived, abandoning the faith handed down by father Abraham, and committing apostasy of the highest degree.

> *"Do not suppose that I have come to bring peace on the earth. I did not come to bring peace, but **a sword**. For I have come to turn a man against his father, a daughter against*

her mother, a daughter in law against her mother in law —a man's enemies will be the members of his own household. Anyone who loves his father and mother more than me is not worthy of me; anyone who loves his son or daughter more than me is not worthy of me; and anyone who does not take his cross and follow me is not worthy of me. Whoever finds his life will loose it, and whosoever loses his life for my sake will find it." Matthew 10:34-39

The Early Church:

It is estimated that approximately 1 Million Israelites believed by the end of the first century, but the nation as whole did not. The early Jewish church sent shockwaves through Israel, as faith in Jesus Christ was the *sword* that clearly *divided* between belief and disbelief in Israel. Hebrew families persecuted their own people, families, removed and disinherited them. Many were even killed by zealous religious leaders such as Saul. (Acts 1-11) After Saul's/Paul's conversion to faith in the Messiah he likewise suffered greatly for his faith. The Messianic church was scattered form Judea to Samaria, driven out of Israel, even unto the ends of the earth, which in turn brought us gentile nations the Gospel. (Acts 1:8; 8:1)

The Nation of Israel:

The *unbelieving* nation of Israel left behind suffered greatly as Jesus had prophesied: *"They (Israel) will fall by the **sword** and will be taken as prisoners to all the nations. Jerusalem will be trampled on by the Gentiles until the times of the Gentiles are fulfilled."* (Luke 21:24) And so it was that in 70 AD the Temple in Jerusalem was destroyed by Rome, many were put to death by the sword, others taken as prisoners, while others survived and were scattered all over the earth. A small remnant remained.

Great Tribulation:

The words of Christ declaring division within families, losing lives for His sake, will be once again the lot of the church at the end of the age, as Jesus spoke of near and far prophecy. He said, *"He who stands firm to the end will be saved."* (Matthew 10:22) A day will come when Jew and Gentile will enter the Great Tribulation and must choose between faith in the Messiah or Allah. Nothing has changed. Jesus is still the "Sword that divides", causing persecution.

Those who reject Allah will face the Sword of Islam.
There will be no other option, no neutrality offered.
It is either the mark of the Beast or the mark of God!
Islam will not give you the option to say: "No thanks!"

AWAKE CHURCH!

Islam is not peace, but a **Sword** of death. Allah is not God, but the father of lies. He is a ferocious beast seeking to destroy in order to rule the earth. Islam is the ancient root of the Anti Christ belief system that renounces Jesus Christ as the Son of God, seeking to destroy Jews and Christians.

How does the shoe fit?

Second coming: The SWORD of Christ

May we keep the faith and know that the **Sword of Jesus Christ** will judge the **Sword of Islam** and its allies. He will come, not to ferociously murder (ratsach), but defend lives! (nakah) (Revelation 19: 21)

May the true God please identify Himself! Is it Allah, who demands your sons to die for him, or the God of Abraham, Isaac and Jacob who sent His Son to die for you? Is it Allah, who demands to rule the earth and kill those who will not submit to him, or the God of Abraham, Isaac and Jacob who promises His children to rescue them and become co-heirs with His Son Jesus Christ, if indeed we serve and suffer with Him?

> *"The Spirit Himself testifies with our spirit that we are God's children. Now if we are children, then we are **heirs—heirs of God and co-heirs with Christ, if indeed we share in His sufferings in order that we may also share in His glory.** I consider that our present (or future) sufferings are not worth comparing with the glory that will be revealed to us. The creation awaits in eager expectation for the sons of God to*

be revealed. For the creation was subjected to frustration, not by its own choice, but by the will of the one who subjected it, in hope that the creation itself will be liberated from its bondage to decay and brought into the glorious freedom of the children of God. (Romans.8:18-21)

CHAPTER 19

Babylonian Kingdoms, or God's kingdom on earth?

Nimrod: Genesis 10: 8-12

> *Cush was the father of Nimrod who grew to be a mighty warrior on the earth. He was a mighty hunter before the LORD; that is why it is said, "Like a mighty hunter before the LORD. The first centers of his kingdom were Babylon, Erech, Akkad and Calneh, in Shinar. From that land he went to Assyria, where he built Nineveh, Rehoboth Ir, Calah and Resen, which is between Nineveh and Calah, that is, the great city.*

Nimrod and the Tower of Babel: Genesis 11:1-9

God commanded man to be fruitful and scatter all over the earth. Under Nimrod's kingdom people opposed God, united, gained in power, to form the first world empire. He was not only a mighty hunter of beast but of men. *Now the whole world had one language and common speech.* (It is believed they were survivors from the flood, and their descendants -NIV Bible foot notes) *As men moved eastward they found a plain in Shinar and settled there. They said to each other," come let us make bricks and bake them thoroughly.*

They used bricks instead of stone, and tar for mortar. Then they said," Come let us built ourselves a city, with a tower that reaches to the heavens so that we may make a name for ourselves and not be scattered over the face of the earth.

Nimrod was the prime mover of the Tower of Babel. At Babel rebellious man undertook a united and godless effort to establish for himself, by a titanic human enterprise, a world renown by which he would dominate God's creation. It was built before his death in the land of Shinar, located in Babylon, today's Iraq. The typical Mesopotamian Temple tower, known as a ziggurat, was square at the base, had sloping and stepped sides that led upward to a small shrine at the top to worship the constellations, the sun, moon and stars.

When God saw what they had done He came down and said: *"If as **one people** speaking **the same language** they have begun to do this, then nothing they plan will be impossible for them."* God confused their language and scattered them all over the earth. He was merciful, and provided yet another chance for mankind rather than destroy them. (Genesis 10: 5-9)

More rebellion:

Throughout the world we have evidence with numerous archeological discoveries of temples to the sun god, moon and stars, and their idols. The names of the Babylonian gods changed from language to language, country to country, city to city, even within short distances, but were always the same false gods.

He was Bel in Babylon; Baal in Canaan (Israel); Beelzebub in Ekron / Philistines; Chemosh of Moab; Eshmun of Sidon; Horus of Egypt; Jupiter /Mercury in Rome; Mal'cham Ammon/ Tyre equated with Molech, Moloch, Milcom, Melqart, Marduk, Melqart often called Baal; Mith'redath / Mithra of Persia (Iran); Nergal in Samaria; Ra in Egypt. _Zeus the supreme deity and sun god of Greece_ was also known as Orpheus, Bacchus Dionysus, Achilles, Hercules, Theseus, Perseus, Jason, and Prometheus. He is _Helios on the Greek island of Rhodes._

"Teotihuacán, the City of the gods," arose as a new religious centre in the Mexican Highland around the time of Christ, with pyramids/ and numerous ziggurats to the sun and moon god. http://archaeology.la.asu.edu/teo/intro/intrteo.htm

A lot of bull around the world:
There is truly nothing new under the sun. The worship of these gods was evil. It involved the sacrificing of children, grotesque sexual immorality and all other kinds of depraved behavior. It was no other than an ancient form of Satanism. All Babylonian kings were spiritual successors of Nimrod of Babylon, the founder of secret societies. Like Nimrod they wore a *"crown of bull horns"*, to simulate the spires of the sun, and were worshipped as sun-gods; human representatives of the sun. All over the world and the ancient Middle East we find references to *the bull*, used as a symbol of strength and fertility, as well as to *"bull gods."* Cattle cults among the Cushite peoples of Ethiopia and India are prevalent to this very day.

Enough bull:
After 400 years of Egyptian bondage God heard their cry and led the Hebrews out of Egypt in a mighty deliverance by the hand of His servant Moses. Soon they rebelled and worshipped the golden *calf / bull*, thus a return to the old pagan practices and worship of Egypt. God judged that generation as they wandered for 40 years in the wilderness before God would grant entrance into the Promised Land. (Exodus 32)

The God fearing remnant of the Hebrew people knew it was bull. To this day they only use a ram's horn. It is not only a reminder of the blood of the Lamb that delivered every firstborn in Egypt (Exodus 11-12), but of the deliverance of Isaac by the ram caught in the thicket. (Genesis 22:13). It furthermore is a clear picture pointing to the Lamb of God that takes away the sins of the world. (John 1:29) For those of us who believe in Jesus Christ we look back in faith to Calvary, to His once and for all sacrifice for sin.

Semiramis, queen of Babylon, the Harlot!
In addition to Nimrod's ruthless rule, his wife queen Semiramis was a corrupt and immoral woman. After Nimrod's death and deification to "Sun-god", she claimed to have become impregnated by

one of his sunbeams. This miracle birth of her son Tammuz was believed to be Nimrod reborn, a savior. People worshipped her over Nimrod, as she gained control of the Babylonian Kingdom by her seductive and licentious ways. Her dominion is typified by the *Harlot / Prostitute, sitting on and riding the bull, thus united with, but controlling the beast.*

At her death she was deified as the *'Queen of Heaven'*, the moon goddess, and goddess of fertility. Her children were the stars. The woman appears in different ways throughout various cultures and times just as Nimrod, but remains the same corrupt and satanic counterfeit religious system and global power. Archeological excavations have found temples and idols to the moon goddess throughout the earth.

She is Isis in Egypt, Indrani in India, Cybelle in Asia, Venus in Rome, Ceres in Greece, Shing Moo in China, Hertha in Germany, Sisa in Scandinavia. But the woman was really Semiramis, the queen of Babylon, the queen of heaven. In the New Testament scriptures she is Diana of Ephesus (Acts 19: 24- 34).In the Old Testament amongst ancient pagans she is the goddess of the Sidonians (1 Kings 11:1-5).

Baal and Ashtoreth in Israel.

You are what you worship. Israel was to be a Holy nation, devoted to God who is Holy. However, Israel was not exempt from the satanic deception and power of the Babylonian gods, their religion and self- rule. She was and still is the most desired object of his satanic goal of hatred, because He knows that through Jesus, the Jewish King, God will bring about his ultimate destruction to set up His Kingdom forever.

When they fell away from God and sought to make a name for themselves they became corrupt and built altars to worship Baal (Molech etc. etc.) and Ashtoreth, the queen of heaven. They burnt their sons in the fire, even set up their detestable idols in the house of the LORD. They became corrupt in every way just as Nimrod (Baal), and Semiramis / Ashtoreth, *the queen of heaven,* the king and queen of Babylon. Numerous passages speak of the Israelites, their rebellion and worship of the sun-god. We also learn of the consequent judgments upon Israel. (1 Kings 11; Jeremiah 7; 44; Judges 2.)

A righteous King, the days of Glory: (2 Samuel)
God chose a shepherd boy named David to rule as King and made Jerusalem the capitol of his kingdom. The enemy of God deceived David and he sinned with beautiful Bathsheba, even arranged for her husband's death. While God judged him for his sin, he was a man after God's own heart, repented of his sin, and never forsook his God to worship the other gods of the nations *round about Israel*. He protected his people like a shepherd and ruled over his kingdom during the days of Glory for Israel.

A Kingdom divided cannot stand:
David's son King Solomon, of whom it was said to be the wisest of all Kings, who built the Temple for God, tragically fell away in his old age to worship Baal and Ashtoreth, the gods of his many pagan wives.(1 Kings 11). God judged and divided the Kingdom, beginning in 930BC.
God raised up numerous Kings to rule over Israel. Some remained faithful to their God others were deceived, and fell into idolatry to worship Baal and Ashtoreth. (1 and 2.Kings) Through His righteous king Josiah, he ordered all the removal of its perverse and idolatrous practices from the land (2 Kings 23:1-30). No sooner was he dead that other kings were overcome by deception. No righteous king was found, as they all did evil in the sight of the LORD. (2 Kings 23: 31-37). Just as kings were divided, so the kingdom was divided from 930-586 BC.

The Kingdom falls: 586 BC (2 Kings 24- 25)
Without repentance they were doomed to end up in bondage and fall into the very hands of the ruthless Empire, the ungodly system and values they embraced. Not only were they doomed, but so was the Kingdom. God gave Israel over to the very Babylonian system they worshipped. They lost their freedom, blessings and protection from God, were captured and taken into captivity by King Nebuchadnezzar, many brutalized, tortured, and taken to Babylon.

Many died. The Temple treasures were taken and during the second siege Jerusalem and the Temple was destroyed. The Kingdom fell. (2 Kings 24 and 25.)

No King:

Since 586 BC no divinely appointed King of the tribe of Judah has ruled from the throne of King David. It has been gentile rule over Israel for *"2500 years."*

The Kings first coming: A Spiritual Kingdom

Outside of the believing remnant, the rightful King of Israel was rejected by His *nation*. They did not repent of their sin, nor receive Him. In turn Jesus established his spiritual kingdom with the believing remnant. He calls this kingdom His church, made up of believing Jews to whom Gentiles are added. *NOTE:* In Matthew chapter 1, we see the lineage of mother Mary. Even though Joseph was only our Lord's legal father, because God was His Father, Joseph was likewise of the royal lineage. God made sure that skeptics don't have any argument. (Luke 3: 23-37).

The Promise: God's Covenant with King David:

God promised King David a King to come that would rule from his throne *forever*. In His second coming He will conquer Jerusalem and make it His capitol. He, like King David, will destroy Israel's enemies and bring about glorious days for Israel when He shepherds His people with justice. Thank God we serve a Covenant keeping God. He has the title deed to the earth, to rule it with righteousness and justice, and has the birthright, - not Allah. He was <u>*born*</u> King of the Jews, of the royal lineage of King David, of the tribe of Judah. He is the rightful heir and King. Give Him Praise!

2 Samuel 7: 5 -16

Go and tell my servant David, This is what the LORD says: Are you the one to build me a house to dwell in? I have not dwelt in a house from the day I brought the Israelites up out of Egypt to this day. I have been moving from place to place with a tent as my dwelling. Wherever I have moved with all the Israelites, did I ever say to any of their rulers whom I commanded to shepherd my people Israel, "Why have you not built me a house of cedar?" "Now then, tell my servant David, this is what the LORD Almighty says: I took you from the pasture and from following the flock to be ruler over my people Israel. I have been with you wherever you have gone, and I have cut off all your enemies from before you. Now I will make your name great, like the names of the greatest men of the earth. And I will provide a place for my people Israel and will plant them so that they can have a home of their own and no longer be disturbed. Wicked people will not oppress them anymore, as they did at the beginning and have done ever since the time I appointed leaders over my people Israel. I will also give you rest from all your enemies.

'The LORD declares to you that the LORD himself will establish a house for you: When your days are over and you rest with your fathers, I will raise up your offspring to succeed you, who will come from your own body, and I will establish his kingdom. He is the one who will build a house for my Name, and I will establish the throne of his kingdom forever. I will be his father, and he will be my son. When he does wrong, I will punish him with the rod of men, with floggings inflicted by men. But my love will never be taken away from him, as I took it away from Saul, whom I removed from before you. **Your house and your kingdom will endure forever before me; your throne will be established FOREVER!"**

In the meantime Beasts and Harlots:

Israel was set apart as God's Covenant nation. When Israel kept Covenant she was the recipient of boundless blessings. She was to draw mankind to her true and living God. While there was and is a godly remnant, the nation sadly failed. God chose His church. She was to draw men to Christ. While there was and is a godly remnant, she has often failed as well. But Jesus, the Messiah of Israel, and Savior of the world never fails. He will assure the destiny of both.

God chose Israel to bless the world, but the world has cursed her because the enemy is always at work. But God neither sleeps nor slumbers. He has His eyes on Israel. The world was blessed when He came to Israel to pay for sin, and will be blessed forever when He returns to Israel to overthrow Satan's kingdom, to set up His kingdom that will last forever. (Psalm12; Zech.14)

Until the Lord comes to rule the earth, the world was and will be infiltrated by Babylonian systems. As world rule began with Nimrod and Semiramis, and wont fall until Jesus Christ comes to rule the earth. Babylonian Beast kingdoms have used and will use their power to gain control over the earth in their ruthless quest, thus typify Nimrod the bull, while the Harlot does so by her seductive ways. Yes, a team indeed! Together they defy God, and usurp God's rule on earth.

Now that we have established that literal Babylon of old was a powerful empire, not merely a religion, that sought to rule the earth, rebelled against the God of Holy Scripture, built high towers, worshipped Babylonian gods, sacrificed their children, and practiced all kinds of grotesque immorality, let us examine Daniel's prophecy and John's revelation given by Jesus Christ.

CHAPTER 20

Beast kingdoms that rule the earth

The Bible focuses upon Kings and kingdoms that rule the earth, specifically how they affected Israel. Once we get that in our heads, it is not so confusing anymore. God has His eyes on the whole world, but Israel is the apple of His eye because through her He has determined to save the world and bring history to a close. She is God s' prophetic time clock.

The book of Daniel and his prophecies are sealed until the time of the end. But God is a Father who wants to protect His children. As time goes on we will gain more and more insight to His prophetic word, as He will reveal it, but in order to do so we must read it, in order for God to bring it to mind. In this chapter we will examine Daniel, and then Revelation. Why?

The test of scripture is always the same. The Old Testament is revealed in the New and the New Testament was concealed in the Old. Although Daniel was written in the Old Testament and Revelation in the New, by people who did not know each other, they are companion books and complement each other. Therefore, people that follow one man who claims to be a prophet and comes up with new revelations, new books, are asking you to check your brains out at the door. God doesn't! You should never listen to such!

In the following dream of king Nebuchadnezzar we see a large statue. Daniel describes four gentile/non Jewish Empires. They represent gentile dominion of the earth from the time Israel became a *"nation."* Daniel declares the head of Gold to be no other than King Nebuchadnezzar of Babylon himself. He was the *"first"* ruthless gentile King / kingdom/ empire, to bring **gentile rule over the throne of Israel.**

The Dream of Nebuchadnezzar: Daniel 2: 31-43

"You looked, O king, and there before you stood a large statue—an enormous, dazzling statue, awesome in appearance. The head of the statue was made of pure gold, it's chest and arms of silver, it's belly and thighs of bronze, it's legs of iron ,it's feet partly of iron and partly of baked clay. While you were watching, a rock was cut out, but not by human hands. It struck the statue on it's feet of iron and clay and smashed them. Then the iron, the clay, the bronze, the silver and the gold were broken to pieces at the same time and became like chaff on a threshing floor in the summer. The wind swept them away without leaving a trace. But the rock that struck the statue became a huge mountain and filled the whole earth.

Interpretation of Dream: Daniel 2: 36-43

"This was the dream, and now we will interpret it to the king. You, O king, are the king of kings. The God of heaven has given you dominion and power and might and glory; in your hands he has placed mankind and the beasts of the field and the birds of the air. Wherever they live, he has made you ruler over them all. You are that head of gold.

"After you, another kingdom will rise, inferior to yours. Next, a third kingdom, one of bronze, will rule over the whole earth. Finally, there will be a fourth kingdom, strong as iron—for iron breaks and smashes everything—and as iron breaks things to pieces, so it will crush and break all the others. Just as you saw that the feet and toes were partly of baked clay and partly of iron, so this will be a divided kingdom; yet it will have some of the strength of iron in

it, even as you saw iron mixed with clay. As the toes were partly iron and partly clay, so will this kingdom be partly strong and partly brittle. And just as you saw the iron mixed with baked clay, so the people will be a mixture and will not remain united, any more than iron mixes with clay.

Nebuchadnezzar's Dream

Object:	Material: Daniel 2	Beast: Daniel 7	Kingdom / Empire	Duration:
Head	Gold	Lion	Babylon	626-538BC
Chest	Silver	Bear	Medo-Persia	538-329BC
Belly and Thighs	Brass /Bronze	Leopard	Greece	329- 62BC Antiochus Epiphane 168-165BC
Legs	Iron	Terrifying / frightening	Rome	63 BC-approx. 400 AD
Feet and toes	Iron and Clay	Same	Rome and ???	Future: 42 months
Divine, not of human hands	Stone / Rock	Becomes Mountain	Rock smashes all gentile Empires	Eternal Kingdom

When you compare Daniel chapter 2 and then chapter 7, we see the following:
1.) Babylon, the head of *gold*, a **Lion.**
2.) Medo Persia, the chest of *silver*, a **Bear**
3.) Greece, the Belly and thighs of *brass/ bronze*, a **leopard**
4.) Rome, the Legs of *Iron*, **terrifying and terrible.**

Notice they are all ruthless BEAST kingdoms / empires.
Notice they diminish from gold to iron.
Notice that each medal is stronger than the other.
Considering that Satan is getting more ferocious in his attempt to rule the earth and destroy Israel as time goes on, these are perfect pictures.

The last Gentile Beast Empire to rise is a return of Rome/ Iron, mixed with something else, *clay*. It is comprised of 2 feet, indicating separation, yet made up of 10 toes, thus smaller Kingdoms to unite to become a mighty ruthless Beast Empire. It is described to be a **union of people** so different that they *cannot bond*, no more than IRON can bond with CLAY. (Daniel 2: 40-43)

The Rock is coming!
While all of these empires fell in succession from power, the statue stands until the "Rock" smashes the feet and then comes crumbling down. Thank God for the Kingdom of Rock not made of human hands, but divine, to smite this damnable statue that represents their ferocious and ungodly control over the throne of Israel and the earth.

Notice what Daniel writes: Daniel 2: 34- 35

While you were watching, a rock was cut out, but not by human hands. It struck the statue on its feet of iron and clay and smashed them. THEN the iron, the clay, the bronze, the silver and the gold were broken to pieces at THE SAME TIME and became like chaff on a threshing floor in the summer. The wind swept them away without leaving a trace. But the rock that struck the statue became a huge mountain and filled the whole earth.

The Kingdom of the ROCK! Daniel 2: 44- 45

"In the time of those kings, the God of heaven will set up a kingdom that will never be destroyed, nor will it be left to another people. It will crush all those kingdoms and bring them to an end, but it will itself endure forever. This is the meaning of the vision of the rock cut out of a mountain, **but not by human hands, a rock that broke the iron, the bronze, the clay, the silver and the gold to pieces.** *The great God has shown the king what will take place in the future. The dream is true and the interpretation is trustworthy."*

The Revelation of Jesus Christ to John:
Now let us compare the vision of Daniel chapter 2 and 7, which describes *"four Beast Empires"* ruling from the throne of King David, with Revelation which describes a total of *"eight."*

This calls for a mind of Wisdom: Rev. 17: 9-11
*The **seven heads** are **seven hills** on which the woman sits."*
*They are also **seven kings, five have fallen; one is.***
*The other has not yet come; but when he does come, he must **remain only a little while."***
*The <u>beast</u> that once was and now is not is an **eighth king.***
***He belongs to the seven** and is going to his destruction."*

The 7 heads on 7 hills have often been taught and thought to be the 7 hills of Rome. However, the text *clearly* identifies these 7 heads on 7 hills *as 7 KINGS.* Since kings have kingdoms, or empires, or what we call coalitions today, this harmonizes with Daniel and all of scripture, as hills and mountains are used as metaphors for kingdoms. Furthermore, these *7KINGS* are to be followed by an *EIGHTH KING* to come, who is the <u>*Final Beast and EIGHTH KINGDOM to rise out of the SEVEN before it.*</u>

Therefore, all eight have the same characteristics of a BEAST, just as the four in Daniel chapter 2 and 7, because they are ferocious and beastlike in their actions. If we keep in mind that the Hebrew people and Israel are the center of prophecy, these are no other than the <u>totality</u> of beastlike kings and kingdoms that have attempted to destroy the Hebrew people. This revelation, given to John, by Jesus Christ, is more comprehensive than Daniel, as the LORD gives him not merely empires that have ruled over *"the <u>throne of</u> Israel <u>after</u> she became a nation"*, but includes *"all"* of the Gentile empires that have persecuted *"the Hebrew people from the beginning of time, to the end of the age."*

Kingdom / Empire 1- 5:
From John's perspective and timeframe he writes that *5 have fallen.* (Rev 17:10)

The 5 empires listed in scripture that existed prior to his time and fell, were: *1.) Egypt; 2.)Assyria; 3.)Babylon; 4.)Medo Persia; 5.)Greece.*

Timeframe: From the Old Testament, including the 400 years between the Old and New Testament recorded in the Apocrypha.

Kingdom/ Empire 6:

The 6th empire during his lifetime was *Rome,* thus John writes, *"one is".*

Timeframe: 1 century, New Testament. John wrote during his exile on the island of Patmos and his suffering under Rome. This is the beginning of the church age, recorded in the New Testament.

Kingdom/ Empire 7:

John describes a 7th Beast, which has *not yet come, but when he does come must remain only a little while.* Rev. 17:10b. Once again it was written from his timeframe. I believe that this 7th *Beast did come,* and was *Nazi Germany.* It lasted *only a little while*. All other empires lasted between 200-400 years, Nazi Germany only from 1933-1945. (Thank God)

Timeframe: Between our Lords first coming and prior to the re-establishment of Israel. This is the mystery age to Israel. Remember that Israel did not exist since 136 AD, was renamed Palestine, and did not come into existence again until May14.1948, no less than out of the ashes of the Holocaust.

Kingdom/ Empire 8: The LAST Beast with 10 horns.

Timeframe: Do the math! Since the 8th Beast empire has to rise *after the re-establishment of Israel,* because the Great Tribulation will beak out in Jerusalem, we are now at the *end of age.* This time of the beast is also known as the *"Time of Jacob's / Israel's trouble."* (Matthew 24: 15; Jeremiah 30:7; Daniel 9:27)

As we saw, the prophet Daniel described this last beast empire as a return of Rome/ Iron, but mixed with something else, clay. It is comprised of 2 feet and 10 toes, which are smaller Kingdoms to unite to become a mighty ruthless Beast Empire. Rather than 10 toes, the apostle John describes a beast with 10 horns sitting on it, thus again a power to unite. *Revelation 17:12-14: The 10 horns that you saw are 10 kings, who have not received a kingdom, but for one hour will receive authority as kings. They have one purpose and will give their power and authority to the Beast."*

Compare Daniel with Revelation

Daniel 2 and 7: Empire:	Revelation 17:9-14 Empire	Beast/Material:	Timeframe	4000 years
Before Establishment of Israel	1. Egypt 2. Assyria		Old Testament	"
After establishment of Israel				
1. Babylon	3. Babylon	Lion/Gold	"	
2. Medo Persia	4. Medo Persia	Bear/silver	"	
3. Greece	5. Greece	Leopard/bronze	Between the Testaments	
FIRST COMING:				
4. Rome	6. Rome	Terrifying and Frightening / IRON	New Testament	
				2000 years
Israel changed to Palestine Scattered amongst the nations	Holy Roman Empire Muslim Empire Nazi Germany Stalin's Russia		Israel's Dispersion	
Israel' reestablished 1948; Ezekiel 36	8. ???	Final Beast 10 horns/ 10 toes IRON and CLAY	Israel's ingathering Birth pangs Great Tribulation Time of Jacob's Trouble Resurrection/rapture God's wrath	
				subtotal 6000 years
SECOND COMING: Israel delivered		God's Kingdom on earth	PEACE, Israel exalted	+ 1000 years Total 7000 years

Prophecy according to Ezekiel:
37 One nation under one King
38; 43 New Temple and Temple area
43 Glory returns to Temple
45; 48 Redistribution/ Division of Promised Land
47. The river flows from Temple

CHAPTER 21

European Union, or EURABIA?

Revelation 17: 3-5

*Then the angel carried me away in the Spirit into a **desert**. There I saw a **woman** <u>sitting</u> on a **scarlet beast** that was covered with **blasphemous names** and had **seven heads and ten horns**. The woman was dressed in purple and scarlet, and was glittering with gold, precious stones and pearls. She held a golden cup in her hand, filled with abominable things and the filth of her adulteries. This title was written on her forehead:*

MYSTERY
BABYLON THE GREAT
THE MOTHER OF PROSTITUTES
AND OF THE ABOMINATIONS OF THE EARTH.

I will explain to you the mystery of the woman and of the Beast she <u>rides.</u> (Rev.17:7)
Now the focus changes from the Beast, to "a woman, a harlot, or prostitute" who <u>sits</u> on all 7 Beast empires and <u>rides</u> the final and "eighth." For centuries believers have attempted to identify "Mystery Babylon." Many have taught her to be the Roman Catholic Church, once gain due to Rome's location on 7 hills, her corruption and power. She is furthermore accused of accepting numerous

Babylonian pagan practices. The Babylonian worship of the sun, and the worship of Mary with sun beams streaming from her head, a crown depicting her as the queen of heaven has been additional reasons that many believe she is *"Mystery Babylon, the Great, the mother of prostitutes, and of the abominations of the earth"*. They see this religious system as one of corruption, the ultimate expression of Babylonianism.

From what I see, we are still talking *"kings and kingdoms"* here, thus *consecutive* Empires, and this one is in power just prior to the end of the age, because she *rides on the LAST Beast, thus controls it*. Literal Babylon was in power in the beginning, **thus the first licentious , Harlot empire** who defied God, verses this "Mystery Babylon" is the **Harlot empire** in power at the **end of the age.** John knew about ancient Babylon, but this one is a mystery to him, yet compares her to literal Babylon of old as she like it, is very corrupt, rich, forsaking the true and living God. By addressing her as "Mystery Babylon", they both embrace the same values, or lack of them. He sees people uniting from many languages and nations, making a name for themselves, thus leaving God out of the picture. (Revelation 18)

A people so different, yet united:

Remember that Daniel speaks of the final Empire consisting of **2 feet** indicating **division,** yet unity, and 10 toes made up of *IRON and something else -CLAY.* We know Iron was Rome - but we don't know who the clay is, not yet! All we know is this: *They are of a people so different that they cannot bond, no more than Iron can bond with clay.* (Daniel 2: 40-43).

European Union:

Many prophetic teachers state that the European Union is the fulfillment of the revived Roman Empire, but is it? Today there are many more than 10 nations. I believe the answer lies in the fact that the ancient Roman Empire was not merely comprised of western European countries, but many Eastern European nations, which in recent history were part of the Soviet Union, and many nations located in today's Middle East. They conquered the northern portions of

Morocco, Algeria, Libya, and Egypt, located on the southern shore of the Mediterranean Sea, the northern border of Africa. They also conquered all of Jordan, Iraq, Syria, Lebanon and Turkey. Outside of Israel these are all Islamic nations today. Therefore the Roman Empire was clearly a union of "East and West."

Map of the Ancient Roman Empire

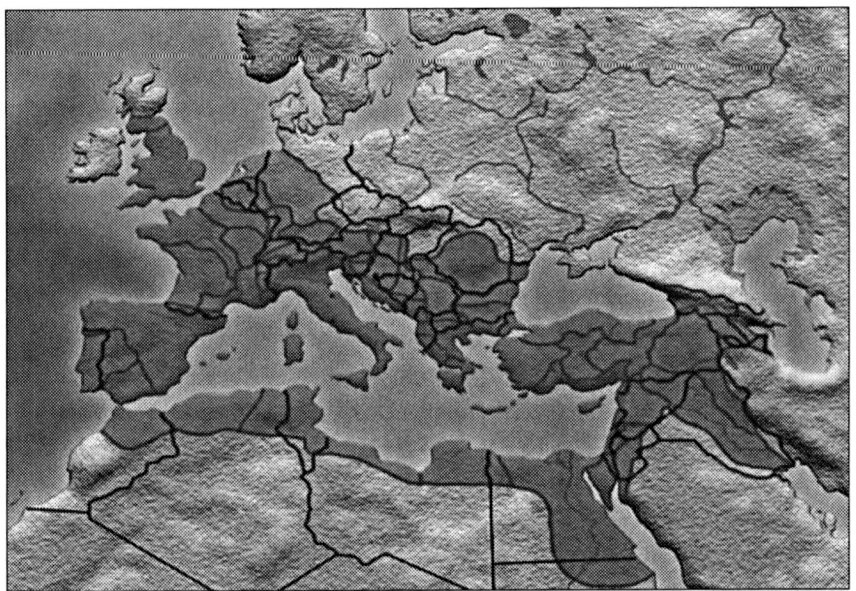

What is EURABIA?
Charles De Gaulle of France already sought to break away from the USA as her ally in the 1960's, making alliances with Arab nations. *The cost?* Large numbers of Muslim immigration and the elimination of Israel. Germany and Belgium joined France after the 1973 oil crisis. They are the troika of European Union leading towards the formation of what Bat Ye'or coins *"Eurabia"*. Read her article *"European Fears of the Gathering Jihad."* Front Page Magazine, February 21, 2003. http://www.frontpagemag.com/articles/ReadArticle.asp?ID=6262

EAST and WEST:

Since the Roman Empire was clearly a union of East and West, it remains to be seen which 5 European countries will break away from the EU and what 5 Arab nations will unite with them to form the last day Beast Empire. But one thing I can say with confidence, it is shaping up fast. The tragic fact is that several nations in Western Europe have large Muslim populations and are expected to come under Islamic rule within short order. Just for the record, France, Germany, England, Belgium, and Spain are living in fear of JIHAD. As the saying goes," if you can't beat them, join them!" After all, they need their oil to economically survive. I therefore expect a union of a people and nations part EAST and part WEST. Whether it will be a willing break away from the EU to secure oil and form a coalition with Arab nations, or a succession of power due to Islamic threats remains to be seen.

The 10 horns that you saw are 10 kings, who have not received a kingdom, but for one hour will receive authority as kings. They have one purpose and will give their power and authority to the Beast." (Revelation 17:12-14)

Tower of Babel:

Since the tower of Babel means defiance and rebellion against God, a people uniting seeking world power, it is more than stupefying to discover that in the year 2000 the new Parliament building for the EU opened in Strasbourg France, and is modeled after the famous artwork of the "Tower of Babel", by Peter Bruegel. The new building appears to be unfinished just like the painting.

Tower of Babel, artwork by Peter Bruegel, year 1563
  Museum Vienna Austria

The new tower of Babel! Year 2000
European Parliament seat: Strasbourg France

There are 3 buildings that comprise the headquarters of the European Union. They are 3 distinct buildings located in 3 locations, but considered as one. The Parliament's seat is in Strasbourg where the one-week plenary sessions are held once a month. The parliamentary committees generally meet for two weeks a month in Brussels, for ease of contact with Commission and Council. The third week is set aside for meetings of the political groups and the fourth for the plenary session in Strasbourg. Parliament also holds plenary sessions in Brussels. The Secretariat is located in Luxembourg.— http://www.europarl.eu.int/abc/visit/stras/default.htm

European Union poster:
"Europe, many tongues, one voice."

European Union currency and stamp.

Here we have a woman riding the *"Bull."* Her name is *"Europa" and she had the continent of Europe named after her.* The coin has her riding over many waters while the stamp pictures her over seven hills. According to ancient mythology, the pagan god Zeus (Baal) seduced a beautiful young maiden *"Europa"*, by transforming himself into a tame *"bull"* to gain her trust. When she sat on him he carried her on his back to Crete where he raped her, thereby fathered several half-god, half-human children with her. Europa became known as the Cretan *"moon goddess"* referring back to her "Babylonian roots." Numerous artwork that depict *"Europa riding the bull"* can be viewed at:http://www.ecsel.psu.edu/~rreynold/Europa.htm

Germany "Der Spiegel"- USA "Time magazine."

Both depict the European Union with a modern Europa riding the bull.

Mystery Babylon revealed!

Now, pay attention! The **Harlot sits on and rides /dominates** the Beast, yet is **united** with the beast moving along her merry way, because she controls it, even though she is totally different than the Beast. The Beast gains its power by ruthless control, while the Harlot does so by her licentious ways and enticement, and uses the Beast for transportation. This fits Eastern Islamic and western nations united.

The end time beast/bull (Eastern Islamic nations) was confined within the Middle East like a caged animal with unchanged borders for centuries. Held back, the Beast found a way to get out by deceiving the naïve maiden, the Harlot (Europe /West), to get on its back for the sake of a ride.(oil) Having gained in size and strength from the very hand that feeds and rides it, it now awaits for the right time to attack. How foolish to ride a ferocious beast, but the harlot unites with the Beast for the sake of her lifestyle and power. Having sold her virtue for money, power and riches, she will soon discover that the bull is ferocious, and will buck her off to rape her.

What a picture of European Union. The harlot in her drunken stupor did not realize her danger blinded by her quest for superiority to become first. While some have sounded alarms of warning, she keeps riding the beast. Outside of a small remnant, she has forsaken her God and Savior Jesus Christ, while Islam is growing like wildfire within her. Her churches are empty and she mocks the God of her youth, while Islamic mosques are popping up like mushrooms to fill the spiritual vacuum. She has sold her soul. Both the Beast and the Harlot sacrifice their children; the Beast by strapping explosives on their backs, the harlot by abortion to keep her life of convenience and harlotry. They both hate Israel. What a team! It is just like Nimrod of Babylon who was ruthless in his rule, but his wife queen Semiramis also ruled, and was a depraved harlot. Together they ruled over ancient Babylon, thus ruled the known world at that time.

If the apostle indeed saw the new tower of Babel in France, the huge European Union, uniting many nations, the woman riding a beast / bull as her symbol, the infiltration of the Islamic Empire and its religion in Europe, he would obviously interpret them from his timing, perspective, religious beliefs, and knowledge of history. He was very well aware of the tower of Babel, the rebellion against God, uniting people together to gain in power, the ungodly Babylonian religious system of Baal and the queen of Heaven, sacrificing their children. He would clearly recall that his own people had fallen into this system and were judged by God.

What else would or could he call her, but "Mystery Babylon, the Great Harlot", comparing her to ancient Babylon? She was a mystery to him, much bigger than anything he could have ever imagined. Could there be another?

CHAPTER 22

Woe to the great city!

Israel has suffered hundreds of terrorist attacks since 1948, and most chalk it up to the problems "over there." Many think that September 11. 2001 was our first attack. How tragic! It is time we pay more attention to world news, rather then O.J Simpson, Monika Lewinski, and Michael Jackson, and consider remembering the following:

- 1979: Iran hostages US Embassy;
- 1983 Beirut Lebanon, US Embassy;
- 1983 Lebanon US Marine Barracks;
- 1988 Lockerbie, Scotland US Pan-Am flight to New York;
- 1993 The First New York World Trade Center attack;
- 1996 Dhahran, Saudi Arabia, Khobar Towers US Military complex;
- 1998 Nairobi, Kenya US Embassy;
- 1998 Dar es Salaam, Tanzania US Embassy;
- 2000 Aden, Yemen USS Cole;
- 2001 New York World Trade Center 2001;
- 2001 Pentagon.

Islamic world terrorism was not announced to the *western world* on September 11. 2001 as many would think, but rather on September 11.1972, when 11 Israelis died in Germany at the Munich

Olympics. In the meantime Spain was pressured to withdraw its support from Iraq. England has likewise been attacked by radical Muslim terrorists. France lives in fear with high alerts. Germany has been threatened by the head Imam of Islam to surrender to Allah or else. In the meantime Anti Semitism is on the rise in Europe, as many once again blame Israel.

Being politically correct seems to take priority over facing the truth, as time and again we are told that Islam is peace, because maybe, just maybe, they just don't want us to know the truth, when in fact the Koran teaches that every knee must bow to Allah or die. We watch pictures of Africans dying in Sudan, calloused by the fact they are always in desperate need, and many do not realize that it is due to Muslim warriors forcing starvation and consequent submission to Islam. They have brutally massacred 3 Million Christians for simply refusing Allah. So why don't you who call Islam a peaceful religion, ask Sudan if Islam is Peace? I suppose that the "left" which portrays President Bush as the terrorist, would call Sudan's Christian leaders terrorists as well as they are fighting for their very survival!

How can it be?

How can it be that we as a nation and churches are divided rather than united when we are facing the greatest threat in history, namely WWIII, and the final global attempt at the Final solution that extends to all non Muslims? What will it take for the world and the church to realize that Islamic rule means the same attempt as the Nazis to destroy every Jew first, then the Christians, and then all other infidels? However, this time an ocean away is no longer a safety barrier due to modern technology and nuclear weapons. How can it be that we are ignorant of the Koran that states Jews are descendants of apes and pigs, so that we would remember that Hitler called them rats, and used starvation to eliminate Jews and Christians as well? How can it be that we have forgotten the Holocaust after only 60 years, when they taught young children to hate Jews, as Islam does? How can it be that we simply choose to forget that Nazis raped women and tortured them, and killed their baby's right out of the womb? How can it be that we forgot Albert Speer recorded Hitler's words saying *"Had Germany been a Muslim rather than a Christian nation she would have been more readily suited for ruthless warfare?* -Yet we are told Islam is peace, and in turn put people in a coma or hit the snooze button, and forget that peaceful Germans were not our problem nor help as well to stop the radical Nazis, because many lived in fear and silence, while others who dared to stand up against this satanic system were exterminated as well. How can it be that we have forgotten that while 6 Millions Jews perished in concentration camps, there were also 6 million Christians killed by the Nazis for political reasons including 7,000 Polish priests? The end result was 60 Million dead from WWII.

Many in the western world believe that the only reason the USA is hated by radical Muslims is because of our lifestyle and support of Israel. Think again! Yes, they hate the Jews and then the Christians which the Koran teaches them to do. Yes, they hate our support of Israel but it is much more. Yes, they hate the West, and see the USA as the epitome of the western corruption, but the reason they really hate us is because we are the superpower in their way to gain global control. If indeed they could dethrone us they could go on their satanic global rampage forcing every knee to bow to Allah, or die.

The methods of Islamic warfare have not changed since its inception, and they fit the description in scripture perfectly as they, due to antiquated technology and adhering to Islamic law have not advanced, and therefore were unable to come against western powers. Today we are facing danger due to their riches gained by oil able to purchase weapons. If they can destroy western domination they can get their hands on Israel, dominate the world, and subject it to Islam. It is as simple as that!

Not a BEAST, but a HARLOT!

Satan was unable to make us into a ferocious "Beast" like other empires, but managed to transform us into a" Harlot" forsaking our Christian roots, our first love, and worship freedom rather than the God who purchased our freedom. We have been blinded to believe the lie that we can be like God, by daring to redefine evil as good, and make our own laws defying God.

Since WWII we have increased in power and escalated in moral decline, even more so since we have become the superpower of the earth after the fall of the Soviet Union in 1989. Today, we have largely accepted the theory of evolution and in turn mock those who stand for God. We have become slaves to "freedom at all costs" even if it means bondage to sin and death.

Yet God has extended grace upon grace, seeking our repentance and return to Him. We began as a precious little girl, but sadly forsook virtue for money, practice sexual immorality of all kinds, gone a-whoring after other gods, deny the God that created and sustained us, as well as the Christian foundation on which we were built. We have been blessed like no other nation, but sadly assumed His blessings would continue even when we ignore or defy Him. Today we are witnessing:

1.) The removal of Christian memorials.
2.) The attempt to remove God from our pledge of allegiance.
3.) Forbidding Christian displays during Holidays, which once were "Holy Days"
4.) Sexual immorality and depravity, expecting Christians to tolerate it all in the name of love.
5.) Attacks on the God ordained institution of marriage by the approval of gay relationships, marriages, adoption, even practicing gay pastors.
6.) The murder of millions of unborn children.
7.) The removal of God and Christ from schools and history, even though 52 of 55 of our founding fathers were devoted Christians, and the other 3 as well recognized the Holy Scriptures as our nations' foundation, which are clearly mentioned in many of their writings.
8.) While we forsake our Christian roots and deny the God who made us, we accept every demonic belief system as a valid religion; even grant tax exempt status to satanic cults.
9.) We ignore that the only God our forefathers knew was the God of Holy Scripture, not Allah, nor Buddha, or any other invented or self-proclaimed deity.
10.) Our founding fathers would shudder. Thomas Jefferson once asked: "Can the liberties of a nation be secure, when we have removed the conviction that these liberties are the gift of God?" The obvious answer is "No!"

11.) Have we forgotten that Pilgrims were Christians who came not merely for a better way of life, nor used our government for selfish gain, but most of all freely honor the true and living God, and His Son Jesus Christ? The point of separation of church was to keep government out of the church, not the church out of government", but was never meant to keep prayers out of school, and God out of public office. It also never meant to make freedom our idol and god, nor preach hatred against our country, never mind destruction. We all know Christians came to build our country with gratitude towards God, yet today we permit Muslim schools and mosques that teach hatred against Jews, Christians, and the West, even our own destruction. This is perverted freedom without boundaries, dangerous complacency, and utter insanity resulting in bondage.

America is First!

We must realize just how much is at stake, knowing that complacency, apathy, and arrogance is the greatest danger to our freedom. Today we are the superpower of the earth and have become arrogant thinking we are invincible. However, history proves otherwise, as every empire that thought likewise fell. Not only did they fall, they all fell for the same reasons. It was power, affluence, immorality, and depravity, arrogantly thinking they were invincible, and last but not least rejected God.

Let us consider the following. About the time our original 13 states adopted their new constitution, in 1787, Alexander Tyler, a Scottish history professor at the University of Edinburgh, had this to say about the fall of the Athenian Republic some 2,000 years prior:

"A democracy is always temporary in nature; it simply cannot exist as a permanent form of government. A democracy will continue to exist up until the time that voters discover that they can vote themselves generous gifts from the public treasury. From that moment on, the majority always votes for the candidates who promise the most benefits from the public treasury, with the result that every democracy will finally collapse due to loose fiscal policy, which is *always* followed by a dictatorship. The average age of the worlds

greatest civilizations from the beginning of history, has been about 200 years. During those 200 years, these nations always progressed through the following sequence:
1. From bondage to spiritual faith;
2. From spiritual faith to great courage;
3. From courage to liberty;
4. From liberty to abundance;
5. From abundance to complacency;
6. From complacency to apathy;
7. From apathy to dependence;
8. From dependence back into bondage "

September 11, 2001: Judgment or warning?

Many within Islamic nations danced in the streets and proclaimed September 11, 2001, Allah's judgment on the USA for her depravity. Was it? Let us compare Satan, the false god to the true God. Satan is a beast that attacks with cunning and without warning, to devour his victims. This is the exact behavior of terrorists as they with deception plan their attacks in order to destroy and rejoice at terror and death. In contrast the God of Abraham, Isaac, and Jacob, is a Shepherd that desires to protect, warn, and save. He will ultimately judge because He is Holy, but He always seeks restoration first before judgment.

Therefore, I believe that in order to get our attention, He lifted His hand of protection over us for a mere moment in order to expose the satanic spirit of Islam. He showed us their hatred, and ultimate desire to destroy America in order to get their hands on Israel, and send out their Muslim warriors around the world making every knee bow to Allah. It was a last ditch effort, an outcry from the heart of God, that tragically cost us the lives of over 3000 Americans, in order to warn us and possibly save our nation seeking our repentance. It is more than tragic that it took such an awakening, as many have been asleep, most in a coma, some drugged and drunk, ignoring the warning signs for years. As a result people seemed to seek God, but it proved to be a facade, as repentance requires a change of attitude towards sin. Sadly, we went back to our old ways and worse.

God bless America?

There is a faithful remnant of godly, kind, and caring people, and I feel a lump in my throat just thinking about all the wonderful people I have met, but our sins as a *"nation"* are piling up. We are intoxicated with unbroken success, consumed with our lifestyle, and do not even realize our danger. We think we are invincible and sweep our sins under the rug, while many don't even recognize them as sins anymore. Yet we sing "God bless America!"

An important question we must ask ourselves: "What makes us think we can presume on God's blessings upon our nation, since to bless is for God to place His goodness upon it?" Repentance is a prerequisite for blessing. God is HOLY not some winking Santa Claus in the sky! The true and living God cannot bless what His Holiness condemns! To put it bluntly; just because a harlot is generous and still has a soft spot in her heart, she is still a harlot sleeping around. She must come to terms with the reality of who she has become, because sooner or later she must face God. If God indeed never changes, a time is coming when we like Israel in the Old Testament will fall into the hands of the very system we have embraced. I have said for years, that in the end our warped interpretation of freedom is going to cost us our freedom. Soon the cup of iniquity will be full, when God will be unable to hold back judgment any longer, and lift His hand of protection over us. May we repent before it is too late!

Once again let us look at Revelation 7: 9-11

> *This calls for a mind of wisdom:* ***The seven heads are seven hills*** *on which* ***the woman (harlot) sits.*** *They are also* ***7 kings.*** *Five have fallen, one is, the other has not yet come; but when he does come, he must remain for a little while. The Beast who once was, and now is not, is* ***an eighth king.*** *He belongs to the seven and is going to his destruction.*

Heads, like any head, are in charge of something, in this case, a kingdom. Hills typify the location. Now let us look once more at the *"Woman sitting on seven of them."* What seems to be in view here is that 7 Beast kingdoms rule the earth, then the Harlot kingdom comes to power *"sitting on - thus controlling all seven"*, a superpower; then the last and 8th Beast Empire to rule the earth. In order for the 8th beast to rule the Harlot must fall from power.

From Babylon to the shores of America!

"The ancient Colossus of Rhodes:" There once stood a gigantic statue dedicated to the sun god Helios, the Babylonian sun god Bel, former Nimrod.

Location: The island of Rhodes is located at the entrance of the harbor of the Mediterranean Sea, in Greece. The capitol city, also named Rhodes, was built in 408 BC, and was designed to take advantage of the island's best natural harbor on the northern coast.

Construction: The architect was Chares Lindos, a Rhodian defender and citizen, a sculptor who was experienced in large-scale statues. His teacher was Lysippus, who constructed the 60-foot high likeness of the pagan **god Zeus**, also known as **Helios.** The Colossus of Rhodes was not only a gigantic statue, but also a symbol of freedom and unity of the people who inhabited that beautiful Mediterranean island. It took 12 years to build. The exterior of the statue was constructed from melted down bronze from the many war machines Demetrius had left behind. The gigantic siege tower became the scaffolding for the project. It was finished in 282 BC.

Description: It stood on a 50-foot pedestal approx. 33 meters high from head to toe. It is often depicted with its legs spanning the harbor entrance so that ships could pass beneath, but was actually posed in a more traditional Greek manner: "Upright, nude, wearing a spiked crown depicting sunrays, shading its eyes from the rising sun, with its right hand raised up, holding a torch and a cloak over its left.

Destruction: A strong earthquake hit Rhodes about 226 BC. The city was severely damaged, and the Colossus was broken at its knees and never rebuilt, although Egypt (her ally) offered to cover all restoration costs. Rhodians feared that somehow the statue had offended their god Helios, *(the Babylonian sun god)*, causing the earthquake to throw it down. Then, almost a millennia later, the Arabs invaded Rhodes in 654 AD and disassembled the fragments. They were sold to a Jew and said to have been transported to Syria on the backs of 900 camels.

Dedicatory inscription:

> *"To you, O Sun, the people of Dorian Rhodes set up this bronze statue reaching to Olympus when they had pacified the waves of war and crowned their city with the spoils taken from the enemy. Not only over the seas but also on land did they kindle the lovely torch of freedom."*

The New Colossus, "The Statue of Liberty":

French sculptor Auguste Bartholdi was inspired by the ancient Colossus of Rhodes and is best known by his famous work *"The statue of Liberty."* It was completed under the supervision of structural engineer Gustave Eiffel by the year 1884. She was to symbolize the friendship of France and the United Sates, freedom and fraternity, and the foundation of the republican form of government.

Dedicatory inscription on the Statue of Liberty:

" *The New Colossus* ", a poem by Emma Lazarus (1849 - 1887)

> ***Not like the brazen giant of Greek fame,*** *with conquering limbs astride from land to land; here at our sea-washed, sunset gates shall stand a mighty woman with a torch, whose flame is the imprisoned lightning, and her name Mother of Exiles. From her beacon-hand Glows worldwide welcome; her mild eyes command the air-bridged harbor that twin cities frame. "Keep, ancient lands, your storied pomp!" cries she with silent lips. "Give me your tired, your poor, your huddled masses yearning to breathe free, the wretched refuse of your teeming shore. Send these, the homeless; tempest-tossed to me, I lift my lamp beside the golden door!"*

Compare the New Colossus with the Old:

The obvious difference is their gender. The male is naked holding a cloak, while she is wearing a Roman Toga, as we are indeed an extension of *Rome, Europe, the Western mind, with its laws, culture, and architecture.* The statue of Rhodes was constructed of bronze plates over an iron framework, very similar to the Statue of Liberty, which is copper over a steel frame. Both stand at the gates of freedom of their perspective country in time and history. Both hold the torch of freedom in their right hand. Both wear a spiked crown depicting sunrays. Both are the same size from head to toe, approx. 33 meters, but the Statue of Liberty stands higher because of the taller pedestal and upraised torch. The Colossus of Rhodes honors the sun god Helios (Zeus, Baal), who's birthday is December 25. The crown or forehead of the Statue of Liberty has 25 windows, which are said to be symbolic of all the gemstones in the Earth.

Two depictions of the original Colossus, and one of the new

The tower of Babel was actually a Ziggurat, a Babylonian Altar. The Statue of Rhodes and the Statue of Liberty stand on Ziggurats and are actually towers. President Grover Cleveland accepted the statue of Liberty on behalf of the US stating: *"We will not forget*

*that Liberty has here made her home; or shall her chosen **altar** be neglected."*

Ziggurat and temple area.

What did the apostle John see?

While travelers and citizens of America in the 21st century cherish Lady Liberty, and look upon her as amazing work of art, a symbol of freedom we hold dear, John would not look upon her from a *western* viewpoint, but with an *eastern* mind, and no understanding of 2000 years. He, an educated Hebrew would have been quite aware of the pagan Babylonian religion, the tower of Babel, Nimrod, the sun god Helios known as Baal, and the statue of Rhodes, as it was built in recent history from his perspective. He would have had no clue about a man named Bartoldi who was inspired to use the Colossus of Rhodes as a model for the Statue of Liberty for the most powerful nation of the 20th and 21st century. In the mind of the apostle John, Lady Liberty would be no other than an idol of the depraved and corrupt goddess of fertility, the wife of Nimrod, the deified moon/sun goddess, queen Semiramis, the queen of heaven, who dared to proclaim to have given birth to a savior. The utter horror, as he was the one who penned by the power and inspiration of the Holy Spirit: - *"In the beginning was the Word and the Word was with God and the Word was God. He was with God in the beginning, and the word became flesh and made His dwelling among us. We have seen His glory, the glory of the One and only, who came from the Father, full of grace and truth!* (John 1: 1-14)

He knew the fate of his own people recorded by the Prophet Jeremiah, when Israel was severely judged by God as they forsook Him, built high places and worshipped the queen of Babylon, the goddess of fertility, filled with licentious immorality and corruption, the "Queen of Heaven." (Ashtoreth/Semiramis, Jeremiah 7 emphasis verse 18 and 31; 44 emphasis verses 7-19)

And now, Jesus Christ is giving him a vision of the end-time Harlot to be judged.

1.) He sees a "Great City", unlike anything he has ever seen before, or could imagine.
2.) He is aghast as he believes he sees a huge idol standing on a Babylonian Ziggurat.
3.) He sees a huge female statue, the exact size of the ancient Colossus of Rhodes.
4.) She is surrounded by a huge star, and he knows the Babylonians worshipped the constellations.
5.) She holds her torch of freedom in her right hand just like the ancient Colossus.
6.) She likewise wears a crown with sun-spires coming from her head, just as the kings wore crowns with bullhorns to honor the sun-god.
7.) He sees her standing at the entrance of this *"Great City* "surrounded by water, welcoming all to her shore, proclaiming freedom, just like the ancient Colossus of Rhodes stood at the island of Rhodes, surrounded by the Mediterranean and Aegean sea.
8.) He describes her as *sitting* and *riding* the final and 8th beast, just as a rider *controls /dominates* its beast for the purpose of transportation. (Rev. 17: 3, 7)
9.) She is rich, covered with glitter and gold, intoxicated / drunk on the wine of her adulteries, focused on preserving her lifestyle.(Rev.17:4)

10.) He does not know who she is, thus calls her *"Mystery Babylon the GREAT", the mother of prostitutes (harlots) and of the abominations of the earth."* (Rev 17: 5)

11.) John describes her as sitting on 7 hills and 7 kings, thus depicts her as "The Superpower" at the end of the age *controlling* the earth. (Rev 17: 9-10)

12.) He sees 10 nations unite to make up the last days' Beast Empire. *The 10 horns you saw are 10 KINGS who have not received a kingdom, but for one hour will receive authority as kings along with the Beast! They have* **one purpose** *and give their power to the Beast!* (Rev. 17: 12-13)

13.) John sees a multitude of peoples, rebelling against God. *Then the angel said to me: The waters you saw; where the prostitute sits, are peoples, multitudes, nations, and languages.* (Rev.17:15)

14.) The question is "How many will repent of their harlotry,- and return to the lover of their soul? How many will experience the judgment of God as He proclaims these horrifying words! *For God has put it into their hearts to accomplish His purpose by agreeing to give the beast their power to rule, until God's Words are fulfilled.*(Revelation 17: 17)

15.) He describes her as "The Great city", the largest economic power at the end of age. - *The woman you saw is "The Great City" who* **rules** *over the kings of the earth.* (Rev.17: 18)

16.) He sees her riches and global trade, knowing Rhodes was a rich and important economic center in the ancient world. *- For all the nations have drunk the maddening wine of her adulteries. The kings of the earth committed adultery with her, and the merchants of the earth became rich from her excessive luxuries.* (Rev. 18:3)

17.) This beast **"hates"** the harlot, seeking to buck her from power. - *The Beast and the 10 horns you saw will hate the prostitute, they will bring her to ruin, and leave her naked; they will eat her flesh and burn her with fire.* (Rev 18:16)

18.) She is charged with infecting the whole earth with her ways. *"By her magic spell the world's great men were seduced."* (Rev. 18:23)

19.) God cries out to a remnant of people within her: *"Come out of her **my** people, so that you will not share in her sins, so that you will not receive any of her plagues; for her sins have piled up to heaven and God has remembered her crimes."* (Rev. 18: 4)

20.) Tragically the "Great city" thinks nothing can dethrone or destroy her. In arrogance she answers: *"I sit as a queen and shall never mourn."* (Rev. 18: 7)

21.) God permits her destruction, according to her pride and greed. *"Give her as much grief as the glory and luxury she gave herself. Rev.18: 6—7. "Therefore in ONE day her plagues will overtake her, death mourning and famine. She will be consumed by FIRE —for great is the LORD who judges her.* (Rev.18: 8-10)

22.) Those who watch her judgment condemn her for her arrogance and wealth, even though they themselves became rich through her. They mourn, but for themselves. *They will say, the fruit you longed for is gone from you. All your riches and splendor have vanished, never to be recovered. The merchants who sold these things and gained their wealth from her will stand far off, terrified at her torment. They will weep and mourn and cry out: 'Woe! Woe, **O great city**, dressed in fine linen, purple and scarlet, and glittering with gold, precious stones and pearls! In one hour such wealth has been brought to ruin. Every sea captain, and all who travel by ship, the sailors, and all who earn their living from the sea, will stand far off. When they see the smoke of her burning, they will exclaim, 'Was there ever a city like this great city?' They will throw dust on their heads, and with weeping and mourning cry out: 'Woe! Woe, O great city, where all who had ships on the sea became rich through her wealth! In one hour she has been brought to ruin!* (Rev. 18: 14-19)

23.) This great city, known for her riches, size and power, her magic spell, lights, music, weddings and workman, is no more. *—Then a mighty angel picked up a boulder the size of a large millstone and threw it into the sea, and said:*

> "With such violence the great city of Babylon will be thrown down, never to be found again. The music of harpists and musicians, flute players and trumpeters, will never be heard in you again. No workman of any trade will ever be found in you again. The sound of a millstone will never be heard in you again. The light of a lamp will never shine in you again. The voice of bridegroom and bride will never be heard in you again. Your merchants were the world's great men. By your magic spell all the nations were led astray. (Rev. 18: 21-23)
>
> **24.)** *Rejoice over her, O heaven! Rejoice, saints and apostles and prophets! God has judged her for the way she treated you.* "(Rev. 18: 14-20) **In her were found the blood of the saints."** (Rev. 18: 24).

While many would agree that Europe's history has been responsible for the martyrdom of a multitude of Christians, I could not see for the longest time see how the USA could be part of "Mystery Babylon", because we have never been persecutors of the church. But then it dawned on me that "never been" speaks of the past, but John is looking into the *future*.

Outside of a faithful remnant of Christians within *western* nations still standing on the Rock and Savior Jesus Christ, I ask myself this question. Since it is becoming increasingly unpopular to be a Christian, could it be that after the destruction of New York City and the economic collapse of our nation, we will be forced to enter an agreement with Arab nations in order to economically survive, thus unite with the Beast just like Europe/Eurabia, and accept the mark of the Beast? If so, this would mean selling out Christians and Jews who refuse to bow to Allah.

Do the math again! The harlot kingdom and her system must fall and be dethroned or destroyed in order for the 8th beast King and kingdom to come to power. John calls this Harlot, the "mother" of harlots, as a mother pictures someone who births someone or something, thus responsible for its existence, in this case her harlotry. Without a doubt, the Beast / Islamic nations look upon the USA with hatred, as they see us as a whore, the ultimate "source" of W*estern* corruption.

The scarlet Beast in the desert: Revelation 17: 3-4

> *Then the angel carried me away in the Spirit into a **desert**. There I saw a woman sitting on a **scarlet beast** that was covered with **blasphemous names** and had seven heads and ten horns. The woman was dressed in purple and scarlet, and was glittering with gold, precious stones and pearls. She held a golden cup in her hand, filled with abominable things and the filth of her adulteries… Revelation 17:16 The beast, and the 10 horns you saw will **hate the prostitute**, They will bring her to ruin and leave her naked. They will eat her flesh and burn her with fire*

I have come to the following conclusion.

The above scriptures identify the <u>Beast in the desert</u>. They are no other than the <u>Muslim Arab nations</u> that <u>hate Israel and the WEST</u>. It is <u>scarlet,</u> because it is <u>covered with blood</u>, a ruthless <u>beast </u>seeking to <u>devour Israel and the whole earth. It blasphemes God, because Allah demands he is the only god, cursing the God of Israel.</u> The <u>Harlot riding the Beast</u>, with all her riches are the <u>western nations</u>. Thus the <u>WEST </u>is sitting on, riding and controlling the <u>EAST. The arrogant queen city is</u> <u>New York</u>. The <u>European Union</u> and the <u>USA</u> are the final composite <u>western superpowers</u> of the earth, with the European Union seeking to gain superiority over the USA, while we fight the Beast to retain our position as the number one superpower of the earth.

Just as Semiramis, the queen of heaven dared to proclaim to have given birth to a savior but was a counterfeit, immoral, and enticed her people into her lifestyle, we must finally come to grips with the fact that we are not the Savior of the world, nor have His righteous integrity, and have become a harlot. Gratitude is honorable and proper, but many nations including Israel have made the USA their idol, worship and place their trust in her, rather than the God who has established and sustained us. I am afraid that we will be dethroned for our pride and harlotry, to make people look to Him, as we have come to the point of no return.

I remember a woman in Europe that helped me when I was young and needy, and I am forever grateful to her. But I will likewise never forget the disappointment to discover she was a prostitute and even tried to entice me into her lifestyle. Thank God I ran the other way! We as a nation have become a harlot, still kind in many ways but corrupt. We need to run the other way; repent of our sins, and return to our Father. But I am afraid that will not happen. While there is a remnant of godly people, we have sadly been on a slippery slope picking up speed, accepting anything in the name of tolerance. May God pour out His Spirit on many before it is too late, to receive the only Savior Jesus Christ our LORD!

We have ridden the bull, but will soon discover the ride is over. The tragic truth of scripture is that God not only judges man for his individual unrepentant sins, but also nations at the end of the age. It will be Beast powers for their ruthless and ferocious actions, hatred of Israel, and rejecting the God of Israel and His Son Jesus Christ. The Harlot will be judged for her corruption, abandoning Christ, whoring after other gods, and pressuring Israel to exchange land for peace to maintain her lifestyle. The nation of Israel will be judged but preserved. All others will be burned up and destroyed, to prepare the earth for renewal. I weep as I write these words. Jeremiah 30:11.

May you have hope in the fact that the LORD promises the following for those who repent: *Then I heard another voice from heaven saying: "Come out of her my people, so that you will not share in her sins, so that you will not receive any of her plagues, for her sins are piled up to heaven and God has remembered her crimes." (Rev.18:4)*

He is not speaking of running away to other countries for all will be judged. God wants you to turn around just like the prodigal son who recognized his foolishness, having squandered his inheritance, lived immoral and ended up eating with pigs. We like this son need to come to our senses, remember we have a Father, and that means we are a daughter of the King, not a whore. (Luke 15:11-24)

CHAPTER 23

September 11 and the number 11

According to research by "September 11.com", the study of September 11th in history uncovers many anomalies and perhaps significant prophetic signs. Here are just a few.

September 11, 1609
  The explorer Henry Hudson sailed into New York Harbor and discovers Manhattan and the Hudson River.

September 11, 1777
  A failed peace treaty with the British.
  Also the first day the American flag was used in battle at the Battle of Brandywine.

September 11, 1922
  On November 2nd, 1917 Britain had promised under the Balfour declaration a homeland for the Jewish people. Despite Arab protests, a British mandate is proclaimed in Palestine on September 11, 1922 that came into effect at the end of September.

September 11, 1941
  Construction officially began at the Pentagon.

September 11, 1944
> President Roosevelt, British PM Winston Churchill, and Canadian PM Mackenzie meet in Canada, at the Quebec conference. Also, the US Army 1st crosses the border to Germany.

September 11, 1972
> The world was introduced to terrorism at the 1972 Olympics in Munich Germany. There were 121 participant countries, 11x11=121, and 11 Israeli athletes were killed.

September 11, 1990
> President George Bush (Sr.) made a dramatic speech to congress, outlining the US position in the Kuwait crisis, and the preliminary steps the US was taking towards the Gulf war.

According to many, the Hebrew calendar, September 11, 1999 was the <u>6,000 anniversary of Adams creation, and year 1 on the Hebrew calendar.</u>

September 11, 2001
> Exactly 11 years after President George Bush (Sr.) made his speech to congress, the USA was attacked. The Twin towers and Pentagon were destroyed, exactly 29 years after the first terrorist attack in Munich. (2 +9=11)

LAST but not LEAST: September 11, 3 BC.
Many biblical scholars, theologians, historians, and astronomers state that the Star of Bethlehem, signifying the birth of Jesus Christ, can be calculated to within a few hours of September 11, 3 BC; based on the celestial charts and alignments for that time. Historian Dr. Ernest L. Martin's first article appeared in 1976, and in 1981 he published his research in "The birth of Christ recalculated." In 1991, the book was re-released as "The Star that astonished the world." Dr. Martin revealed in his book, that the "signs" in the sky on the night of Jesus birth occurred exactly on September 11, 3 BC between 6.15 p.m. and 7.49 p.m. EST.

The number 11:

We learned earlier that in Hebrew the letter Aleph is the equivalent of number 1 and means beginning. The letter Yod = 10 and opposes. Therefore in Hebrew when you add Aleph and Yod you have 11, which means END!

WWI the war to end all wars, ended at the 11th hour of the 11th day in the 11th month. After four years of bitter war, from 1913-1917, an armistice was signed. It was End, End, End! I find that rather interesting!

New York and the number 11

The number 11 is extremely special to New York, as she is the 11th state of the union. The first state quarter of 2001 belongs to the Empire State New York. The quarter has eleven stars, which again represents New York, along with the first 11 states of the Union. The statue of liberty stands on an 11-point star shaped structure named fort Wood, built in 1811 for the defense of New York. Fort Wood is also known as "Star Fort". The statue contains 354 steps, which lead from the entrance up to the crown. A Lunar year happens to be 354 days long with a difference of <u>11</u> days to the end of a solar year. The actual height of Lady Liberty from heel to head in feet is 33.86 Meters = 111'1" (www.endex.com/gf/buildings/liberty/libertyfacts.htm)

September 11 and the number 11

The dominance of the number 11 makes it even more mysterious, considering the horrifying picture found in the cloud of smoke from the burning Twin towers, depicting an evil face, and yet a large metal cross found standing in the ruins of the world trade center.

God has been trying to warn us over and over again.-Why would He do that? If we remember that all other Empires listed in scripture were ferocious Beasts that ruthlessly conquered the earth and persecuted Israel, but we are like the Harlot, a young woman gone corrupt, but we have indeed blessed Israel and her people. No other nation has been the safe haven like we have, where Jews live in peace and prosper. We like no other nation have helped other nations, and sent the Gospel throughout the earth. I believe that God has for that very reason blessed us beyond measure, and likewise has held off judgment after judgment, waiting to the very last minute until He cannot hold back any longer. If you ask me about the God I serve, He would extend His grace to a harlot many times before He would to a beast. At least a harlot has a heart!

It has been said, that if God does not judge America soon, He will have to apologize to Sodom and Gomorra. I don't know how much longer He can hold on, because I know He is a Holy God and judges sin when the cup of iniquity is full. But I also know He loves us and wants us to repent and come to Him to save as many as possible. My heart breaks when I think of the agony God must have felt when He had to remove His hand of protection over us for a moment to expose the satanic sprit of Islam to our nation and the world. The cost was high, but how else were we going to pay attention? After all, how many times were we already attacked in numerous US embassies, military installations, on a jet plane, ships, even the world trade center back in 1993, and most of us didn't even get it?

The number 11 on September 11, 2001

Besides the constant repetitions of September 11 in US history, I believe that God had His hand all over the tragedy of September 11.2 001. The number 11 is everywhere screaming out End, End, End! It was our LORD calling to our nation screaming: *"LISTEN TO ME! The end is coming!" Come back to me!"*

September 11, or 9.11, (9+1+1=11)
September 11th is the 254th day of the year: (2+5+4= 11)
After September 11th there are 111 days left to the end of the year.
Flight 11, 92 on board. (9+2 =11)
Flight 77, 65 on board. (6+5 = 11)
119 is the area code to Iraq and Iran (1+1+9= 11)
911 is the emergency number in the USA. (9+1+1 =11)
Twin towers standing side by side, looks like the number 11
The first plane to hit the towers was flight 11
State of New York, the 11th State added to the union
New York City, 11 letters.
Afghanistan, 11 letters.

The Pentagon, 11 letters.
Ramzi Yousef, 11 letters (convicted of the attack on the WTC in 1993)

Does the number 11 mean that we the USA are the LAST Empire to rule before the final Beast takes control, to bring about the return of Jesus Christ? Interestingly, in English our Lords name Jesus and His title Christ equals 11 letters. I find it prophetic that our president said we are the last bastion, meaning a strong defense. If indeed this is so, could it be that Allah the moon /war god was exposed by Jesus Christ on September 11th, the very day that Dr. Ernest claims to have calculated the exact date of Jesus Christ's birth based upon the famous star of Bethlehem and the celestial stars for that area?

CHAPTER 24

The Seat of Satan

Isaiah 14:12-14

How you have fallen from heaven, O morning star (Lucifer), son of the dawn! You have been cast down to the earth, you who once laid low the nations! You said in your heart, "I will ascend to heaven; I will raise my throne above the stars of God; I will sit enthroned on the **mount of assembly,** *on the utmost heights of* **the sacred mountain.** *I will ascend* **above the tops of the clouds;** *I will make myself like the Most High."*

Satan's goal is to rule from heaven and earth. The mount of assembly, on the utmost heights of the sacred mountain, was Mt. Zaphon also called Mt Casius which the Canaanites considered the home and meeting place of the gods, much like Mt. Olympus for the Greeks, where the **sun god Zeus** was worshipped.

To the Church in Pergamum *Revelation 2: 12-13*
John wrote under direct revelation of Jesus Christ the following words: - *To the angel of the church in Pergamum write: These are the words of him who has the sharp, double-edged sword. I know where you live—***where Satan has his throne.** *Yet you remain true to my name. You did not renounce your faith in me, even in the days*

of Antipas, my faithful witness, who was put to death in your city— **where Satan lives.**

Pergamos is located in today's Turkey, former Asia Minor. In this town was first discovered the art of making parchment, called "Pergamena." The city was greatly addicted to idolatry, and its grove, which was one of the wonders of this place, was filled with statues and altars. Pergamos became a city of temples, devoted to *sensuous worship*. And here was one of the seven churches of Asia. The Jews and Christians viewed it as the **"Seat of Satan"** the ultimate location of satanic ritual. The primary pagan god and altar located in Pergamos was the **altar of Zeus, the pagan god of light.**

From Babylon to Berlin:

1878-1886: The German engineer and archaeologist Karl Humann worked in Turkey (Asia Minor). He directed the railroad construction for the Turkish government and did extensive excavations in **Pergamos,** under the direction of the Berlin Museum. In **1898** the Germans took two significant things from Babylon and Turkey, **"The great altar of Zeus"**, a masterpiece of Hellenistic art, and **"Ishtar Gate from Babylon."** When the Jews went into captivity in Babylon they had to pass through this gate. The gate had pictures of 337 demons, the Babylonian snake-gods. The number 337 in Hebrew numerical equivalent means "Hell." Therefore Jews called this gate the "Gateway to Hell." This altar and gate were rebuilt in Berlin.

1913 The reconstruction of the **Pergamon altar** was completed in Berlin in 1913 and was followed by a tremendous opening ceremony of dedication. Within one year Germany was at war. 10 million die as Germany invades Belgium and begins World War 1. (1914-1918)

Pergamos Altar "Seat of Satan in Berlin"

Ishtar Gate with 337 demons "Gateway to Hell"

1934: Before WWII, Hitler's architect Albert Speer designed the Zeppelin grandstand, ("Zeppelintribuehne"). It was inspired, by the

Pergamon altar, the Seat of Satan, for Nazi rallies in the city of **Nuremburg.** It was massive. The grandstand alone held 150,000 people. The stadium where a million and a half faithful supporters breathlessly waited is where Hitler made some of his famous speeches including the one declaring the extermination of the Jews. The columns were three times as tall as those of the **Acropolis.** They were surmounted by eagles of granite and joined together by tens of thousands of flaming banners with swastikas turning in their **solar disks.** For nighttime "Party Rallies", Albert Speer designed a **Cathedral of Light,** ("Lichtdom") around the field. Their **beams of light** rose up very high and very straight in the night like the pillars of an **unreal cathedral.** It was quite a fabulous imaginary construction, **worthy of Zeus, master of light and of the night of the heavens. Then, like a prophet, Hitler came forward.** The **ceremony** unfolded with an almost **religious aspect.** When the people went home they were captivated and won over.

Zeppelintribuehne http://www.thirdreichruins.com/nuernberg2.htm
Barnes review http://www.barnesreview.org/html/nuremberg.html

1944 Russia: When the Communists in the Soviet Union were going to build the mausoleum of Lenin on the Red Square in **Moscow**, the architect Aleksej Sjitusev / Alex Shchusev used the main altar of ZEUS **in Pergamos** as a model for the new building. Pieces of the Pergamon Altar were carried to Leningrad Russia, resulting in the reign of terror of Lenin and Stalin. http://www.aha.ru/~mausoleu/m-hist_e.htm

1944 Back to Germany: A German military detachment traveled to Turkey and removed additional parts of altars from Pergamos that were erected in Berlin.

1944 Back to Russia: When the Soviet army entered Berlin, special forces retrieved this altar and secretly moved it to Moscow, where it was set up in Lenin's mausoleum. The Soviets lost track of how many they killed, but Stalin was to brag to Churchill in August 1942, that "ten millions" of peasants had been "dealt with."

1945 Hitler was defeated: Holocaust of the Jews **6** Million dead, including **6** million Christians, with **60** million from WWII. "**6 6 6**" It is clear that the Babylonians, Romans, Nazis and Communism tried to evoke Satan's power to gain rule and dominion of the earth by bringing the Seat of Satan to their place of rule.

1947: Marshall Plan sets a United Europe in motion.

1948: Israel became a nation on May 14.

1959: The Pergamon Altar returned and was *re-erected* in the *Pergamon Museum in East Berlin* where it can be seen today. Therefore one cannot avoid the truth that for a short time Satan resided in the air over Berlin, and that he later moved to Moscow, now back in Germany. See Pergamon Museum http://pergamon-museum.foosquare.com/

1967: Israel gained control of Jerusalem in the 6 day war, thus for the first time in 2500 years came under Jewish authority, but relinquished the "Temple mount" under Arab pressure.

1989: Fall of the Soviet Union. The wall is removed between East and West Germany, and Germany unites as **one** nation.

1999: Germany's capital was moved from the city of Bonn **back** to Berlin. This is amazing, yet utterly frightening and disturbing! In the heart of a "United Germany", with a "root of Anti Semitism", in a "United Europe", in the "Capitol city of Berlin", resides the "altar of the seat of Satan" and the "Babylon gateway to hell", in the "Pergamos Museum."

As a Christian and German born I find it "very interesting" and more than odd that Germany has arisen out of the destruction of WWII, at the same time Israel rose out of the ashes of the Holocaust. In addition, Arab nations have gained in power due to oil. Never mind the fall of Communism, the rise of Militant Islam, and the threat against the USA vowing our destruction, there is just too much "coincidence" here! When we examine history and the Bible, every power that ever came against Israel and or the Jewish people, has become a non-issue as far as world economics and power. Yet, there arose Germany, not only alive and well, but as the economic engine of Europe, with a lifestyle to be envied by most, and sadly filled with arrogance, pride, and Anti-Semitism. Now things are beginning to look not quite as rosy, and if you think they are willing to consider the thought of loosing their cushy lifestyle, think again. One cannot help but remember that Germany blamed the Jews for all their problems before.

Many thought Hitler was the Anti Christ, and he does the fit the bill quite well. However our Lord and numerous scriptures tells us that the Anti Christ must come to power when Israel exists as a nation, must have a temple in order to enter it in Jerusalem and cause the outbreak of the Great Tribulation.

The Miracle: Israel and Jerusalem

Since this is impossible **without** a temple and the control of Israel and Jerusalem by the Jewish people, let us remember that king Nebuchadnezzar took control of Jerusalem in **586 AD** established gentile rule and dominion over Israel ever since. No divinely appointed king of the royal lineage of King David has ruled from Jerusalem since. The Temple was destroyed again in 70 AD by Titus of Rome, and Hadrian of Rome renamed Israel Palestine in 136 AD. *Then came May 14, 1948, when Israel became a nation after 2,000 years, then 1967 the control of Jerusalem after 2 500 years.* These are "phenomenal" events of historical, biblical, and prophetic magnitude. Yet multitudes of Christian are sleeping, oblivious due to teachings that ignore the vital role of Israel.

Why do the Jews want a Temple?

Since there is no temple to offer sacrifices, and many Jews to this day are in unbelief because they reject Jesus as their Messiah, there has been no atonement for the sins of the people for 2000 years. Therefore, committed religious Jews to the law are yearning to reestablish the sacrificial system *until Messiah comes*. As of today, the priesthood is trained, the garments are sewn, and the implements are ready. Just recently 71 Sanhedrin were chosen. The ashes of a perfect Red heifer are required to mix with the old ashes. (Numbers 19) For several decades ranchers throughout the world have been contracted to seek out and selectively choose cows to produce this perfect animal. Some say they have it. They also need the Ark of the Covenant. Various rumors say they have it as well. I don't know! But what they ultimately need is the Temple mount to locate the Holy of Holies, and rebuild. A group called the "Temple mount faithful movement" is committed. For current updates log on to http: //www. Templemountfaithful.org/

But before Messiah comes, the Anti Messiah (Christ) will come. In order to better understand, let us first of all examine the difference between Anti Christ's and false Christ's.

FALSE Christ's came along saying:
I am an **Israelite / Hebrew/ Jewish**
I am a son of Abraham.
I am a son of David.
I am of the tribe of Judah.
I am the anointed one.
I am the promised one.
I am your Messiah.
I am your deliverer.
I am your King.
I am going to usher in the Kingdom age and bring peace to Israel.

They were not Anti Christ's, but false Messiahs', or false Christ's.

ANTI Christ's are different!
These came along in Jewish history in *opposition* to the biblical belief of a Messiah. They were *Gentile* political leaders under the banner of a false religious system.
They did NOT claim to be the Messiah, but rather said:
Forget your belief in your God.
Forsake your hope of a Messiah.
Forget about a Kingdom to come under his rule.

Abandon what you have believed and hoped for.
I am a powerful King.
I can bring peace to Israel.(1Thess: 5:3)
Sign a Covenant with ME!

Israel has experienced many false" Messiahs" (Christ's), and "Anti Messiah's" (Christ's). The abomination to come is not a false Christ, but rather the *ultimate Anti Christ,* - thus *against, and in place of, the true Messiah/Christ.* Before the deliverance of Israel will come, Jesus said the worst is yet to come. *There will be Great Tribulation, unequaled from the beginning of the world until now and never to be equaled again.* (Matthew 24: 21)

The Revelation of the true Christ:
The apocalypse is the "Revelation of Jesus Christ", the unveiling, a disclosure, a taking off. From this word we get the word burlesque. Jesus is truth, He had nothing to hide when He came to Jerusalem in His first coming; nor did He hide the future as He revealed it to John. The prophets and the Holy Spirit always point to Him in order to authenticate Him as the Messiah and His message of truth. Therefore, the truth about the end of the age will become clearer to us, as we approach the Great Tribulation and the Day of the LORD.

Anti Christ, the counterfeit:
The Anti Christ will come first, joined by his partner, the false prophet to authenticate his false message. He will offer a Covenant of peace to deceive, and the world will think he is the savior, having produced peace in the Middle East. They will follow him, deceived by numerous signs, wonders and miracles. He will conceal his true agenda to gain followers, until it is too late.

The unveiling of the Anti Christ:
Scripture does not indicate that Anti Christ will be known for his true identity when he is born, nor when he comes to power, nor when he confirms his 7-year peace Covenant, but rather when he *reveals* himself in the Temple in the middle of the 7-year period, breaks his Covenant of peace, and causes the desolation of the Temple, the

outbreak of the Great tribulation. (Daniel 9:27; Matthew 24: 15-22) So let me point out the following:

Hitler deceived a nation as he concealed his true agenda in the beginning, to gain followers. The Anti Christ will do likewise but will deceive the world!

Hitler transformed people into His image.

Hitler declared the Final Solution to Jews *and united with an Arab leader, supported by Arab nations* in their demonic attempt to gain world control to destroy Jews and Christians. Anti Christ and the false prophet will do likewise.

Hitler announced his "Third Reich" which means a "1000 year kingdom" under His rule, killing Jews and Christians, in direct satanic opposition to the 1000 year Kingdom of peace ruled by Messiah promised to Israel in Holy Scripture.

Hitler came to power in 1933, but the Holocaust began in 1938, and ended in 1945. This compares to the 7 year time frame of the Tribulation. It seems it was a preview of what is to come, since the Great Tribulation, a.k.a. the "Time of Jacobs trouble," is no other than the last ditch attempt at the "Final solution" to Jews, and those who hold the *testimony of Jesus*. (Revelation 12:13-17, emph.v17; Jer.30: 7; Daniel 9: 25, Obadiah 12; Zephaniah 1: 15; Matthew 24: 21; Mark 13: 19)

Hitler's death is shrouded in mystery. How intriguing that no one was able to get rid of him for such a long time, even though many tried his assassination.

ATTENTION!

Hitler's VISION OF THE DESTRUCTION OF NEW YORK ALIGNS WITH TODAYS VISION OF ISLAM.
Albert Speer recorded in his "Spandau Prison journals" an amazing event. He recalled an **"astonishing"** *scene towards the end of the World War II. Adolf Hitler, in a kind of delirium, pictured for himself and for us the destruction of New York in a hurricane of fire. The Nazi leader described skyscrapers being turned into "gigantic burning torches,*

collapsing upon one another, the glow of the exploding city illuminating the <u>dark sky.</u>

Notice it said "NIGHT SKY!" This means September 11 2001 was only a preview, a test run in the daylight. *http://www.sullivan-county. com/id4/if.htm*

Why not a counterfeit resurrection and second coming?

How tragic that few were *astonished* when Jesus Christ rose from the dead and most to this day still dispute His claim. For 2000 years the world has rejected the true resurrected Christ, because they won't believe the Gospel that requires a humble heart, repentance of sin, and eyes of faith. How befitting that the world would accept a lie, and in turn be *astonished* when they see the Anti Christ. But what would be so *astonishing* when they see him, unless it is someone who is well known? - Could it be that the Anti-Christ will stage a *counterfeit resurrection* to deceive the world? What if it is Hitler or just someone made to look like him, since it says *"One of the heads (leaders) of the Beast* (10 nation coalition) *"seemed" to have had a fatal wound, but the fatal wound had been healed. The whole world was astonished and followed the beast.* (Revelation 13:3) - What a shock, as Israel and the world would immediately know his agenda.

Why not have the Anti Christ rise/ resurrect out of Germany with a three- piece suit and European polished appearance, while the world is afraid of the Middle East, never thinking he could be our enemy to lead the final satanic coalition of 5 western and 5 Arab nations? Everyone would think he would have the best interest in mind for Western nations, as he comes up with the seemingly perfect solution to make peace in Israel and secure oil for Western nations. This would lull the world into thinking peace, peace, when in fact it will turn into a covenant/ treaty of death. Why not change his hairstyle, color it a bit darker, and then add that peculiar mustache to his upper lip the day he reveals himself in the Temple to announce his true agenda? You may think I'm crazy, but I have learned that Satan does not have the capability to create new thoughts.

Satan is the deceiver and master counterfeiter.

Satan has his own trinity and kingdom, patterned after the true and living God, but in satanic opposition. Remember when God declared His will; Satan said, "I will."

Satan is the god and father of lies, rather than truth. (John 8:44)

Satan has a son, the Anti Christ, demanding to be first, rather than the only Christ, the Son of God who came in human likeness who made Himself last. (Rev.13, Matthew 24:15)

Satan produces the spirit of deception and false prophets, and the ultimate false prophet, rather than the prophets of God and Holy Spirit. (Matthew 23: 23- 26, Revelation 19:20)

Satan announced a 1,000 year kingdom through Rome and Nazi Germany that caused death to the Jews, rather than the 1,000 year Messianic kingdom of peace and righteousness. (Rev.20)

Satan marks his followers with the mark of the beast that will end in destruction, while God marks His for salvation and redemption. (Revelation 13: 16-17; 19:20; Ephesians 4:30)

Satan's followers will join him in his kingdom of hell, while believers in God and His Christ will be co-heirs with Him in His kingdom.

The team from hell:

Why not have Hitler's "twin" and his friend the "Muslim Mahdi" whom Muslims expect to bring about the Day of Judgment, unite to become the team from hell? Don't you know it would have been Hitler's and Arab leaders utmost of pleasure to step into Jerusalem and declare his rule from the Temple, then attack Jerusalem and all of Israel, but she did not exist until after WWII? Don't you know Satan is seething and foaming at the mouth remembering 24 hours a day, every minute of the day that he was stopped, and Israel was actually raised out of the ashes of the Holocaust? Last but not least Hitler did call himself *"The Fuehrer"*, no less than master, exalting himself above God. With him and the false prophet of Islam united what a team they would make.

Here is what the apostle Paul prophesied and wrote in 2 Thessalonians 2:3-5 *"He will oppose and exalt himself over every-*

thing that is called God or worshipped, so that he sets himself up in God's Temple, proclaiming he is God. Don't you remember that when I was with you I told you so?

> Daniel 11:36-39 *"The King (Anti Christ) will do as he pleases. He will exalt and magnify himself above every god and will say unheard things against the God of gods. He will be successful until the time of wrath is completed, for what has been determined must take place. He will show no regard for the gods of his fathers or for the one desired by women, nor will he regard any god, but will exalt himself above them all. Instead of them, he will honor a god of fortresses, (WAR, Allah), a god unknown to his fathers he will honor with gold and silver, with precious stones and costly gifts. He will attack the mighty fortresses (Jerusalem) with the help of a <u>foreign god</u> (Allah) and will greatly honor those who acknowledge him. He will make them rulers over many people, <u>and will distribute the LAND (Promised Land) at a price!</u>"*

Notice that the Anti Christ will honor the god of war, and continue the division of the Promised Land during the Great Tribulation, a natural progression of what we are watching today, —and have been watching since the rebirth of Israel in 1948. Notice the satanic trinity in the following passage doomed to hell. Since Satan wanted to rule from heaven and earth, his throne and dwelling place will be in hell forever. (Rev 21:10) *And the **devil**, who deceived them, was thrown into the lake of fire burning with sulfur, where the **Beast** and the **false prophet** had been thrown. They will be tormented day and night forever and ever! (Revelation 21:10)*

One, two, three strikes you're out at the LORDS ball game!

I cannot ignore the fact that *Berlin is once again the capitol of Germany*, which houses *the altar of the seat of Satan* spoken of in Revelation chapter 2, and the *Babylonian Gate of Ishtar* known as the *gateway to Hell*, in the *Pergamos museum*, in a *united Berlin*, in a *united Germany*, in a *united Europe!* Since Germany started WWI and WWII, I will eat my hat if they don't start WWIII. After all Hitler did declare the final solution from Nuremberg and didn't quite make it. I am no prophet, but have learned that history repeats itself. We cannot overcome what we are unwilling to confront whether in our personal lives or nations, thus are doomed to repeat it unless we are willing to face the truth, repent and change. Mankind unwilling to bow to Jesus Christ is doomed. While there are good people and a faithful remnant of Christians in Germany, the nation as a whole is too stiff-necked, proud, and arrogant, to bow to Jesus Christ, and repent of her Anti-Semitism. All I can say is "Watch!"

I call it all loss:
I hope I am wrong, but fear that I'm not, as I take no pleasure in thinking, never mind believing that my country of birth will be the leader of a coalition to once again be the source of horror in this world. I loved my country, and remember the day when I fell deeply in love with my beloved Bavaria. There I sat in a lush green meadow on a hillside overlooking this paradise, a picturesque village with its beautiful homes, looking as if they grew from the land to enhance the natural beauty. I heard the church bells ringing, and smelled the fragrance of alpine flowers. It was indeed a sight so grand for this heart of mine, that I could not contain it. I wept as it had touched my heart from the deepest recesses of my soul.

After immigrating to the USA I missed the charm of the Alpine region, my culture and traditions. During my first trip home I sat and looked over the same spot. It was a beautiful day, with the sun on my back, listening to the church bells once again. But my heart was heavy as I could not fathom and understand how such a beautiful place could have been part of the Holocaust and produced such evil people. I furthermore noticed that many of the surviving generation of Germans exposed to this time of evil, were arrogant, demanding, critical, even brutal. External perfection superseded relationships, controlled by a Spirit of domination that disturbed my Spirit. I wept deeply, as I realized I was raised by such a father, who almost destroyed my life, and although the war was long over, it was still affecting people and their children.

In 1986 I came to know Jesus Christ in a most powerful way. Then I read these words: *"Oh Jerusalem, Jerusalem, you who kill the prophets and stone those sent to you, how often I have longed to gather your children, as a hen gathers her chicks under her wings, but you were not willing. You're house is left to you desolate. For I tell you, you will not see me again until you say, "Blessed is he who comes in the name of the LORD!" (Matt. 23:37-39)*

I wept bitterly! Yes, I knew the feeling. How utterly heartbreaking for my Savior to look down upon his beloved country, the city of Jerusalem, the beautiful Temple, yet filled with many leaders who's hearts were hardened, often vicious, with no compassion and mercy for the common people, not knowing their Messiah's love, nor how to forgive others, and consequently never learned to forgive themselves and be free.

In 1991 God gave me a vision of Germany that was most disturbing. I was looking at old postcards from Berlin, given to me by a beloved friend. My eyes were drawn to the black bear, the symbol and city crest of Berlin. All of a sudden it moved out of the postcard as if I were using a magnet in slow motion. It startled me, but I chalked it up to needing eyeglasses.

Soon after I visited a German club, and there was a crest of Berlin with its symbol the "Black bear" on a large plaque hanging on the wall. As I looked, the bear moved rapidly out of the picture as if to devour me, but stopped just in time. It rattled and shook me up so terribly, causing my body to tremble uncontrollably in fear. I ran to the restroom shaking. While sitting on the toilet seat trying to get my composure I found myself crying out: "Oh no God, - not again!"

Back then I had little understanding of scripture, as prior to my conversion in 1986 I had never opened a Bible. But I knew that God not only showed me that Germany would be a major player in the end times, to cause the persecution of the Jewish people once more, but was asking me to let go of my dream to live once more in my beloved Bavaria, because I needed to identify myself as an American for a work that He had prepared for me to do. I did not know what, but soon after that experience I became a citizen renouncing all loyalties to my country of birth, and cried out to God: "My citizenship is in Heaven!"

But I was devastated and felt like a traitor. My husband knew my struggle and already planned to take me to a restaurant overlooking the city. As I was sitting there, numb, and sad, looking out into the distance, with hot tears rolling down my face, I was all of a sudden flooded with a peace beyond comprehension and explanation. Joy filled my spirit and the burden lifted. Then I knew without a doubt I had done exactly what God asked me to do.

I had lost it all; my birth family, adoptive family, my inheritance, my son, my country and almost my mind. The last thing was a paper that said German citizenship that guaranteed my return. Now it was gone, all gone. On that day I knew what Abraham felt like, who had left his country, his people, his household, to go to the land God promised. On that day I understood what Paul said: *"I consider everything a loss compared to the surpassing greatness of knowing Christ Jesus my Lord, for who's sake I have lost all things. I consider them rubbish, that I may gain Christ, and be found in Him, not having a righteousness of my own that comes from the law, but that which is through faith in Christ-the righteousness that comes from God and is by faith."* (Philippians 3:8-9)

When I left everything behind to come to the USA, I lost it all, but gained a wonderful husband who has modeled Jesus Christ to me for many years. In His grace God brought me here to hear the Gospel, to find Jesus Christ. He has used all my pain of the past to open up His Word. What Satan meant for destruction, God meant for good. I indeed call it all loss, in order to gain Christ!

CHAPTER 25

Exempt from Tribulation or *GOD'S WRATH?*

*"For God did not appoint us to **suffer wrath**,*
but to receive salvation through Jesus Christ our Lord."
1 Thessalonians 5: 9

Some say: *"It does not matter if Pre-Tribulation is right or not, what ever happens, it will all pan out at the end."* This statement reflects the confusion and frustration in the body of Christ pertaining end times. I know, as I used to come back after prophetic seminars more confused than before I went.

A man I highly respect said something like this: *"An army prepared to face the front lines does not compare to the reserves. Those ready to go to battle are trained for war. The Pre-tribulational view has left the church unprepared as it has given Christians an anesthetic putting many to sleep, expecting to be whisked out of here on beds of ease. I am afraid the church will walk into a spiritual Pearl Harbor!"*

The Pre-Tribulational rapture of the church:
While I believe with every part of my being that the church is not appointed unto wrath but rather unto salvation, the pre-tribulational position concludes that the wrath of God and Great Tribulation are

one and the same, thus teach exemption from it. They divide the first 3 1/2 years as the tribulation period, and the last 3 1/2 years as the Great Tribulation. In order for Pre-tribulation to stand, it rises and falls on 3 points. The rapture must be silent; sign-less, and imminent. By that they mean "any moment", with no prophesied events to precede it.

What is God's Wrath?

We musk ask ourselves this important question: *"What exactly is God's wrath?* So let us begin!

Israel: Throughout scripture we see how God in his anger/wrath judged the *"NATION"* of Israel for her sin and apostasy, by removing His protection over His Covenant nation and people. As a result they fell into the hands of *pagan nations* that sought their destruction by war and captivity. But God always preserved a remnant of His people according to His grace and Covenant promises.

World: When God judged the *"WORLD"*, *He removed the righteous and poured out his wrath upon the wicked directly from "HEAVEN!"* In the case of the days of Noah and Lot, His wrath had nothing to do with war, but rather God's purging and cleansing of the earth from sin by the direct outpouring of His wrath from *"HEAVEN."* It was by water during the flood at the time of Noah, and by fire and brimstone from *"HEAVEN"* in the times of LOT.

Notice the big difference!

The Great Tribulation is directly caused by Satan, through Anti Christ, his armies, and followers. They will make war and cause the most severe persecution of Israel and believers. While God will permit it to bring history to a close, He is not the direct cause of it. The church is not exempt, because it is not God's wrath, but rather the final and greatest persecution at the end of the age, thus our LORD called it the "Great Tribulation", never to be equaled again. (Matthew 24: 12)

God's wrath is directly caused by God poured out from <u>*HEAVEN!*</u> It is in <u>*direct response and opposition*</u> to the Great Tribulation to <u>*stop it*</u>, as God intervenes to <u>*cut it short*</u>, or in context <u>*"no believing flesh would survive."*</u> (Matthew 24: 22) He will do so by <u>*resurrection and rapture*</u>, then proceed to pour out His wrath from "*HEAVEN*" upon unbelievers, during the trumpet and bowl judgments (Matthew 24: 29, Rev.6:12- 17; 8:1). *IT IS AS SIMPLE AS THAT!*

Thief in the night:

Because Jesus is coming as thief in the night, the Pre- tribulational view teaches that the rapture will be a sign-less and silent. However, Jesus will only come as a thief for the *"unbelieving"*, as *"they"* will be caught off guard, oblivious and unaware of their impending judgment.

1 Thessalonians 5:1-11

> *Now, brothers, about times and dates we do not need to write to you, for you know very well that the day of the Lord will come like a thief in the night. While people (unbelievers) are saying, "Peace and safety," destruction will come on **them** suddenly, as labor pains on a pregnant woman, and **they** will not escape. ——**But you, brothers, are not in darkness so that this day should surprise you like a thief.** You are all sons of the light and sons of the day. We do not belong to the night or to the darkness. So then, let us not be like others, who are asleep, but let us be alert and self-controlled. For those who sleep, sleep at night, and those who get drunk, get drunk at night. But since we belong to the day, let us be self-controlled, putting on faith and love as a breastplate, and the hope of salvation as a helmet. **For God did not appoint us to suffer wrath (His wrath)** but to receive salvation through our Lord Jesus Christ. He died for us so that, whether we are awake or asleep, we may live together with him. Therefore encourage one another and build each other up, just as in fact you are doing.*

Noah and Lot were *not caught off guard*, because they were children of light, *"believing, expecting, thus prepared."* Noah a preacher of righteousness cried out for 120 years *"The flood is coming get into the boat!"* Besides his family no one entered the ark, thus indicates the hardness of their hearts, as there was not a single convert in 120 years. Today believers cry out: *"Believe in the Lord Jesus Christ to be saved, He is the open door, come on in, judgment is coming!"* (1Thess 5:1-11; Matt 24:36-51; 25:1-13)

Abraham pleaded with God to hold off judgment if only 10 righteous men could be found. Unbelievers did not change their minds, as only Lot and his daughters were spared. His wife looked back and turned into a pillar of salt. (Genesis 19) In both cases they were *NOT* exempt from Tribulation, but rather from *His wrath poured out from HEAVEN!* In the context of the end of the age Jesus declared: *"It shall be like the days of NOAH and LOT."* (Genesis 6-7; Matthew 24:36-39; Luke.17: 26-30)

Do you believe in a Sign-less and Silent resurrection?

There is a principle, a key in God's Word. Anytime we focus on ourselves *"FIRST"* we are blinded by a spirit of arrogance, and find ourselves the recipients of cursing, not blessing, and at best confusion. *THINK!* If you accept a sign-less and silent rapture, *then you must also accept a sign-less* and *silent resurrection!* This means you must accept that the most awesome day since creation is a *"Sign-less and Silent SWISH."* Ask yourself, do you really believe this, and is it biblical?

The primary passage concerning the rapture or gathering up of the church is found in the letter to the Thessalonian church. However, here we are taught that the dead in Christ rise *FIRST,* because *their* primary concern was "what will happen to our loved ones who have died?" <u>Encourage each other with these words</u> meant don't worry about your loved ones who died, they will precede you and resurrect, thus go *first,* and you *"who are still alive and left",* or as the King James says, *"those who remain",* will be caught up in the air with them, so you will be together. This does not refer to Christians sitting in padded pews, with their thumbs on the rapture button waiting to get whisked out of her on beds of ease, but rather those who, survived, who are left, who remained, until the LORD intervenes. The whole point of the rapture is to intervene on behalf of Christians or none would be left to rapture.

1Thess. 4: 14-18

> *"We believe that Jesus died and rose again and so we believe that God will bring with Jesus those who have fallen asleep in Him. According to the Lords own words, we tell you, that we who are still alive, who are left till the coming of the LORD, will certainly **not precede those who have fallen asleep**. For the Lord Himself will come down from heaven, with a loud command, with the voice of the archangel and the trumpet call of God, and the dead in Christ will **rise first**. After that, **we who are still alive and are left** will be caught up together with THEM to meet the LORD in the air. And so we will be with Him forever. **Encourage each other with these words.**"*

Anti Christ must be revealed in the Temple:

In addition, Paul insisted that in order for the coming of our LORD, and the **gathering up** of the church **(rapture)** to occur, the abomination/Anti Christ must enter the Temple in Jerusalem, and cause the outbreak of the Great Tribulation FIRST! Daniel states that he will cause the sacrifices to cease, so therefore a temple must exist and the sacrificial system must be reinstituted FIRST.(Daniel 11:31)

> 2 Thessalonians 2:1-5 *"Concerning the **coming** of our LORD Jesus Christ, **AND OUR BEING GATHERERED (raptured)** to Him, we ask you, brothers, not to become easily unsettled or alarmed by some prophecy or letter supposed to have come from us, saying that the day of the Lord has already come. Don't' let anyone deceive you, in any way, for that day will not come, until the rebellion occurs and the man of lawlessness is **revealed,** the man doomed to destruction. **He will oppose and exalt himself over everything that***

is called God, or worshipped, so that he sets himself up in God's temple, proclaiming himself to be god. Don't' you remember, that when I was with you, I used to tell you these things?"

What is the sign?

God is the creator of the Zodiac (Hebrew/ Mazzaroth). He has appointed the stars as *signs* in the heavens. *"Let there be lights in the expanse of the sky and separate the day from the night, and let them serve as* ***"signs"*** *to mark the seasons and days and years, and let them be lights in the expanse of the sky to give light on the earth. And it was so"...* (Gen. 1: 14-15)

In keeping with his character, Satan produces counterfeits as all the *signs* of the Zodiac, and other constellations and stars were associated with the various gods of the Chaldeans (modern Iraq) astrologers. The Babylonians worshipped the sun, moon and stars, the created, rather than the creator. Astrology is likewise the counterfeit of Astronomy.

First coming:

God through a miracle produced His Son, and gave the star of Bethlehem as the *"singular sign"* of authenticity at Christ's virgin birth. *The GLORY / BRIGHTNESS of the LORD* shone all around the shepherds.(Luke 2). It was in *DARKNESS* that God gave the world a *BRIGHT LIGHT*, as *the singular sign* of authenticity. The star over Bethlehem identified the true Messiah, versus the numerous counterfeits that had already come to Israel before Him.

Crucifixion:

From the sixth hour to the ninth hour (12 noon till 3 PM) Jesus Christ was crucified. The Earth turned **dark**. (Matt 27:45 Mark 15: 33, Luke 23: 44-45) The Earth **shook** and the **rocks split.** (Matt: 27: 51) **The tombs broke open** and the **bodies of many Holy people who had died were raised to life.** (Matt 27: 52-53). This foreshadows the rapture to come, *preceded* by the resurrection.

What is the "SIGN" of your coming?

When Jesus declared His departure the disciples asked Him in Matthew 24:3, the following question: *"What will be the "sign" (not signs) of your coming?* He concludes with the clear answer: *"The sun will be **darkened, the moon will not give its light, the stars will fall from the sky, and the HEAVENLY bodies will be shaken!"*** *"At that time **"The Sign"** of the son of man will appear in the sky, and all the nations will mourn. They will see the son of man coming in clouds of the sky, with power **and GREAT GLORY (brightness). And He will send His angels with a LOUD trumpet** call and they will **gather (resurrect and rapture) His elect from the four winds, from one end of the heavens to the other."*** (Matthew 24:23-31)

Compare to Revelation 6:12-14

*"I watched as He opened the **SIXTH seal**. There was a **great earthquake.** The **sun turned black** like sackcloth made of goat hair, **the whole moon turned blood red,** and the **stars in the sky fell** to the earth like late figs drop from a fig tree when shaken by a strong wind. **The sky receded like a scroll, rolling up and every mountain and island was removed from its place."***

What happens when the sky recedes like a scroll?

The LORD will illuminate the DARK earth, as the brilliance of the GLORY of God and of the Lamb is revealed sitting on the throne! *(Opening of 6th seal, Rev 6: 12)* Rev. 6:15-17 *"They shall say to the rocks and mountains: "Fall on us, and hide us from the face of **Him who sits on the throne and from the wrath of the Lamb! For the Great day of "THEIR" Wrath has come! And who can stand?"***

Left behind!

Many books and movies portray that the *"left behind"* will stand around wondering what happened to millions of people, as they disappeared silently without a sign. I can't tell you how frustrated I am with this. No way! It will be the most awesome day since creation. They will panic because they are left behind with the removal of *all natural light*, as *the earth shakes* violently and the rocks fall, then will see *His light penetrate the darkness,* more brilliantly than the sun. They wished they were dead, for they know they are *"left behind"* in the hands of an angry God. Notice they will see Him on the throne, and that is exactly why and how every eye shall see Him.

Like NOAH and LOT! Matthew 24: 36-44; Luke 17:26-30

Jesus Christ, Himself, likens His "gathering unto Him" to the time of Noah and Lot. The believers were taken, the others left behind to suffer God's *immediate outpouring of His Wrath!* I am certain that those who were "left behind" during the flood ran for dear life, seeking the highest tree or mountain, anything to escape. Those in Sodom and Gomorra tried to run from the fire and brimstone that rained down from heaven. Neither stood around wondering what happened to Noah and Lot.

Question? Since God never gets tired and never changes, and **immediately** poured out His wrath once the faithful were removed, thus swiftly judged in the days of Noah and Lot, why would God silently remove his people by rapture, and then **need 7 years** to pour out His wrath on the unbelieving left behind? Yet, this is exactly what the Pre Tribulational view expects us to believe.

Confirmed in the Old Testament:
The Feast of Trumpets: (Leviticus 23: 23-25)

The "Feast of Trumpets" is Israel's *dark day.* It occurs on the new moon, on the first day of the 7th month, (September =Tishri), when the primary night light is *darkened,* because the moon is a mere narrow crescent. The Israelites were commanded to *blow Trumpets.* It was Israel's *final wheat harvest.* Jesus often used this metaphor to teach about the final harvest of mankind.

The prophets of old often spoke of this *day of darkness as the Day of Judgment. "The sun shall be turned into **darkness**, and the **moon into blood, BEFORE the coming of the Great Day of the LORD!"** It was associated with the *resurrection of the dead.* Jewish graves are often decorated with a shofar trumpet, the ram's horn. (Joel 2: 31, 3:15; Isa.13: 9-10, 34: 4-8)

The Seals, Trumpets and Bowls:

The Pre-Tribulational view concludes that the 7 Seals, 7 Trumpets, and 7 bowls of Revelation are the wrath of God, thus exempt the church from its events associated with it. I totally disagree, because *ALL scrolls contain their seals on the outside, thus ALL 7 seals* must be broken in order for the scroll to open. The 7 seals are *NOT part of God's wrath*, but rather *CONTAIN* the wrath of God on the *INSIDE*. Therefore, the trumpets and the bowls are blown and poured out *AFTER* the opening of the 7th seal

Examine the seals: (Rev 6: 1-11)

Seal 1: White horse: Conqueror bent on Conquest (Anti Christ)
Seal 2 Red Horse: Bloodshed and war
Seal 3: Black horse: Food shortages, famine .
Seal 4: Pale horse: Death (Natural consequence of the first 3 seals)
Seal 5: Martyrs under the Altar

Is God the author of evil?

The other crucial point is this. If seals 1-5 are part of God's wrath as Pre-Tribulation contends, God would be indeed the author of EVIL and the direct cause of these events, including the martyrdom of His own people. However, they are directly caused by Satan through Anti Christ, a conqueror bent on conquest making war, seeking the "Final Solution" to destroy Jews and Christians.

Seal 6: God's intervention! Rev. 6:12

1.) LIGHTS OFF! No sun moon and stars, earthquake!
The sky recedes like a scroll! —**LIGHTS ON!**
God's GLORY will illuminate the earth!

2.) Sealing the 144,000: Rev. 7:1-8

Before God raptures the church He seals a remnant of Israel. They are *left behind and protected from God's wrath*, as it is about to commence. The Holy Spirit is not gone at the rapture of the church, but handed off like a baton to Israel, as they are sealed, preserved, and protected to experience a mighty deliverance at the literal return of Christ to Jerusalem. (Revelation 7:1-17, 19:11-21; Zechariah 14.)

3.) The resurrection and rapture of the church: Rev. 7:9-17

> *"After this, the sealing of the 144,000, I looked and there before me was a great multitude that no one could count, from EVERY NATION, tribe and people and language, standing before the throne and in front of the Lamb. They were wearing white robes and were holding palm branches in their hands. And they cried out in a loud voice: "Salvation belongs to our God who sits on the throne and to the LAMB ...."*
>
> For God did not appoint us to **suffer wrath**, but to receive salvation through Jesus Christ our Lord." 1 Thessalonians 5: 9

Imminence:

Pre - Tribulation teaches an imminent any moment rapture. But does imminence mean any moment, or in our lifetime, "if" certain prophetic events occur? Think again! They say no prophecies need to be fulfilled before the rapture can occur, but if Pre-tribulation is true, it would have been true when Christ taught it 2000 years ago. However, the LORD said that many things must occur. (Matthew 24, Luke 17; Mark 13)

The gospel must be preached in all the world, the earth must experience wars and rumors of wars in relationship to Israel, thus must exist as a nation. *The Anti Christ must be revealed*, and Great Tribulation must commence, in order to *cut it short*. Cosmic disturbances must occur, with the *darkening* of the earth. A huge earthquake and the *sign* in the heavens will be seen. The Trumpet will blow. <u>*The resurrection of the dead must precede the rapture of the living*</u>.

Jesus said: *"Therefore keep watch, because you do not know the day nor the hour!" (Matt. 25:13)*

> May I point out, that it is impossible to *watch*,
> for a "Sign-less and Silent" event,
> to occur at any moment,
> with no prophesied events to proceed it!

While the Pre-Tribulational view may be well meaning, teaching escape rather than endurance, it is in reality not well meaning at all, leaving believers comatose with false expectations, ready to tiptoe through the tulips, but unprepared to stand firm even unto death. I personally have found nothing to substantiate its beliefs from solid, biblical evidence, but based on assumptions, and wishful thinking. It will indeed result in a spiritual Pearl Harbor, as it will shake the faith of millions and question what else they were wrong about.

Am I brave? No! Ask me if I would like to be exempt from Tribulation. You bet! Yes, I would love to be exempt from persecution and suffering, but what makes us think we will be exempt from the last Beast Empire, since God never exempted Jews from any other, nor raptured Christians from Rome or Nazi Germany? Why doesn't God remove the Christians in Sudan by rapture right now, enduring a "Hidden Holocaust", a "preview of the Great Tribulation" at this very time of history, having endured the martyrdom of 3 Million Christians? What makes us any better than all those who suffered and still suffer persecution and martyrdom? What makes us any better than Jesus Christ? No servant is above His master!

Our debt is due!

Why would the church want to be gone, when she is needed the most? When the enemy of mankind and God will deceive the world like never before, we are an army needed like never before! Not only are we to be witnesses for Christ to a dying world, but to Israel at the end of the age. While God called upon the natural branches of Israel to stand firm in the first century, bringing us Gentiles the Gospel, He is calling upon the wild branches, the Gentile Church to love Israel and the world at the end of the age. Our debt is due!

We have done a lousy job so far, by either persecuting or ignoring Israel. But we cannot escape the fact that the Gentile Church has been given the mandate to love Israel and arouse them to jealousy.

We have the responsibility and privilege of sharing the Gospel. We must care for the least of his brethren, the despised Jew, giving them food, drink, and clothing, as the world will blame and hate them once again. Maybe this time they will actually believe us when they see us love and suffer with them during their darkest hour. (Romans 11; Matthew 26:31-46)

John 15:12-17

> *My command is this: Love each other as I have loved you. Greater love has no one than this; that he lay down his life for his friends. You are my friends if you do what I command. I no longer call you servants because a servant does not know his masters business. Instead, I have called you friends, for everything I learned from my Father I have made known to you. You did not chose me, but I chose you and appointed you to go and bear fruit - fruit that will last. Then the Father will give you whatever you ask in my name. This is my command: Love each other!*

CHAPTER 26

The Wrath of God

The Seventh seal is opened! There is silence in heaven for half an hour! Why? Because heaven knows God is ready to go to war and pour out His wrath! The contrast is amazing! The Trumpet blew, the earth shook with a violent earthquake, millions of graves opened, a multitude of people are resurrected and raptured in heaven, praising God from every nation, and now it is beyond silent, with an eerie nothingness for 1/2 hour. There is a hush beyond description as heaven holds its breath knowing the Day of the LORD is about to commence.

The Wrath of God commences with the 7 Trumpets, followed by the 7 Bowls poured out directly from HEAVEN, executed by *"FOUR angels."* (Revelation 8) In direct contrast and response to the *"FOUR horsemen"* of the Anti-Christ, that caused war, starvation, death and martyrdom, now God repays with a Holy vengeance. It is eye for an eye, tooth for a tooth as vengeance is mine says the LORD!" *—And the "FOUR angels" who had been kept ready for this very hour and day and month and year were released to kill a third of mankind."* (Revelation 9:15) Notice the difference once again! God's wrath poured out from heaven is executed directly by His angels. He does not need mans inventions, nor uses mans evil weapons of war. His wrath is HOLY.

Let my people go!

Anti Christ is beyond furious, because the church is safe as God intervened by resurrection and rapture, and now in a last-ditch effort marches against Jerusalem in an attempt to destroy the hiding remnant of Israel. At this point, the Great Tribulation runs side by side with the wrath of God to continue to the end of the 70th week of Daniel. NOTE: *Keep in mind that God is now dealing with the kingdom of Anti-Christ and His eternal will and deliverance for Israel.*

Just as in the days of Moses, God pours down plague after plague, as the trumpet and bowl judgments are saying, *"Let my people go!"* But the Anti Christ and his followers only curse the God of Heaven. (Rev 8: 9; 16) He is the fulfillment of Pharaoh, who in pride and arrogance declared he was god on earth. When are we going to understand that such people are demon possessed? God knew he would not repent and therefore hardened his heart in order to bring about a mighty deliverance for Israel.

The 7 Trumpets: Revelation 9

As God's wrath is poured out from heaven,-1/3 of the rivers turn to blood, hail and fire are mixed with blood, 1/3 of land and sea are destroyed, 1/3 of mankind dies. *"The rest of mankind that were not killed by these plagues **still did not repent!**"*

The 7 bowls: Revelation 16

It intensifies! Painful sores break out on people that took the mark of the beast, and everything in the sea dies, as the rivers and springs of water *turn to blood.* The sun scorches them with intense heat, but they refuse to repent and still ***"curse God!"*** They are warned one more time with 100 pound hailstones and a huge earthquake like never before, but—they still *"curse God"* and keep marching. Why? Why not repent and get right with God? I believe that when they accepted the mark of the Beast they submitted to their master Satan, just as a Christian submits to Christ, and is marked by the Holy Spirit.

Who are they?

Who would be so determined to kill Jews and keep cursing the God of Israel and His people, after being warned over and over again with plague after plague? Who would hate with such intense raw hatred? Many think it will be a huge invasion from China. I think not. They are from the East all right, but East in scripture always refers to the Arabs, today's Muslim nations. Remember the Beast is in the desert in Revelation 17:3-4? And if you read Revelation 16 they are coming up the Euphrates river which is still in Iraq not China.

In the days of Noah the people cursed God and refused to repent as well, while Noah built the ark for 120 years and did not have a single convert. Only eight people were saved. "How can this be I asked? What was so utterly evil that God only saved Noah and his family, and Jesus said it would be like in the days of Noah again?" Scripture reveals that *the sons of god intermarried with the daughters of men! They became numerous, powerful and wicked. The inclination of the thoughts of their hearts was only evil **all** the time.* (Genesis 6) Scholars have debated for years as to who they were. I would like to suggest the following.

Since angels are called sons of God, but 1/3 rebelled along with Lucifer, I do agree with many who think they are demons, Satan's counterfeit host and army, just like God has His true angels, and army. In all accounts of scripture we see demons that possess people, thus seemingly cannot function otherwise. It is no other than Satan's way to gain control of people, to produce heirs in his image, to rule and dominate the earth. These were not normal human beings; they were *demon possessed, numerous, powerful and wicked. The inclination of the thoughts of their hearts was only evil all the time.* No wonder God was so grieved regretting He ever made man, needed to destroy the earth and start all over again.

The term evil in scripture is not merely used to explain any sin, but rather the worship of the false gods *surrounding* the nation of Israel, because with it came brutal, licentious and grotesque behavior, including the offering and sacrificing of their children in the fire. It was no other than Satan worship, and therefore God judged the nation of Israel severely when they fell away. He had to, in order to rid the evil from His Covenant land, and furthermore secure Israel's future, all of mankind, the earth, and preserve the Messianic linage. God knew better and commanded the Israelites to destroy all in Deuteronomy 20. Why? In verse 18 the Lord reveals his concern. *"Otherwise, they will teach you to follow all the <u>detestable things they do in worshipping their gods,</u> and you will sin against the LORD your God!* These were not normal people, for you are what you worship, and such were Satan worshippers.

How do demons enter people? I am sure there are various ways, but the most open door I would like to suggest is rejecting God coupled with unrelenting - raw - hatred. While there are many good and peaceful Muslims who claim Allah is God, when we look at the raw hatred of *radical Muslims* they are totally submitted to the image of Satan. Look at scripture and compare how ancient Arab warriors with utter ruthlessness pursued Israel, their detestable practices, and God swore to destroy them all; then watch today's videos of radical Muslim warriors, how they hate Jews and Christians and brutalize people without mercy, while their eyes sparkle and laugh while doing it. This is nothing but the same demonic spirit. When you see mobs in the streets singing death to America and dance as if they are having a party, burn our flag, and rejoice, it is raw hatred. They hate so much that they love to see blood, torture, and death, even eat the meat of their victims in a frenzy such as occurred at the lynching of Ramallah on October 12, 2000, when Avrahami and Novesche, two Israeli reservists, accidentally walked into Palestinian territory. They were beaten, stabbed countless times, their eyes gouged, and literally disemboweled and dismembered with the attackers' bare hands to serve them on platters, while Moslem psychopaths danced and cheered in a frenzied, hideous ecstasy. What can one say to this monstrous barbarism, except "pure evil?" Their hatred even makes them happy to offer their own children to such a god in the fire (explosives) in hopes to blow up those they hate. To watch how they treat Christians in Sudan, cutting off heads, hands, women's breasts, to starve their babies, poison wells and starve them out, bury them alive, or even crucify them for simply refusing Allah their merciful god, this is evil. Such people are devils.

When I watch films of the Nazis and read about what they did to their own people during medical experiments while alive and torture them, yet were utterly unemotional about it,- they were demon possessed. No normal human being can even relate to such behavior. When they can brutally treat and exterminate 6 Million Jews, yet sing "Silent night-Holy Night", and then have my friend tell me that she watched Nazis rip the uterus out of Polish women while they were still alive and smash their babies into tress; they are no longer human beings, they are devils. When I think of what Nazis did to indoctrinate kids in "youth groups", taught them Jews were rats, and even turned on their parents if they so much as said anything against Hitler; then compare it to today's video called "Jihad for kids", and see a Palestinian Television program using a children club forum, with Mickey Mouse no less, but teaches 4 and 5 year olds to hate Jews, the descendants of apes and pigs, sing songs of spilling their own blood for the cause of Jihad, and death to the Jews, it is no less than the same spirit of hell. It's hard enough to raise children and have them turn out to be decent human beings, but when they are raised to hate and be brutal, you have demons on your hands.

If indeed I am right, and 5 European nations and 5 Muslim nations form the last day beast empire under the leadership of the Anti Christ, we have a marriage made in hell! Already Anti-Semitism is rampant in Europe, just wait until the Spirit of Anti Christ takes over. No wonder the LORD has to destroy the earth and start all over, but this time with the redeemed to enter eternity. No wonder God caused the flood and this time will burn up the earth. The LORD was grieved that He made man and his heart was filled with pain. He had to judge man whom he had created in His image. He had to destroy the earth which He called good and given as a gift for an inheritance, and now He has to do it again! What a slap in God's Face! I used to be angry with God, thinking He was brutal for doing such, but now I am thankful.

Oh my God help us to stand strong in these days ahead. Give us the faith and grace to endure our suffering. May you help us like you did Shadrach, Meshach and Abednego, and step with us in the fiery furnace for refusing to bow to false gods. You LORD know those who's hearts are beyond reaching, but may You pour out Your spirit upon people before it is too late. May You bring angels to Muslim people who are not willing to brutalize people, trapped in these totalitarian regimes, as many are already dying at the hands of their own people. May they know You, the true and living God and Savior Jesus Christ who spilled His blood for us all!

Jesus, the Mighty deliverer, like Moses:
Just as the mighty Pharaoh had to learn that he was not god, now it is Anti Christ's turn to experience, that there is but one God, the God of Israel. The LORD even dries up the Euphrates river for him and his armies, so they have a place to march, since roads must be in shambles from the severe earthquake.(Revelation 16). As they approach Jerusalem like a swarm of locust, the people seem doomed to destruction. However, God pours out His Spirit upon the house of David to save Israel, and Jesus Christ steps down on the Mount of Olives to split it in half to provide a way of escape for His people, just like Moses! (Zechariah 12: 10; 14:1-11)

They sing a song nobody else can sing but the Jews. This is recorded in Revelation 15:3-4. But it is quoting Exodus 15. It has been sung by them, for 3500, on Sabbath evenings in the synagogue to celebrate *Israel's great deliverance from Egypt*. It is no other than the **Song of MOSES and the song of the LAMB"**

"Great and marvelous are your deeds, LORD God
   Almighty
Just and true are your ways, King of the ages.
Who will not fear you, O LORD, and bring glory to your
   name?
For you alone are HOLY. All NATIONS will come and
   worship you,
for your righteous acts have been revealed."

Jesus, a conqueror, like Joshua (Zechariah 14:12-15)
Now that the remnant of Israel is delivered and safe as well, God is ready to treat His enemies according to their *own measure,* and avenge the blood of His people. They have been crying out for justice. *And I saw under the altar the souls of those who had been **slain** because of the Word of God and the testimony they had **maintained**. They called out in a loud voice and said: 'How long O*

*Sovereign LORD, Holy and true, until you judge the inhabitants of the earth and **avenge our blood?**'* (Revelation 6:10)

While God's wrath was poured out on the earth from HEAVEN, Jesus and His heavenly army is coming to EARTH in fury to avenge the blood of the saints and destroy the armies that came against Jerusalem. **Anti-Christ** was in view at the opening of seal 1-5; riding a **white horse** to conquer the earth, causing terror and war, starvation, death and the martyrdom of His people, now in perfect justice it is *"eye for eye and tooth for tooth, according to their own measure."* **Jesus Christ** is coming on **His white horse**, and their blood will flow and **repay** for the blood they spilled and the hunger they caused, as the birds of the air gorge themselves on their flesh." The LORDS robe is dipped in blood, this time not in His own, but in the blood of those who dared to reject His love, and martyred His people. **The SWORD of Allah/ Islam is now judged by the SWORD of Jesus Christ!**

The Rider on the White Horse Revelation 19:11-21

> *I saw heaven standing open and there before me was a white horse, whose rider is called Faithful and True. With justice he judges and makes war. His eyes are like blazing fire, and on his head are many crowns. He has a name written on him that no one knows but he himself. He is dressed in **a robe dipped in blood**, and his name is the **Word of God**. The armies of heaven were following him, riding on white horses and dressed in fine linen, white and clean. Out of his mouth comes a sharp **SWORD** with which to strike down the nations. "He will rule them with an iron scepter." He treads the winepress of the fury of the wrath of God Almighty. On his robe and on his thigh he has this name written: **KING OF KINGS AND LORD OF LORDS**. And I saw an angel standing in the sun, who cried in a loud voice to all the birds flying in midair, "Come, gather together for the **great supper of God**, so that you may eat the flesh of kings, generals, and mighty men, of horses and their riders, and the flesh of all people, free and slave, small and great." Then I saw the*

beast and the kings of the earth *and their armies gathered together to make war against the rider on the horse and his army. But the* ***beast (Anti Christ) was captured****, and with him* ***the false prophet*** *who had performed the miraculous signs on his behalf. With these signs he had deluded those who had received the mark of the beast and worshiped his image. The two of them were thrown alive into the fiery lake of burning sulfur. The rest of them were killed with the* ***SWORD*** *that came out of the mouth of the rider on the horse, and* ***all the birds gorged themselves on their flesh.***

Jesus, a King like King David: Jesus Christ will establish His Messianic Kingdom on earth, when Israel will finally be exalted and Jerusalem the praise of the earth. The Temple will be rebuilt, and the Shekinah glory shall return. The Promised Land will be allocated and divided according the 12 tribes of Israel just as Joshua did. (Eze.40-43, Zech.14, Rev. 2; Isa. 2; 62:7.Eze 37: 15-27)

> *"Of the increase of His government and peace there will be no end. He will reign on David's throne and over His kingdom, establishing and upholding it with justice and righteousness from that time on and forever. The zeal of the LORD Almighty will accomplish this."* (Isaiah 9:7)

PRAISE GOD!

CHAPTER 27

Six days

How close are we to Christ's return? That has been the question in every generation. Most often it has been tragic as people follow leaders like sheep led to slaughter. I am not here to set dates. I wrote this book so that you may see that Israel is God's prophetic time clock, not mine. Considering the global events, we like no other generation need to have our wicks trimmed.

The apostle Peter wrote concerning the return of the Messiah, and assured believers it was not due to slowness, but rather His patience desiring that all men come to repentance. He stated: *"With the Lord a day is like a thousand years, and a thousand years like a day."* (2 Peter 2: 8-9) This is a quote from Psalm 90:4. While God's timing is never our timing, I now believe this refers to God's timing of creation in **6 days,** and recreation / restoration in **6000 years.**

Prophecy concerning Israel's restoration: Hosea 6:1-2

The prophet Hosea wrote: *"Come let us return to the LORD. He has torn us to pieces but He will heal us; He has injured us but He will bind up our wounds. After* **two days** *He will revive us; on the* **third day** *He will restore us that we may live in His presence."*

- From Genesis to Christ's first coming, was approx. **4000 years.** From Christ's First coming until today, we have approx. **2000 years** when Israel was torn to pieces, the nation owned by numerous enemies, scattered and persecuted, thus brings us to a total of approx.

6000 years . The coming **1000 year** millennial kingdom, will be Israel's /earths Sabbath rest, and brings us to the end of **7000 years**. Notice I said "approximately", so don't go off setting dates!

Six days later, -a preview of the LORDS second coming:

In the Scriptures, mountains/ hills represent *kingdoms.* Jesus said to His disciples: *"Truly I say to you, there are some of those who are standing here who shall not taste death until they see the Son of Man coming in His kingdom."* And **six days** later Jesus took Peter, James, and John, and brought them up to a high mountain. He was transfigured before them, and His face shone like the sun. His garments became as white as light."* (Matt. 16:28-17:2). Along with Him appeared Moses and Elijah. Here in this passage we see that after **six days** they saw the LORD in all of His Glory in His kingdom, thus beheld a preview of what is to come.

Lazarus is raised from the dead: John 11

When Lazarus was sick and his sisters asked Jesus to come He said: *"This sickness will not end in death. No, it is for God's glory so that God's Son may be glorified through it."* (v. 4) Jesus loved Martha and Mary and Lazarus but deliberately stayed in Bethany **two more days.** (v. 6) It seemed like a cruel joke when He told his disciples in v 14 *"Lazarus is dead, and for YOUR sake I am glad I was NOT there, so that YOU may believe. But let us go.*

Upon His arrival Lazarus was already in the tomb **four days.** (v.17). He said to Martha *"Your brother will rise again."* She thought it was at the resurrection at the end of the age. (v.23-27). Martha was in anguish over His "late" arrival and said" *Lord, if you had been here, my brother would not have died.*(v32-33) It is my personal conviction that Lazarus was not dead **four days** but rather **six days.** He was in the **tomb four days**, but had died **two days** before His burial, and was raised on **day six**. The LORD was not late but right on time. The reason Jesus delayed His coming by **two days** and said to His disciples that Lazarus was dead, and was for *"their"* sake that He was not there; was to display the Glory and Power of God and the timing of the future resurrection of all the dead after **6000 years** on the "Day of the LORD."

The law of redemption: Leviticus 25

The law permitted **6 years** of planting, but the **7th year** was to be a Sabbath year of rest for the land. In case you lost your property it remained with the new owner for a period of **six years,** but in the **seventh year** you could purchase it back. Within a scroll were written the requirements and then sealed. At the time of redemption the scroll would be opened to show your ability to pay the price. If you were unable to redeem it, then a close relative, or near-of-kin, called a ``Kinsman Redeemer', or "Goel" could step in your place. If no redeemer was found, then it was lost, and would permanently remain with the new owner.

God gave the earth to man as an inheritance but forfeited it to Satan on the **6th day.** Since then, man has been a slave to sin, and the earth has remained under its new owner for a period of **6,000 years**. Jesus Christ the redeemer paid the price **4000 years** ago not with corruptible things such as silver and gold, but with His precious blood. 1 Peter 1: 18-19. For **2000 years** He has extended the Good news, His invitation to redeem mankind from under the yoke of sin and their old taskmaster, Satan. As we approach the end of the **sixth millennium**, the time of redemption is almost over. Soon He will return and take possession of the earth.

The apostle John wept when he was unable to find one "worthy" to open the scroll, for indeed it was the title deed to the earth that contains the term of redemption. To his relief, Jesus the "kinsmen redeemer" was found. (Revelation 5) Once the **sixth seal** is opened, which was prefigured by the end of the **sixth year**, the kinsmen redeemer intervenes as He preserves a remnant of Israel and resurrects and raptures His church. (Revelation 6: 12 through ch.7:17) After the **seventh seal** is broken, the scroll opens. (Rev.8.) If we are redeemed we are His forever, if not, we must remain with the old owner forever as his slave. This was foreshadowed in the redemption of slaves. If you were sold into slavery, you would remain a slave for **six years**, but in the **seventh year** you would be set free.

Jesus humbled Himself to become human to redeem us; the least we can do is humble ourselves to be spiritually reborn to become children of God. The question you must ask yourself "Is He your kinsmen redeemer?" The period of the right to redemption is almost up. The time of the gentile dominion of the earth is about to end, when Israel's Redeemer will rule the earth from Jerusalem. In order for you to enter His rest, you must know the "Prince of Peace" and follow Him today if you are to enter into His kingdom in His day of glory."

Jesus says: "COME!"

CHAPTER 28

In my Father's House

The apostle John recorded the following words of Jesus Christ. *"Do not let your heart be troubled, trust in God; trust also in me. In my Father's house are many dwelling places (rooms); if it were not so I would not have told you so. I am going there to prepare a place for you. And if I go and prepare a place for you, I will come back and take you to be with me that you also may be where I am. You know the way to the place where I am going."* (John 14:1-4)

The Lord in speaking to His disciples guaranteed a place to call home with their "Heavenly Father" in the *"FATHER'S House."* What good news as they were rejected, abandoned and persecuted by their own. But Jesus assured them by using the common picture of a bridegroom and his bride to describe the relationship between Him and His church, as it was Jewish custom for the bridegroom to prepare a place for his bride, by adding a room unto his father's house for a dwelling place. It was not until it was completed that the marriage took place. Likewise, our heavenly Father is permitting His Son to add rooms for His bride, the church. When it is ready, it's time to celebrate the wedding supper of the LAMB. Unfortunately, much Tribulation has come and gone for Israel and the church, and sadly we must suffer again.

Tribulation: (Rev. 6:1-11)

Besides loosing it all for the sake of His beloved Savior—from status, family, inheritance and friends, John faced abandonment again, loosing his church family as he was exiled to the Island of Patmos by the Roman Empire. There he is given the Revelation of Jesus Christ. He records an overview of the events, centered around the end of the age. Seal 1- 5 describes "A conqueror deceiving the earth riding a white horse, war, famine, pestilence, death, and the martyrdom of believers! Can you imagine the discouragement?

Had it not been enough to suffer for his firm conviction that Jesus was the Messiah of Israel, the Word made flesh? Now, abandoned and under the yoke of the Roman Empire, he is persecuted and exiled on an island for his faith, and faces a bleak future. Had it not been enough for him to know Israel's history, when power after power sought Israel's destruction, and conquered the earth, and now this? Had it not been enough to know that the majority of his nation had rejected their Messiah, and he was living with the hope of their deliverance, and now this? Had it not been enough to lose family, friends, land, country and now sees the persecution of his people, nation and his church? Now, God, as if in a terrible nightmare, shows him the worst persecution ever. The Great Tribulation!

Triumph:

It is here that Jesus Christ reveals to His beloved Apostle the encouragement he needs to endure.

1.) *The remnant of Israel preserved.*

He sees God place a seal upon 144,000 Israelites. 12,000 from every tribe, as God is about to repay with vengeance against the demonic powers who attempted to destroy Israel and conquer the earth for their false god. (Rev 7:1-8)

2.) *The resurrection and rapture of the church:*

What he sees now is far beyond anything he could have ever imagined, as he beholds a multitude in heaven so great that no one could number, believers who were not merely a small number from Israel—but from *"every nation, tribe and people and tongue in*

HEAVEN praising God." (Rev.7: 9-17) Place yourself in his shoes! All he knew was a small beginning, a fledgling, persecuted, struggling church.

3.) God's Wrath!
Then, John goes on to describe God's outpouring of His wrath from heaven to stop the Beast power on Earth, which caused horrific destruction of the earth. (Rev. 8 and on)

4.) Messiah's literal return to JERUSALEM:
He describes the Lord's return to earth, whose name is the Word of God, to save Israel and consequently the world. (Rev.19: 11-21)

5.) The Millennial Kingdom:
He sees the Messianic Kingdom on earth that endures for 1000 years when Israel is finally exalted, and Jerusalem as the praise of the earth. (Rev.20, Isa. 2, 62:7)

6.) The destruction of Satan, the Beast/ Anti Christ and the false prophet. (Rev. 20: 7-10)

7.) The final judgment of the wicked. (Rev.20:11-15).

8.) New heaven and earth, and the New Jerusalem: Revelation 21

When all is said and done and the 1000 year kingdom on earth is complete for Israel, they will have produced as many descendants as <u>the sands on the seashore</u> for father Abraham, because no one will try to exterminate them anymore. They are the redeemed of the <u>earth</u> after the rapture, along with the surviving gentiles. (Rev 20; Isaiah 65: 17-25; Zechariah 14) When God brings the New Jerusalem <u>down to the new (renewed) earth, we,</u> the church, as <u>numerous as the stars in the sky (heaven),</u> are united with the <u>sands on the seashore (earth),</u> to enjoy Gods new heaven and new earth together forever. The Temple is no other than the very Gate of Heaven to connect the new heaven and new earth! Then and only then is God's promise to

Abraham complete. (Genesis 22:16-17; 26;4; Exodus 32:13; Rev. 21)

Aware of the very words that Jesus spoke and John himself penned, he now sees the Fathers house with rooms prepared by Jesus Christ for His church / bride. Now all the suffering is forgotten, as with joy beholds it in all its glory, and he writes:

v.9-11: It shone with the Glory of God, and its brilliance was like that of a very precious jewel, like jasper, clear and crystal.

v.12-13: It has a great high wall. There are 4 exits made up of 3 gates each, named after the 12 tribes of Israel. Each is described to be 4,500 cubits wide, equaling 6,750 feet, approx. 1.3 miles.

v.14: The wall of the city has 12 foundations, and on them are the names of the 12 apostles of the Lamb.

v.15: He describes it as a perfect cube, as was the Holy Place and Holy of Holies in the Temple on the Temple mount, the earthly dwelling place of God. (1 Kings 6- 8; Rev 21: 15)

v.16: The city measures 12,000 stadia *square;* which is approx.1400 miles high, wide and deep. It has 12 floors. Each floor is just short of 2 million square miles. This means the Fathers house is as high, wide and deep, as southern California up to the State of Washington. (If you only like little churches, you better get ready!)

v.17: The walls are 144 cubits thick, which is approx. 200 feet.

v.18: The walls are made of jasper. This stone is a material exceedingly hard and almost indestructible. Pillars made of this stone have lasted some thousands of years and have appeared to have suffered scarcely anything from the tooth of time.

v.19 - 20: Each floor / foundation is made of precious stones.

v.21: Each gate is made of a single pearl. The main street is made of gold, as pure as glass.

v.22: The city has no temple. Sacrifice is over! God and the Lamb are the Temple.

v.23: The city requires no light, for God the Father is the Light and Jesus the Lamb is the Lamp, and they both illuminate the Holy City with their Glory.

v.24: There are no more wicked kingdoms / empires, and kings to rule the earth, only the Kingdom of God. They will submit themselves to His rule, and bring him honor. *The kings of the earth will bring their splendid into it.*

v.25: The gates will never be shut. No night there, no enemy to be found of whom to be afraid.

v.26: The glory of the honor of the nations will be brought into it.

v.27: Nothing impure will enter it, nor will anyone who does what is shameful or deceitful, but only those whose names are written in the Lamb's book of Life.

The river of life, Eden restored:

If that were not enough, now John is permitted to see *the **Promised Land restored unto Eden!*** Revelation 22:1-2 states: *"Then the angel showed me the RIVER of the water of life as clear as crystal, flowing from the throne of God and of the Lamb down the MIDDLE of the great street of the city.*

The prophet Joel prophesied about the water, which will flow out from the hill of the house of God / Temple, in the time of the redemption of the people and land of Israel, expressing this in a very unique and beautiful way. *Joel 4:18-21 "And it shall come to pass on that day, that the mountains shall drop sweet wine, and the hills shall flow with milk, and all the streams of Judah shall flow with waters, and a fountain shall issue from the house of the Lord, and shall water the valley of Shittim. Egypt shall be a desolation, and Edom shall be a desolate wilderness, for the violence done against the people of Judah, because they have shed innocent blood in their land. But Judah shall remain forever, and Jerusalem from generation to generation. For though I have acquitted them, I have not acquitted those who shed their blood. And the Lord dwells in Zion."*

The prophet Ezekiel in chapter 47 speaks of it extensively: *"And he brought me back to the door of the house (God's house/Temple); and, behold, waters flowed from under the threshold of the house eastward; for the front of the house faced to the east, and water run out from beneath the right side of the house, at the south side of the altar. And he brought me out by the way of the gate northward, and led me around the way outside to the outer gate by the way that faces to the east; and, behold, there ran out water on the right side. And when the man who had the line in his hand went out eastward, he measured a thousand cubits, and he brought me through the water; the water reached the ankles. And he measured a thousand, and brought me through the water; the water reached the knees. And he measured a thousand, and brought me through; the water reached the loins. And he measured a further thousand; and it was a stream that I could not pass over; for the water had risen, water to swim in; a stream that could not be passed over. And he said to me, 'Son of man, have you seen this?' Then he brought me, and caused me to return to the edge of the stream. And when I had returned, behold, at the bank of the stream were many trees on one side and on the other. And he said to me, 'These waters flow out towards the eastern region, and go down to the Arabah, to the sea; and when they enter the sea,(dead Sea) the waters shall be healed. And it shall come to pass, that every thing that lives, which moves, wherever the streams shall come, shall live; and there shall be a very great multitude of fish, because these waters shall come there; for they shall be healed; and every thing shall live where the stream comes.'"*

"And it shall come to pass, that the fishers shall stand upon it from Ein Gedi as far as Ein Eglayim; they shall be a place for spreading nets; their fish shall be according to their kinds, a great many like the fish of the Great Sea.(Mediterranean Sea) But its

swamps and its marshes shall not be healed; they shall be left for salt. And by the stream, upon its bank, on this side and on that side, shall grow all trees for food, whose leaf shall not wither, nor shall its fruit fail; it shall bring forth fresh fruit every month, because the waters for them flow from the sanctuary; and their fruit shall be for food, and their leaves for healing. Thus says the Lord God: 'This shall be the border, according to which you shall divide the land for inheritance to the twelve tribes of Israel; Joseph shall have two portions. And you shall inherit it, one as well as another; concerning which I raised my hand to give it to your fathers; and this land shall fall to you for inheritance. And this shall be the border of the land toward the north side, from the Great Sea, by the way of Hethlon, as you go to Zedad; Hamath, Berothah, Sibraim, which is between the border of Damascus and the border of Hamath; middle Hazar, which is by the coast of Hauran. And the border from the sea shall be HazarEnan, the border of Damascus, and the north northward, and the border of Hamath.'"

"'And this is the north side. And the east side you shall measure from Hauran, and from Damascus, and from Gilead, and between the land of Israel and the Jordan, from the border to the east sea. And this is the east side. And the south side southward from Tamar, to the waters of MeribotKadesh, to the river, as far as the Great Sea. And this is the south side towards the Negev. The west side also shall be the Great Sea from the border, as far as opposite the entrance to Hamath. This is the west side. And you shall divide this land for yourselves according to the tribes of Israel. And it shall come to pass, that you shall divide it by lot for an inheritance to you, and to the foreigners who sojourn among you, who shall father children among you; and they shall be to you as those born in the country among the people of Israel; they shall have inheritance with you among the tribes of Israel. And it shall come to pass, that in whatever tribe the foreigner sojourns, there shall you give him his inheritance, says the Lord God.'"

Nations are healed from the leaves in Eden:

On each side of the river stood the tree of life, bearing twelve fruits every month. And the leaves of the tree are for the healing of the nations. No longer will there be any curse. Rev.22:3

The church in the Fathers house *reigns* over the earth!

*The throne of God and of the Lamb will be in the city and his servants will serve Him. They will see His face, and His name will be on their **foreheads**. There will be no more night. They will not need the light of a lamp or the light of the sun, for the LORD God will give them light. And they will **reign** forever and ever. The angel said to me: 'These words are trustworthy and true. The LORD, the God of the spirits of the prophets, sent his angel to show his servants the things that must soon take place.'* Rev.22:4-5

Can you imagine?

Having lost it all for the sake of following Jesus Christ His beloved Savior, can you imagine how John felt seeing God's faithfulness? No wonder John wrote: *"Blessed is he who keeps the prophecy in this book - **I, John,- am the one who heard and saw THESE things!"*** (Rev.22: 7)

John was there when Jesus took the cup of redemption during Passover before His crucifixion and instituted communion. But Jesus would not drink the fourth cup, "the cup of acceptance", because His joy would not be complete until He drinks it when He comes into His Kingdom, when His bride the church is with Him, when Israel as a nation is redeemed and receives Him as their King, the earth is renewed, and His country is restored to Eden. Jesus said: *"I WILL take you as my own people, and I will be your God!"* (Exodus 6: 6-7 Matthew 26:28) Can you imagine John recording this awesome promise on a scroll, recalling every detail of what he saw and wrote, while suffering in exile? I am positive the original is drenched in tears of praise, thanksgiving, and living hope.

I can only imagine!

CHAPTER 29

An everlasting Love!

I did not suffer my tragic losses due to persecution, but I can identify with John's pain. I know what it is to be rejected, abandoned, and abused. When I think back, I do not understand how I ever managed to get through without faith. Little did I know God preserved me all along! In His Grace and foreknowledge He used all of my pain to identify with the pain of the Hebrew people, with a burden I cannot even describe. I cried out to Him: *"Why God? Have You really forsaken Israel and given all Your promises to another, the church? If You have, then Your word means nothing? Then You are no better than my earthly birth father, and adoptive grandfather who did not keep their word, who abandoned me and threw me away, who abandoned my mother and grandmother. If You have truly forsaken them, then I cannot serve You, for You and your Word cannot be trusted! You just might forsake me! Please Father, help me to understand!"*

This prayer was the clear and decisive moment in my walk of faith, when God like a flood-gate, began to open my eyes to the depth of His word in a way I had never known. He began to bring sources and overwhelming clarity of His absolute commitment to restore Israel. Oh what joy it was to discover it, as for me it meant His absolute commitment to restore me, and bring about the plan of redemption for the world. Sadly, I could hardly find anyone that shared the enthusiasm of my new discovery. Many even thought I was more concerned about Israel than the church, as they were trained to apply all the word to themselves, and wanted to hear nothing else. I wept! If they only knew that His will to restore Israel, is His will to restore everything He has created and called good.

Then one day I discovered I could actually place my thoughts on paper, something that had been futile and a burden before. I began to send letters to churches. No response! Although technically challenged I purchased a computer so I could type, to correct my many mistakes, as to this very day I only pick at the key board. I used email as my source of spreading the Word, but wanted to speak in churches to talk to my family, my brothers and sisters in Christ, to share my heart and God's love for Israel, and warn them of the Holocaust to come. Being a woman and an unknown proved to be discouraging. I am thankful to the few who have listened, and permitted me to speak and teach.

But I was so frustrated, and felt like I was going to burst inside, getting on the roof and screaming: *"Listen everybody, there is a Holocaust coming. We are not exempt from tribulation, we are the target, the first being Israel!"* I shared my frustration with a friend who said: *"Do not underestimate the power of the pen. Look at the Bible - it is the most powerful tool in God's hands!"* These words were instantly branded into my Spirit.

I began to send hundreds of emails, wrote numerous lessons, stayed up late searching the scriptures, as God drove me deeper and deeper into His Word. Information and resources seemed to come out of nowhere. I began to have thoughts about writing a book. Years of depression were unable to stop me because I knew without a doubt it was God's will for me. Although riddled with anxiety attacks, chronic fatigue and depression, whenever I wrote it was like taking a drug that empowered me and gave me strength. Tears of joy would flow as God revealed new nuggets of gold in Scripture. Over and over I would fall on my knees to thank Him for *"His everlasting love for Israel."*

"I WILL!"

Whenever God says, "I will", it is His will, and as good as "law." He cannot erase it, nor replace it, it must come to pass. God is committed and determined to save and restore Israel not only by His Covenant promises, and for His Name sake, but because people matter to God. He Promised the Garden of Eden to be our inheritance, set Israel aside to secure it, in order to live with us forever. So it is written, so it shall be done.

Disciplined, yet preserved: Jeremiah 30:11

*I am with you and **will** save you,' declares the LORD. 'Though I completely destroy all the nations among which I scatter you, **I will** not completely destroy you. **I will** discipline you but only with justice; **I will** not let you go entirely unpunished.'*

An Everlasting love Jeremiah 31: 3-14

*The LORD appeared to us in the past, saying: "I have loved thee with an **everlasting love**; I have drawn you with lovingkindness. Sing with joy for Jacob (Israel) shout for the **foremost of the nations**. Make your praises heard and save the remnant of Israel." **See, I will** bring them from the land of the north, and gather them from the ends of the earth. Among them **will** be the blind and the lame, expectant mothers and women in labor; a great throng will return. **They will** come with weeping; **they will** pray as I bring them back. **I will** lead them beside streams of water on a level path where **they will** not stumble, because **I am Israel's father**, and Ephraim is my firstborn.*

Israel you are MINE! Isaiah 41:8-16

*"But you, O Israel, my servant, Jacob, whom I have chosen, you descendants of Abraham my friend, I took you from the ends of the earth, from its farthest corners I called you. I said, 'You are my servant'; I have chosen you and have not rejected you. So do not fear, for I am with you; do not be dismayed, for I am your God. **I will** strengthen you and help*

*you; **I will** uphold you with my righteous right hand. "All who rage against you **will** surely be ashamed and disgraced; those who oppose you **will** be as nothing and perish. Though you search for your enemies, you **will** not find them. Those who wage war against you **will** be as nothing at all. For I am the LORD, your God, who takes hold of your right hand and says to you, Do not fear; **I will** help you. Do not be afraid, O worm Jacob, O little Israel, for **I myself will** help you," declares the LORD, your Redeemer, the Holy One of Israel. "See, **I will** make you into a threshing sledge, new and sharp, with many teeth. **You will** thresh the mountains and crush them, and reduce the hills to chaff. **You will** winnow them, the wind will pick them up, and a gale **will** blow them away. But **you will** rejoice in the LORD and glory in the Holy One of Israel.*

Messiah will:
Every age since the fall of creation has been part of the age of sin and death. But there is a greater age to come, the Messianic Age, a period of time of peace and righteousness during the King Messiahs reign.

Messiah will bring an end to sin. (Ezek. 36:25-27, 33, 37:23-24, Zeph.3:13, 3:15, Job 3:17, Isa. 60:21, Jer.50:20)

Messiah will bring an end of suffering. (Isa. 65:19)

Messiah will bring universal and eternal peace and tranquility.(Isa. 2:4, 9:6, 11:6-9, 65:19, 25, Zech. 9:10, Micah 4:3, Hosea 2:18)

Messiah will bring one creed and one religion. (Isa. 2:2, 14:1, 45:14, 22-24, 52:1, 60:2-6, 14-16, 66:23, Zech. 8:23, 14:9, Psalm 86:9, Mall 1:11, Joel 3:17, Jer. 31:34)

Messiah will bring the inauguration of one kingdom and one kingship (Isa. 11:12, 43:5-6, 60; Dan. 2:44, 7:27, Ezek. 37:21-22, 39:28, Zech. 14:9)

Messiah will release the resurrection of the dead (Isa. 26:19, Dan. 12:2, Deut. 32:39)

Messiah will abolish all idolatrous images and false prophets (Isa. 2:18, 42:17, Zephaniah 2:11, Psalms 97:7)

Messiah will slay all the wicked (Isa 11:4, Zechariah 14)

Messiah will cause the restoration and regathering of the tribes under her Davidic king. (Ezek. 37:21-22 and 47-48);

Messiah will end the battle of Gog and Magog (Ezek. 38 and 39)

Messiah will cleave /split the Mount of Olives (Zech. 14:4)

Messiah will build the future temple (Ezek. 40-46)

Messiah will release living water from the site of the temple (Ezek. 47: 1-12)

Messiah will bring the renewal of the Covenant with Israel as sanctification for the Israelites (Ezek. 37:26-28)

Messiah will bring the going up of the remnant of the nations to Jerusalem to worship Him. (Zech.14:16 - Isaiah 2)

Messiah will cause Jerusalem to be safely inhabited (Zech. 14:11- Isaiah 32:18)

Messiah will cause the Temple to be the desire of the nations. Hag. 2:7 - Isaiah 2

Messiah will bring the messianic kingdom stretching from sea to sea (Zech. 9:10, Psalm 72:8, Dan. 7:14).

A matter of inheritance!

There are always those who think they can get an inheritance by force, even if it means to kill and destroy. But anyone knows you have to be a son or daughter to receive an inheritance; that your name has to be written in the Fathers will. Furthermore any Last Will and Testament cannot be in effect until the owner dies. Muslims don't believe in the God and Father of Abraham, Isaac and Jacob, nor His Son, nor His death never mind resurrection, so how can they be heirs? Last but not least, it's up to the owner to decide who gets the inheritance. It's time for them to reconsider and adjust their attitude, because my Father would never permit me to kill to get an inheritance, but disinherit me.

It is God's desire to gain as many heirs as possible to live and rule with His Son Jesus Christ in His Kingdom. In order to do so you must humble yourself, repent of your pride and sin, and receive Jesus as your Savior, your Forgiver and LORD. You must enter second birth to become a co- heir with Him. It is up to you. You have a choice. You can stubbornly insist on being first and receive nothing, or accept second birth.

It's all about family!

God is our Father who desires to save His family. Jews and Muslims are cousins related to Jesus in His humanity. Christians are the bride and Christ is our bridegroom. Satan is the father of lies out to destroy the heirs, and for centuries managed to pit us against each other. He hates the natural and the spiritual family because both are God's design. It is time to wake up! I believe Jesus says, *"Come! Through the blood of Adam you were infected by sin, but through my blood you are made acceptable. The only way to be one family is by adoption."* STOP THE FAMILY FEUD!

Sunrise -Sunset:

It has been the worship of the sun, moon and stars, false earthly gods, bull gods and their numerous names, satanic empire after empire, declaring the will of Satan to rule the earth. They have conquered and killed under the ensign of their false gods, slaughtering millions, attempting to exterminate the messianic lineage. They have renounced the God of Holy scripture, demanded their rule from high places, and sought to destroy Israel. Some have even dared to rule from the Temple mount in Jerusalem.

It has been "Sunrise, Sunset, Sunrise, Sunset", but soon, *the sun and moon will not give its light, the stars shall fall from heaven, (as they are no gods at all) - and the sign of the Son of man shall appear in the sky.* (Matthew 24:29-30) When the cup of iniquity of man's sin and arrogance is full, and man has refused the gracious provision of Jesus as their only hope and redeemer, not only individuals, but gentile kingdoms will crumble, and find themselves in the hands of an angry God.

Stand firm even unto death!
Hang on to the faith! Jesus is coming SOON!
"Blessed are the poor in spirit, for THEIRS is the Kingdom of HEAVEN!
Blessed are those who mourn, for THEY will be comforted!
Blessed are the Meek, for THEY shall INHERIT the EARTH!"
Matthew 5:3-5

Bibliography

Apocrypha. New Jerusalem Bible

Babylon, Mystery Religion. Ralph Woodrow

Daily life at the time of Jesus. Miriam Feinberg Vamosh

Inside Islam. Reza F. Safa

King James Bible.

Inside the Third Reich. Albert Speer

Jewish New Testament Commentary. David H. Stern

Koran. Translation by Abdullah Yusuf Ali

NIV study Bible.

Our Father Abraham. Marvin R. Wilson

Our hands are stained with Blood. Michael L. Brown

Spandau: The Secret Diaries. Albert Speer

Strange scriptures. Barbara M. Bowen

Unger's Bible Dictionary. Merrill F. Unger

The complete works of Josephus. Josephus Flavious, Translated by William Whiston, Grand Rapids; Kregel publications, 1960

The Feasts of the LORD. Kevin Howard and Marvin Rosenthal

The Kingdom of the Cults. Dr. Walter Martin

The Islamic Invasion. Dr. Robert Morey

The Pre-wrath rapture of the church. Marvin Rosenthal

The Rise and the Fall of the Third Reich. William L. Shirer

Index

Covenant Land Grant
Genesis 13:14-17; 15:18-21; 17:7,8,19; 35:11-12;
Exodus: 23:31
Numbers 34:1-12
Deuteronomy 1:8; 4:31.
Joshua 1:2-4
Psalm 105: 7-11
Ezekiel 47:13-22, 48

Warning of dispersions
Leviticus 26: 32-37
Deuteronomy 4:27-30; 28:15; 30:1; 37; 64-68
2 Chronicles 7:19
Jeremiah 2:7, Jeremiah 16:18 .
Zechariah 7: 8-14
Luke 21:24; 19:42-44

Preserved, re-gathered and restored.
Deuteronomy 30:3-6;
Psalm 53:6-7; 69:35-35; 106:47; 107:2-3; 126;
Isaiah 10:20-21; 11:11; 14:1-2; 27:6; 12-13; 35:1,10 ; 41:8-10; 43:5-7; 9-13; 16-19; 44:26; 45:20; 46:3-4; 49:22; 51:3;11; 58:12,14; 60:4-5; 8-9

Jeremiah 3:12; 14-18; 12:14-15; 16:14-15; 23:3-8; 24:6-7; 27:22; 29:11-14; 30:3; 30:10-18, 31 7-28; 32:37-41; 33:7,14-16 46:28; 50:19; 51:5-6; 45; 50;
Lamentation 4:22
Ezekiel 11:17-19; 20: 25-29; 28:25-26; 34; 36-37; 39:22 to ch.45;
Hosea 2:14-23; 3:5; 6:11; 8:10; 14:7;
Joel 2:18-19, 32; 3:17,20.
Amos 9:11-15
Obadiah 1:15,17,19-21
Micah 2:12; 4: 1-2; 6-7; 10-13.
Nahum 1:15
Zephaniah 3:19-20
Zechariah 2:6-8,10-13; 8:1-8,13,20-23; 9:16; 10:6,8-10; 12:10; 13:8-9; 14:14
Romans 11:25-36,

Arab nations, Judgments and destructions: (Partial list)

AMMAN / JORDAN
Ammon, Moab (Isaiah 15; Jeremiah 25:2; Zephaniah 2:9))

ARABIA/ SAUDI-ARABIA. Kedar son of Ishmael (Isa 21:13-17) Also know as Edom / Idumea / land of Seir Arabia, birthplace of Islam.
Composite judgment against all Arab nations (Ezekiel 29-32; 34; 35; 36; Jeremiah.25: 21)

EGYPT
(Isaiah 19-20; Ezekiel 25-32; Jeremiah 25:19).

IRAN, Persia
(Ezekiel 27:10.)

IRAQ
Assyria / Babylon (Isaiah 14: 24-32, Jeremiah 50 and 51, Isaiah 14: 15-27; 21).

LEBANON
   Sidon and Tyre (Jer.25: 22; Isaiah 23; Ezek.27-28; Joel 3).

LYBIA
   Put, North Africa, (Ezekiel 30:5).

PALESTINE
   Philistia / Philistines (Joel 3:4; Ezek 25:15-17).

RUSSIA, N/E EUROPE
   Gog and Magog, (invades Israel Ezekiel 38 - 39).
   (Rise of Islam within them today)

SUDAN / ETHIOPA
   Cush, (Isaiah 18; 19; Ezekiel 30:5).
   Sudan ancient Christian nation, Muslim conquests, today's Christian Holocaust.

SYRIA
   Damascus capitol city in Syria (Isaiah 17

TURKEY
   Lydia, Asia Minor (Ezekiel 27:10)

Printed in the United States
56822LVS00005B/145-195